Canada's Lost Plays

Volume One

The Nineteenth Century

Edited by Anton Wagner and Richard Plant

CTR Publications
Toronto
1978

Series Editor: Anton Wagner

Copyright © 1978, CTR Publications. The editors wish to thank Wintario for financial help in the preparation of this manuscript. CTR Publications operates under special grants from the Canada Council, the Ontario Arts Council, Alberta Culture and York University. Printed in Canada by Page Publications Limited. ISBN 0-920644-46-5 (hardcover); 0-920644-48-1 (paperback).

Contents

Introduction

Reclaiming the Past

The *Bibliography of Canadian Theatre History 1583-1975,* its 1978 *Supplement* and *The Brock Bibliography of Published Canadian Plays in English 1766-1977* record source material documenting almost 400 years of live theatre in Canada and 2,000 Canadian plays published over a period of two centuries. The *Canada's Lost Plays* series will attempt to reclaim a small part of this past for Canadian playwrights and producers, for critics seeking to place our theatre in an appropriate historical context and for scholars wishing to identify Canada's early theatrical history.

The plays published in this and subsequent anthologies should correct the misconception that English-Canadian theatre and drama are largely a product of the post-Canada Council 1960's and 70's and that playwrights are only now addressing themselves to issues of concern to all of Canadian society. The fact that *The Female Consistory of Brockville, Dolorsolatio, Santiago, The Fair Grit, H.M.S. Parliament* and *Ptarmigan* discussed women's rights, religious and political corruption, and national and cultural survival already a century ago is significant, for as Northrop Frye reminds us, "literature is itself an active part of the historical process". Far from being "dead" theatre, these plays can be as immediate to us today as they were to the audiences of their time when viewed from within their theatrical conventions.

In *The Critical Path,* Frye notes that "the critic has to establish a pattern of continuity linking present culture with its heritage, and therefore with its inheritors, for a culture that is careless of its past has no defences against the future."[1] The absence of such a strong theatrical and dramatic tradition in Canada has been commented on by playwrights and critics alike. George Ryga has observed that "the emergence of our contemporary theatre owes less to esoteric tradition than it does to political and economic realities outside the stage door. . . . As a dramatist, I wish it had been otherwise — that some continuity might have been maintained to enrich and deepen the field in which we work."[2]

Surveying the theatre and drama from 1920 to 1960 in the *Literary History of Canada,* Michael Tait similarly concludes:

> the overriding impression one receives from the last four decades of drama in Canada is of a group of playwrights, some with considerable gifts, separated primarily not by space and time but by the absence of a common dramatic tradition, a tradition that may be accepted or challenged, but within which action produces reaction. In an important sense, the playwright in this country has hardly anything either to follow or to repudiate. He must begin each time to build from the bottom and in such circumstances it takes a dramatist of formidable energy and skill to build very high.[3]

Tait's often quoted survey of nineteenth century English-Canadian drama, "Playwrights In A Vacuum", published in *Canadian Literature* extends this lack of a common dramatic tradition for another century. His analysis is representative of much of current critical opinion which states that nineteenth century Canadian drama was dominated by a colonial impulse to imitate which resulted in only derivative closet verse dramas:

> This early period offers the anomalous spectacle of Canadian dramatists writing in total isolation from the most energetic popular theatre Canada has ever enjoyed. Of course, as most of the players and almost all the plays were imports, this vitality was, in a sense, specious. For want of even a minority demand for the performance of native plays, these would-be dramatists were compelled willy-nilly to write for the closet rather than the stage. Denied a vitalizing contact with the coarse realities of stage presentation, they produced works at once petrified and undisciplined.[4]

Apart from ignoring a great deal of writing for the theatre, simply stating that there was no common indigenous dramatic tradition in the nineteenth century fails to account for the great number of dramatic compositions that were published and performed. Nineteenth century Canadian drama has mixed origins influenced by two separate but interrelated traditions: the literary, including poetic drama and largely unskilled native verse; and live theatre activity, both the local amateur and professional stage and the large imported professional touring productions. The literary tradition, supported by several centuries of British dramatic writing, accounts in large part for the works of such earlier British North American dramatists as George Cockings' *The Conquest of Canada* and Robert Rogers' *Ponteach or the Savages of America* of 1766 and Adam Allan's *The New Gentle Shepherd* of 1798.

The large body of Canadian native verse published in the early eighteen hundreds includes numerous dramatic sketches, dialogues and dramatic fragments that precede by over three decades Charles Heavysege's *Saul* of 1857, commonly viewed as the first notable drama in Canada. Eliza Lanesford Cushing alone wrote eight dramatic sketches in addition to her three-act romantic tragedy *The Fatal Ring,* all published in the *Literary Garland* from 1839 to 1845. Besides the evidence of these dramatic fragments and sketches, the fact that Canadian poets often turned to drama is further indicated by more sophisticated plays such as "Bertram and Lorenzo" in Charles Sangster's *The St. Lawrence and the Saguenay and Other Poems* of 1856, and George Washington Johnson's "The Columbiad", "The Count's Bride" and "Grantly Granville" in his *Maple Leaves* of 1864.

The British tradition was, of course, not confined to serious poetic drama but also included the popular stage play and dramatic satire as is clearly reflected in John Simpson's "Captain Plume's Courtship" in his *Canadian Forget Me Not for 1837* and Lynch Rawdon Sharpe's *The Viceroy's Dream; or, The Government Not "Wide Awake"* of 1838. Precursors of the satires by "Caroli Candidus", "Sam Scribble", Nicholas Flood Davin, William Henry Fuller and Jean Newton McIlwraith contained in this volume can be found already in the early newspapers and periodicals of the colony. Samuel Hull Wilcocke published dramatic sketches satirizing Montreal high society in his notorious *Scribbler* from 1821 to 1827. In St. John, the *New Brunswick Courier* published "The Triumph of Intrigue", a three-act political farce attacking the Lieutenant Governor, in its February 23, March 2 and March 9, 1833 issues. *The British Colonist* in Upper Canada printed a similar satirical "Provincial Drama Called The Family Compact" attributed to its editor, Hugh Scobie, in five issues from June 19 to July 31, 1839.

5

Newspapers played an important role in the cultural life of colonial and post-Confederation Canada by acting as printers and publishers of many dramas and other literary works. The influence of journalistic polemical writing with its direct address to the public is evident in many nineteenth century plays such as Scribble's *Dolorsolatio* and Davin's *The Fair Grit*. One of the origins of contemporary Canadian theatre and drama can in fact be attributed to the conjunction of live theatre and the Canadian focus of the local press in the Canada of the eighteen hundreds. In Toronto, the amateur and professional theatre was much livelier than is generally realized and found strong encouragement in the pages of the *British Colonist*, the *Daily Patriot and Express* and other papers.

When this theatre activity was relatively continuous, as in the actor-manager John Nickinson's management of the Royal Lyceum from 1852 to 1858, the influence on dramatic writing quickly becomes apparent. Nickinson successfully produced *Fiddle, Faddle, and Foozle,* a farce by the second leading actor in his company, George Simcoe Lee, on April 9, 1853 and Lee's second play *Saucy Kate* quickly followed on July 11.[5] Nickinson staged his own *The Fortune of War* at the Royal Lyceum January 13, 1854. It is interesting to note that despite its native authorship, *Fiddle, Faddle, and Foozle* was actually criticized by the editor of the *Daily Patriot and Express* for its too British and not sufficiently Canadian orientation.

The influence of this live theatre activity in Toronto can also be seen in plays not known to have been performed, such as *The Two Elders* and its sequel *The Meal Club Plot* by "Toots" published by the *Citizen* in 1856. Satires of the authoritarian Dr. Robert Burns, pastor of Knox Presbyterian Church in Toronto shown in bitter conflict with his congregation, the two short plays have stage directions and musical accompaniment clearly indicated and are in fact stageable. 1856 is also the year of publication of *The Female Consistory of Brockville,* by "Caroli Candidus", based on a similar contemporary incident, the dismissal of John Whyte, a Brockville Presbyterian minister, through pressure from his congregation. The facts of this case, particularly Whyte's conviction for mistreating his wife, are amply documented in *The Acts and Proceedings of the Synod of the Presbyterian Church of Canada.*[6]

Entitled a "melo-drama in three acts", *The Female Consistory of Brockville* is more reminiscent of the English comedy of manners in its satiric character portrayals, social intrigue, witty dialogue and male-female conflict. With an astute dramatic sense, the anonymous "Candidus" weaves a tale of alleged abuse against a Brockville minister whose circumstances bear striking similarity to the historical John Whyte's. By bribing a number of servant girls to lie about the manner in which the minister has governed himself and his house, the women of the consistory succeed in bringing the minister before a Presbytery inquisition where, on further trumped up evidence, he is found guilty and relieved of his office.

Far from being stylistically imitative, part of the originality of *The Female Consistory* lies in the form its author has chosen to present his Canadian subject. Although partly in verse, the play is feasible on the stage even today without great technical and dramaturgical changes, unlike many other verse dramas of the period. It offers a language and verse style that is plain, functional and surprisingly sophisticated. The play stands apart from the often crude, polemical satires and farces that precede it by presenting both sides of its dramatic conflict, at least indirectly airing the case for women's rights. The climax of *The Female Consistory* is a marvellous scene with a thoroughly modern flavour in which the "body of the victim" is carried in on a litter after the trial. As the apparently victorious women dance ritualistically around the minister's body chanting abuse, a dramatic turnabout takes place and the minister rises from his litter in grotesque triumph, scattering the consistory. Because of its potentially libelous subject matter, *The Female Consistory* probably would never have been performed even had there been amateur and professional theatre activity in Brockville comparable to that in Toronto.

Domestic conflict, but of a different nature, is the subject matter of *Dolorsolatio,* "a local political burlesque" by the also anonymous "Sam Scribble", first performed at the Theatre Royal, Montreal, January 9, 1865. "Scribble", for all his anonymity, was a prolific playwright, the author of at least three other farces. *"Not Dead Yet" or, The Skating Carnival* was performed at the Theatre Royal, February 22, 1865. A second pro-Confederation play, *The King of the Beavers,* "a new original, political, allegorical, burlesque, extravaganza", was staged by the Amateurs of the Garrison at the Theatre Royal, December 26, 1865. All three plays were also published in Montreal that year. "Scribble's" last known work is *Orpheus and Eurydice,* "a classical extravaganza", published in 1866. The text of *The King of the Beavers,* ascribed to "Sam Scribble, Comedian", suggests that, like George Simcoe Lee, Scribble may have been a leading actor with the company that produced his work, the Amateurs of the Garrison in Montreal.

In comparison with the poetic drama of the period, *Dolorsolatio* may appear to be of little literary consequence. The play is of great interest, however, precisely for its revelation of the economic, political and cultural conditions of the time and for its lively theatricality — a combination of musical accompaniment, song, dance, comic dialogue in rhymed verse, and zestful burlesque action and characterization. The descriptions in the *Dramatis Personae* of Master West, Toronto, Ottawa and Montreal reveal not only the Canadian self-perception of the time but also an awareness of regional identities that have remained largely unchanged until today. The play presents in an enlightened fashion East-West economic disparities and cultural differences, taxation, transportation difficulties and a view of the tensions caused by the American Civil War and threatened annexation to the United States which is also reflected in many later dramas.

The frequent use of trapdoors, descriptive music, and other theatrical devices in Scribble's plays reminds us that nineteenth century plays were written for a theatre, and an age, very different from ours, an age of novelty within conventions. The Canadian dramatist of the time wrote either for a theatre of the mind or for the live stage, although often the influences of both were interwoven in the same work. For live performances, the houses varied from make-shift spaces — stables, inns or abandoned churches converted to theatrical purposes — to large and elegant buildings of the second half of the century modelled after European or American theatres. *H.M.S. Parliament, Dolorsolatio* and *Ptarmigan* were all performed in large houses: Montreal's Academy of Music (1,800 capacity), The Theatre Royal in Montreal (2,000 capacity), and Hamilton's Grand Opera House (1,100 capacity), respectively.

Despite the differences in theatre size and the more elaborate style in larger houses, the methods of production which might influence a playwright were much the same. The stage was generally illuminated by gas which had received enough refinement by mid-century to be a significant improvement over the dimmer light of candles and kerosene used previously. Improvements in lighting helped foster the growth of spectacle on the stage so that the stage direction in Canada's last speech in *Dolorsolatio,* "Now then, blue fire! and down curtain" was only made possible by new facilities for blue light. Colours became a kind of convention, blue used for good characters and pleasant scenes and red for evil.

Only very late in the century were the house lights dimmed for the show, a telling comment on the kind of illusion a playwright worked with in the theatre — credibility was important, but not the realism of the naturalists. In set design, the box set and its kind of illusion was rarely used until late in the century. The common practice, which influenced the plays in this volume, involved painted one-dimensional backdrops, and wings and borders that moved in grooves in the stage floor and tracks overhead. The facility with which wings and borders could be changed, combined with the audience's readiness to accept conventions, meant that the playwright did not need to limit the scope of his scenes. To nineteenth century audiences, the scenic demands of *Santiago* would not have been as unusual as we might find them. In fact, the set description, "a shelf of rock in the Andes. Snowy peaks and a volcano in the distance", is in itself almost a convention signalling the imaginative nature of the poetic play and suggesting a kind of scene rather than a specific location.

Above: A nineteenth century 'sensational' drama produced in Canada — 1875.
Right: Marietta Ravel — *the tight rope walk — at Montreal's Theatre Royal in 1863.*

This less restricted dramatic sensibility showed itself in the latter half of the century especially in the playwrights' willingness to accommodate spectacular effects in their plays. Particularly in Europe and to a lesser extent in Canada, audiences saw great nautical dramas in huge water tanks, scenes with exploding ships, burning buildings, and trains on the stage, *Hamlet* done on horseback, and so on. Stages were built with trapdoors and machinery for these effects so that Pepper's Ghost, the Vampire Trap and the Corsican Trap which allowed actors to appear or disappear as if from nowhere are but three illusions easily manufactured in front of the audience.

If there is a chief characteristic of the plays themselves, it is their variety. In an age when the theatre entertained a large cross section of the population — although this was less true of amateur shows whose audiences were largely determined by the nature of the performers — variety was especially important as a means of keeping audiences returning to the theatre. Not only was there variety in the kinds of plays — farce, burlesque, high comedy, adaptations of Shakespeare, melodramas, historical, costume or romance dramas, comic opera, extravaganzas, and so on, but an evening's bill of fare was also multifarious. Until late in the century when the performance of one play per night began to take over, bills consisted of short curtain raisers, main pieces, after pieces, with music, song and dance as added diversions. This in part accounts for the shortness of stage plays such as *Dolorsolatio* and for the prominence of MacDeadeye's Highland fling in *Parliament* and the Letty Salad gavotte in *Ptarmigan*.

The 'Pepper's Ghost' illusion as produced at the Grand Opera House in Hamilton, 1863. A typical effect easily produced.

The boundaries shaping the plays of the theatre of the mind were chiefly those of the creative imagination rather than the physical realities of the stage, although as can be seen in *Santiago,* the influence of the stage was not distant. The central characteristic of such plays, separating them from popular stage plays whose aim was simple enjoyment, was the conscious attempt by the author to comment seriously on life, about great people or life's great moral, religious or philosophical concerns and to express that comment in a language which suited and enhanced the play's lofty purpose. In most cases, these plays were written in verse although a few such as Newcomb and Hanks' *Dermot McMurrough* and *The Fireworshippers* were in prose. Most were written simply to be read although a production of Heavysege's *Saul* was contemplated by Charlotte Cushman and Wilfrid Campbell submitted *Mordred,* as a star vehicle, to Sir Henry Irving.

The main source of inspiration for these poetic dramas was the nineteenth century conception of Shakespeare. Hence the plays, *Santiago* included, exhibit numerous "Shakespearean" qualities, words, phrases, and lines from his plays, blank verse except for the speech of commoners and for serious moments which were rendered in prose, and characters often modelled on memorable Shakespearean figures. Other inspirational sources can be found in the gothic tales of the late eighteenth century and in early nineteenth century romanticism as expressed in the plays of poets such as Byron and Shelley. Later in the century, Tennyson's sententious, rhetorical style became almost as important a model as Shakespeare. In light of the moral cast of the period, Biblical and historical figures were important inspirations.

In terms of critical analysis, poetic drama received a disproportionate amount of literary comment, which has created the impression that poetic drama dominated the age. For this volume to represent dramatic activity of the period, the form must be included here. We have chosen Thomas Bush's *Santiago,* a poetic drama printed in Hamilton and published in Toronto in 1866. Although not Canadian in subject like *Dolorsolatio,* an aspect characteristic of most poetic dramas, the play compares favourably with such generally available works as *Saul* and Mair's *Tecumseh.* *Santiago* possesses a degree of individuality which many other poetic dramas of the period do not. Murray Edwards in *A Stage in Our Past* senses this uniqueness when, in his discussion of poetic drama, he separates *Santiago* from other works. He cites what he admits as only a "slight, but interesting irregularity", the fact that Bush, an author about whom virtually nothing is known, uses as part of his plot an incident contemporary with the play's writing, a disastrous church fire in South America in which 2,000 persons perished. But this individuality goes further than Edwards will allow. More complex than the "melodramatic thriller" Edwards speaks of, *Santiago* presents a serious attack on various forms of evil in the world, particularly breaches of faith and idolatry, with a warning that such transgressions are ultimately punished.

The "storm-ridden realm" we see in the drama, although given a note of contemporary realism by its association with the South American conflagration, is primarily a fictional world which serves as an instructional analogue to the real world of the time. This world is ruled by forces of evil — theft, murder, greed, insolent pride, blasphemy, idolatry and lack of faith are among the vices portrayed. The geographical features of the setting, volcanic mountains, "sepulchres of stone", "vacant chasms" filled with "mouldy skeletons . . . hacked by ravenous beasts;/Hewn by fell murder" seem chosen to reinforce this presence of evil. Its inhabitants are also entirely suited to their environment. "Ghoulish" Avero, Treacher and Gripos are manifest criminals and Sheeram and Pat Scran are almost as evil. In a moral and theological sense, the

Archbishop who admits he has failed to lead his flock in the paths of righteousness and the Pope's Nuncio who, with the Archbishop, sanctions Urangos' hubristic attempt at "eclipsing Rome" and usurping divine power, violate laws. But in Bush's fictional world, evil is eventually punished. After the transgressions are made clear, Vampries, representing an elemental, atavistic force of retribution, swings into action destroying the offenders, and as in the case of the Tower of Shiloam carefully alluded to in the play, some innocent bystanders as well.

Santiago provides a good example of how Canadian poetic drama often mixed the conventions of its literary origin with those of the live stage. Typical of poetic dramas, *Santiago* presents "weighty" topics, often in philosophical "Shakespearean" soliloquies, such as Vampries' musing on the "moral rotteness" and "mouldy superstitions" of man's existence, in a language judged to be suitably elevated for the importance of the subject. Here again Shakespeare is in evidence in Bush's use of blank verse. The play's setting could very well have come directly out of the most gothic of poetic dramas with characters appropriately exotic, particularly Vampries, the mysterious "stranger" with otherworldly powers.

Side by side with the influences of the poetic drama are those of the live stage. One of the most obvious is the "gentleman of colour" whose only appearance in the play is to sing a song "in character" after the fashion of "Jim Crow" performers. Add to this man two other blacks, one of whom is called Bambo, (Tambo was the name of the end man in minstrel shows who played the tamborine), Pat the Irish barkeep, a crafty Jewish tailor, a Dutchman who smokes and a "Yankee" skipper, each of whom speaks his own stage-inspired dialect, and the influence of popular stock characters becomes evident. *Santiago* further draws on elements central to melodrama, the backbone of the nineteenth century stage, when for instance, Credulous is thrown over the cliff yet is saved, or when the love intrigue between Mary and Cortez is introduced. Amid the aspiration for lofty philosophical comment, *Santiago,* like so many other Canadian poetic dramas, displays an air derived directly from the nineteenth century live stage.

Members of the Hogan and Mudge Company wash off blackface after a performance. About 1872.

Still another kind of drama popular particularly in the latter nineteenth century, was political satire in the form of burlesque, farce, musical comedy or operetta. One of the most interesting of this period is *The Fair Grit or The Advantages of Coalition* published in 1876 by Nicholas Flood Davin, a colourful figure in Canadian history. Born in Ireland in 1843, Davin came to Canada in 1872 to begin a career as an author, journalist, lawyer and politician. By 1883, he had founded the *Regina Leader*. In 1884, he published a collection of verse, *Eos, A Prairie Dream,* and in 1887 he was elected to the House of Commons for West Assiniboia, sitting as a Conservative until 1900. But Davin's early success gave way to increasingly serious personal troubles and in 1901 he committed suicide.

A strong critique of government corruption, Davin's *The Fair Grit* stands in sharp contrast to *Dolorsolatio* and its optimistic, conciliatory ending. *Dolorsolatio*'s elixir, whose sole ingredient is "Federation", has by 1876 already failed to be the all-healing remedy for Canada's woes. Through his depiction of the love affair of Angelina, the fair Grit, and George, the son of a Tory, Davin focuses on the divisiveness caused in Canadian society by political antagonisms. Davin satirizes Prime Minister Mackenzie in the figure of Angelina's father, Alexander McPeterson, and brings party patronage and the partisan press under especially strong fire. When the lovers attempt to gain support for their marriage from the Liberal and Conservative newspapers, *Smasher* and *Dasher,* they find the editorial offices filled with satanic torture instruments operated by mad editors.

What obviously outraged Davin was the total disregard of responsibility to the country at large displayed by politicians and political parties. If personal or party gain could be secured at the expense of political integrity or principles, the end justified the means. George's father, a staunch Tory, is capable of switching to the Grits for the sake of a good position at the expense of supposedly important differences espoused by the two parties. The animosity displayed to George and Angelina's proposed marriage becomes encouragement when the "advantages of coalition" in terms of political power for one party are considered. The author's view of the situation may well be presented in Angelina's comment at the end of the play: "The sad suspicion will force itself unbidden/That by both parties country's overridden."

The Fair Grit is only one of many plays which raised a protest against the political and personal opportunism and corruption of the time. *The Great Land Bubble* and *The Land Swap,* Montreal, 1874 and 1875, explored the same subject on a provincial level. William Henry Fuller's *The Unspecific Scandal* attacked the federal government over the Pacific Railway scandal whose participants were further satirized in Fuller's *H.M.S. Parliament, or the Lady Who Loved a Government Clerk* and the anonymous *Sir John and Sir Charles, or the Secrets of the Syndicate* of 1881.

Unlike Fuller's *Unspecific Scandal* of 1874 which the author mockingly stated was performed only "at the Great Dominion Theatre, Ottawa", *H.M.S. Parliament* was given a well received, week-long stage production at the Academy of Music, Montreal, February 16, 1880. The play is a satirical attack on the Conservative government's protectionist economic "National Policy" of high tariffs, on government bureaucracy, political opportunism, patronage, nepotism, and the personal foibles of political leaders of the time. Sir John A. Macdonald, Alexander Mackenzie, and the finance minister Sir Samuel Tilley receive special satirical attention as was noted in the *Canadian Illustrated News* of February 28:

> The making-up of those heads for which the *taps* are intended, is so
> cleverly done that the expression leaves no doubt as to who is meant, and

the striking resemblance of the Canadian household which are busy with grinding axes in the opening scene, indicates that the hits are really good.

That *H.M.S. Parliament* was received as political satire and not merely a parody of Gilbert and Sullivan's *Pinafore* (the Holman Opera Company production of *Pinafore* opened at the rival Theatre Royal, February 19, 1880) is further indicated by reviews in the Montreal *Gazette* which emphasize the thematic content, locale and characters of the play and its Canadian context. The *Gazette* of February 17, 1880 commends the actors for their "realistic" impersonation of the political figures being satirized and praises the "sparkling wit" and "bright and clever" dialogue of Fuller's text and Eugene A. McDowell's lavish production:

The scenery and stage setting were particularly fine: indeed we have never seen on the Academy stage anything to equal in point of realism the two scenes, first the library of the House, and secondly, the exterior of the Parliament buildings by moonlight and as the curtain rose on each the hearty applause testifies to the impression the artists' work made on the audience.

The reviews in the *Gazette* reveal that the actor-manager McDowell and his wife, the actress Fanny Reeves, were well received in the roles of the lovers Angelina and Sam Snifter. In addition to satirizing the bearded old Senators by dressing them as women, McDowell's production burlesqued Mrs. Butterbun, the insatiable monopolist and advocate of the "N.P.", by giving the role to a man. As the *Gazette* reported: "this part Mr. Andrew Waldron endowed with much life" and "Mr. Waldron repeated his success of Monday evening".

Fuller is the most persistent and successful of the nineteenth century Canadian satirists. His strong opinions on economic and other government policies were undoubtedly influenced by his service as a banker in India and his association with the Ontario Bank after coming to Canada in 1870. Fuller has one of the best records of stage productions of nineteenth century dramatists. Following its week-long Montreal run, *H.M.S. Parliament* was toured by the McDowell company to Ottawa, Toronto and over two dozen other cities from the Maritimes to Winnipeg, from February to August 1880.[7] Fuller's musical comedy *Off to Egypt or An Arab Abduction* toured the U.S. and Canada in 1884 and *A Barber's Scrape,* "a musical farcical burlesque", was produced at the Lyceum Theatre in Montreal in 1896.

The conflict evident in *H.M.S. Parliament* between sentimental and historical ties to Britain and economic and political realities requiring closer relations with the United States is further exemplified by Geoffrey Quarles' *Commercial Courtship and Unselfish Union, A Tale of the Borders* of 1888 and Jean Newton McIlwraith and John Edmund Paul Aldous' comic opera *Ptarmigan* first produced, for three performances, at the Grand Opera House in Hamilton, February 15, 1895. Aldous came to Canada from England in 1877 and was a well-known musician and principal of the Hamilton Music School at the time of *Ptarmigan's* performance. He composed the music for at least three other operas, *The Golden Catch, Nancy,* and *The Poster Girl.* Jean McIlwraith had previously compiled *The Days of the Year, or, The Masque of the Months* successfully produced at the Galt Town Hall, Dec. 1893 and in several other cities. *A Book On Shakespeare, A Book On Longfellow,* and a study *Sir Frederick Haldimand* for the Makers of Canada series, were among her publications as well as many historical romances which displayed her knowledge of North American history.

The action of *Ptarmigan* centres around P. Tarmigan, a native of Ottawa, who emigrates to the United States because of greater economic opportunities there, returns to Canada after acquiring American citizenship and discovers economic and cultural conditions much improved. He is at first rejected by his former friends for having deserted Canada and Britain. But he is welcomed back into their society when he expresses a strong desire to be a Canadian again and Hepatica claims he became an American only in an act of madness. Although not as satirically and dramatically sophisticated as *H.M.S. Parliament, Ptarmigan* was received with equal enthusiasm at its premiere when both the libretto and score were singled out for praise. Unlike many operettas of the period, the originality of the work lies partly in its refusal to imitate the Gilbert and Sullivan model and other stage conventions. As *The Hamilton Spectator* of February 18, 1895 commented: "Of the burlesque type of humour which is considered to be a necessary element in the comic opera of the day, Miss McIlwraith has supplied little or none; but there is not lacking in the dialogue and verse bright sallies of wit and gleams of sly humour."

Aldous, who also directed the orchestra and singers, was lavishly praised for his score. "Of the music of the opera much has been said in praise, but not too much. It is far and away the best music of a similar character that has been composed by a Hamiltonian — perhaps it would not be exaggeration to say, by a Canadian . . . most of the musical gems of the evening had to be repeated".

As in *Parliament,* in which Mrs. McDowell played Angelina, Mrs. Aldous played a leading role as Blue Belle, with Mr. Lucas, the stage manager, as Ptarmigan. During the course of the operetta, McIlwraith satirizes many aspects of life in the United States and Canada, particularly Canadian culture. While McIlwraith makes it clear that a Canada exists in which people have refused to acknowledge their Canadian identity, she also satirizes excessive cultural nationalism. McIlwraith's contention is that drawing inspiration solely from foreign sources can never create a truly Canadian society. Nor can running to the United States as Ptarmigan has done. But once again, the vision of a purely Canadian home is compromised by its being seen as part of the British Empire.

This strong nineteenth century English-Canadian identification with British civilization and aversion to American politics and culture is to a great extent explained by the political and economic circumstances of the time. The American constitutional system had been shown to be less than perfect by the Civil War. Corruption among U.S. politicians was known to be rampant on a national and local level. As opposed to Britain's free trade policies, the United States had levied high tariffs on Canadian imports. Furthermore, the expansionist American "Manifest Destiny" not only endangered Canada's western borders but indirectly threatened the economic, political and cultural survival of the new Confederation. As Nicholas Flood Davin observed in his public lecture *British versus American Civilization,* "The Americans . . . do not understand us. They evidently regard us as if we were but a chip on the outer circle of a whirlpool into whose vortex we must inevitably be sucked".[8] Surrounded by an indomitable wilderness in a nation still in the process of formation and crowded by an older, more dynamic and violent neighbour to the south, the nineteenth century English-Canadian naturally looked to the British Empire for his cultural and political security.

In light of such a strong identification with British culture and its imperial *Weltanschauung,* it is not surprising that many English-Canadian playwrights continued to look to the English poetic drama and the English stage for their models of dramatic composition. It is also worth noting that many other prominent playwrights such as Charles Heavysege, Samuel James Watson, John Hutchinson Garnier, John Hunter-Duvar and Sarah Anne Curzon were immigrants from the British Isles and thus had a direct link with British dramatic tradition. The six plays included in this anthology should dispel, however, the widely-held misconception that nineteenth century English-Canadian theatre and drama consisted solely of unstageable poetic drama, or at the other extreme, exclusively foreign dominated popular plays.

Dolorsolatio, H.M.S. Parliament and *Ptarmigan* were staged and published as were other plays with Canadian themes, such as Frederick A. Dixon's *A Masque Entitled "Canada's Welcome* of 1879, George Broughall's burlesque *The 90th on Active Service, or Campaigning in the North West* of 1885 and George Frederick Cameron's opera *Leo, the Royal Cadet* of 1889. Many other plays surviving only as titles, as Murray Edwards points out in *A Stage in Our Past,* such as Charles Handscomb's *The Big Boom* of 1886, George Cameron Rankin's *The Canuck* of the 1890's as well as many other Canadian musical comedies, operettas, revues and melodramas were similarly performed. All the above plays and probably many others yet to be discovered suggest the basis of a Canadian popular theatre and drama with considerable literary, social and cultural dimensions with which a comparison with twentieth century English-Canadian theatre and drama can be made. The many different self-perceptions, regional identities, historical and political events, accents and sentiments of the time displayed by these plays attempt, like so much of contemporary English-Canadian drama, to define that territory called Canada and its inhabitants.

Richard Plant
Anton Wagner

[1]Northrop Frye, *The Critical Path.* An Essay on the Social Context of Literary Criticism. Bloomington, Indiana University Press, 1971, p. 100.

[2]George Ryga, "Contemporary Theatre and Its Language" in *Canadian Theatre Review,* #14, Spring 1977, p. 4.

[3]Michael Tait, "Drama and Theatre" in *Literary History of Canada,* Canadian Literature in English, 2nd Ed. Carl F. Klinck, general editor, Toronto, University of Toronto Press, 1976. V.2, p. 159.

[4]Michael Tait, "Playwrights In a Vacuum, English-Canadian Drama in the Nineteenth Century", *Canadian Literature,* #16, Spring 1963.

[5]Patrick O'Neill, "Fiddle, Faddle, and Foozle — The First Stage Production of a Canadian Play in Toronto" in *Canadian Drama/L'Art Dramatique Canadien,* vol. 3, #1, Spring 1977, p. 20. See also his *A History of Theatrical Activity in Toronto, Canada: From Its Beginnings to 1858.* Ann Arbor, Michigan University Microfilms, 1973.

[6]Presbyterian Church in Canada. Synod. *(Minutes of the Synod of the Presbyterian Church of Canada in connection with the Church of Scotland; together with The Acts and Proceedings of the Synod.)* Sessions XXIII, 1852; XXV, 1854; XXVII, 1855.

[7]For a complete production history of *H.M.S. Parliament* see Robert G. Lawrence's article in *Canadian Theatre Review,* #19, Summer 1978.

[8]Nicholas Flood Davin, *British versus American Civilization,* National Papers, #2, Toronto, Adam Stevenson, 1873, p. 44.

THE

FEMALE CONSISTORY

OF

BROCKVILLE:

A MELO-DRAMA IN THREE ACTS,

BY

CAROLI CANDIDUS, ESQ.,

𝔄 𝔠𝔦𝔱𝔦𝔷𝔢𝔫 𝔬𝔣 𝔠𝔞𝔫𝔞𝔡𝔞.

BROCKVILLE :
PRINTED FOR THE AUTHOR.
1856.

DEDICATION

To the Ladies of Brockville

My Dear Ladies,

To you who are so distinguished in the Province as patrons of the Drama, of Preaching, and of Horticulture — I dedicate this little work.

Your judgment of it will at once seal its condemnation, or open to it the door of popular favour. In either case, I shall have the satisfaction of knowing that I am judged by discerning and impartial judges. None know better than you whether it be true to nature. None know better whether it be true in fact. None know better whether the portraits are drawn from life. None know better whether they are daubs or photographs.

Therefore, with implicit confidence in your usual good taste, fine feelings, and liberal sympathies, I commit it to your patronizing care.

And that you may never lose your patronizing celebrity of waxflowers, preachers, and playactors, is the fervent hope of

Your very humble Servant,

CAROLI CANDIDUS

Glentattle, February, 1856.

DRAMATIS PERSONAE

Sir George Mulish	*Of Half-House Hall,* *Baron of the Court of Contra,* *and Chief Kimbo of the Squatters' Sessions*
Old Mulish	*Father of the Baron*
Squire Waterson	
The Beadle	
Lady Mulish	*Wife of the Baron*
Lady Dowager Mooress	
Madame Waterson	
Madame Noheart	*Wife of the Minister*
Miss Prim Proboscis	*A member of the Baron's family*
Ann Limper	*The Baron's Protege*
Sally Rubknocker	*Nursery Maid*
Marjory Crucklebuck	*Maid-of-all-Work*

ACT I

L'ENVOYE

> *O ye women! which be inclined*
> *By influence of your nature*
> *To be as pure as gold yfined*
> *And in your truth for to endure,*
> *Armeth yourselves in strong armure,*
> *(Lest men assail your sickerness),*
> *Set on your breast, yourself to assure,*
> *A mighty shield of doubleness.*

— Chaucer

SCENE I

Parlour in Half-House Hall. Enter Old Father Mulish and Lady Mulish.

OLD MULISH: I wonder what wud St. Paul say about this female government in the Kirk?

LADY MULISH: St. Paul does not favour the ladies, Mr. Mulish. But, you must know, a great many things have been discovered since St. Paul's time.

OLD MULISH: O Yes, I ken that: the Bloomer costume has been discovered since his time, and twa — three mair sic-like things.

LADY MULISH: Yes, Mr. Mulish; and equality is better understood now than in his days.

OLD MULISH: Na, feint a bit o' that — for he tells us there's nae difference between Jew and Gentile — bond and free — but a' nations are made of one blood.

LADY MULISH: You mistake my meaning, Mr. Mulish; I mean equality of the sexes.

OLD MULISH: Superiority, I rather think ye mean, my Leddy.

LADY MULISH: Superiority, sir, if you will. The Rights of Woman are now beginning to be better understood, and to bring to light her long-buried capabilities. It has lately been discovered that woman is the equal of man: equal in counsel — equal in debate — equal in judgment — equal in eloquence — equal in courage — equal in every quality, but that of brute force — a poor superiority, enjoyed by them in common with the beasts of burden.

OLD MULISH: Na, but ye'd better let the men bear the burden o' the bairns tae.

18

LADY MULISH: That, Sir, is one of woman's inalienable rights — had it not been so, man (the selfish creature) would, I believe, have appropriated it long ere now.

OLD MULISH: That certainly wud be an awfu' greedy stretch of the selfish propensity. That wud be what phrenologists wud ca'a striking illustration of the philoprogenitive faculty. But, what have women to do with Church affairs?

LADY MULISH: Women are of the same weight as men in the Church: indeed, they are its moving spirits.

OLD MULISH: I grant ye they're the *moving spirits,* for, were it no' for them and their movements, especially their tongue movements, all would stand still in peace and quietness. But, what wud John Knox say to this female dominancy in the kirk? You that's a staunch Presbyterian, can ye tell me that?

LADY MULISH: John Knox was a boor, and knew nothing of the delicacy and deference due to the female character.

OLD MULISH: He agreed with you in one respect; he tho'ht them moving spirits; but he wished to blaw them awa'. Ye've heard o' his *Three blasts o' the trumpet against the horrible regimen of women?*

LADY MULISH: Mr. Mulish drop this subject, or you and I shall quarrel.

OLD MULISH: Na, but if ye mean to rule the Kirk, ye maun listen to reason. Ye ken this is the age o' moral suasion — nae physical force noo-a-days: — this is anither thing that has been discovered sin' Paul's time.

Enter Lady Dowager Mooress.

LADY MULISH: I wish you men had only the nineteenth part of the reason that belongs to us women — in church affairs — and all would go as it ought.

LADY D. MOORESS: Yes tell him that — I wonder how you can support a man that kicks his wife, Mr. Mulish?

OLD MULISH: Did you ever see him kick his wife?

LADY D. MOORESS: No—o, —a—hem!

OLD MULISH: How do you know it then?

LADY D. MOORESS: No I never saw him, but a—hem! —hem!

OLD MULISH: How do you undertake to say it then?

LADY D. MOORESS: I asked him one day if he approved of men beating their wives? and he laughed like a hyena, and said, O yes, a beating sometimes drives the dust out of things.

OLD MULISH: And do you call that proof?

LADY D. MOORESS: I would never ask another proof.

LADY MULISH: Where is your reason now Mr. Mulish?

OLD MULISH: Weel that's certainly reasonable. But I think the man must have been laughing in his sleeve when he tauld ye sic a story.

LADY D. MOORESS: Laughing! yes, and that was the strongest confirmation of the proof — What would you ask, for proof, if that be not proof? — reason! indeed.

OLD MULISH: O that's reasonable — very reasonable — a little siller gangs far when it's weel guided. Tak' care o' your proof — hoard it up weel — and it will gather. You'll soon get plenty o' that kind o' proof. There is na doubt a snaw ba' will grow if ye keep rowin' it.

LADY MULISH: We are determined to roll the ball, Mr. Mulish, till the snow melts.

OLD MULISH: O very weel; but tak' care that ye dinna row yersels in tilt — for then ye'll may be carried awa' wi' the flood — like the antedeluvians. — Hah! ha! ha! heh! he!   *Exit shaking with laughter.*

LADY D. MOORESS: We must prepare and set the wheel in order to spin the thread, to weave the web of this unruly fellow's downfall. He'll not be ruled by us, then we must teach him who are masters here. Besides, I owe him a bitter grudge for reflecting on my domestic management. He scruples not to say that these step-children of mine are not properly brought up.

LADY MULISH: Intolerable audacity: it must not go unpunished. — And do you know the girl I hired and sent to the house, he has turned her off alleging she's a thief.

LADY D. MOORESS: What, Jane?

LADY MULISH: Yes, Jane.

LADY D. MOORESS: Our espionage is then foiled?

LADY MULISH: For the present at least. But we must just be all the more reserved and wary; — Jane was dear to me for her sister's sake — they had served me faithfully for years; — and dear to Madame Waterson for her mother's sake — she had been nurse to Madame Waterson in her pleurisy; — and dear to the sovereign for her father's sake — he is the sovereign's chief body servant. But we will be avenged. I've sworn we will be avenged.

LADY D. MOORESS: But how, my Lady, how!

LADY MULISH: Go you — he'll not suspect you — and hire two servants for his house; discharge the old ones; and keep the new in your own hand — you comprehend? From them know everything that passes in the house; and then you'll see what train of consequences will ensue.

LADY D. MOORESS: But how can I accomplish this?

LADY MULISH: Nothing more simple. Make up a case with Madame Noheart, that the present servants must be all dismissed — that their insolence to Madame Noheart cannot be longer borne. Tell him it is the talk of all the town, and as he values the honor of the Church to discharge them without one day's delay. Go and be bold, firm and persevering, and you'll see how it will work.

LADY D. MOORESS: Suppose I threaten to leave the Church?

LADY MULISH: Good! Excellent!

LADY D. MOORESS: And say that you will too.

LADY MULISH: You may — if Sir George does not get word of it. Be cautious!

LADY D. MOORESS: We'll teach him.

LADY MULISH: We will.
He'll find our deep intrigues possess a force
Denied to bone and muscle — man and horse.

They exit.

SCENE II

The Tea-Table of Half-house-hall. Enter Sir George Mulish and Lady Mulish.

SIR G. MULISH: I say, all past experience proves it true. Women have been at the bottom of all mischief since the world began. In the days of the great Comble did not your intrigues all but upset the Kirk?

LADY MULISH: You do speak unadvisedly with your lips. But for my peculiar tact and management, the whole fabric even then had tumbled down. Comble was my near kinsman whom I loved, and for whose sake I could have gone through fire and water. And you know Sir George, my father, brother, grandsire, and many more of my collaterals held office in the Kirk; and therefore it is that I do deem it a sacred duty — a hereditary right — to guide and direct its office-bearers, and to see that they do fulfil their public duties, and order their houses with discretion — and moreover, Sir George, you know 'twas I that made you an office-bearer in the Kirk: but for me and my influence, you had still been in the pews of black Prelacy.

SIR G. MULISH: *Sheepishly.*   That, doubtless, is true. But why should you busy yourself with what is altogether beyond the prerogative of woman?

LADY MULISH: The prerogative of woman! The prerogative of women in Ecclesiastical matters is like the rights of kings — it is a right *divine.*

SIR G. MULISH: Tut! tut! — talk to old maids and shrews about the rights of women. The rights of women are to get wed as speedily and as comfortably as they can.

Enter Lady Dowager Mooress, Madame Waterson, Madame Noheart, and others.

LADY MULISH: O fy! Sir George. But hush! here come the other members of the Consistory to consult. Good evening ladies: just come in the nick of time. Sir George and I have been consulting on the Kirk affairs.

LADY D. MOORESS: You find, I hope, a ground of process?

SIR G. MULISH: *Shaking his head.*   No grounds of process, a man may chastise his wife — if he does it in reason.

All voices at once cry out: O! Sir George, Sir George!

SIR G. MULISH: But I tell you he may. A man's wife is a member of his family. He may whip any member of his family who revolts, or disobeys his lawful commands, — provided he always does it in reason, — that is, breaks no bones and leaves no scars.

LADY D. MOORESS: But, Sir George, is this the law?

SIR G. MULISH: It is the statue law, — and, I fear, the *Common* law too.

MADAME WATERSON: This is dreadful!

LADY D. MOORESS: Dreadful!

LADY MULISH: Most dreadful! — what shall we do?

LADY D. MOORESS: We must not give it up. — Let me see —   *to Sir George.* Sir George, pray tell me this. Have not Kings been suspended in their regal functions for insanity? and why should not ministers? Call in the lawyer and the doctor, you'll find they both pronounce him mad.

MADAME WATERSON: Mad as a March hare!

SIR G. MULISH: *Gravely.*   That is certainly, a ground of suspension. I'll fetch the statutes relative to the case of George the Third.   *Here Sir George fetches down from his library shelves an armful of musty folios. Reads, half looking on, half off.* The first precedent touching insanity — that is regal insanity — as affording grounds for the suspension of George III, is that recorded in act 9th, cap. 12, sec. 3, 1217. This act is dubious, and admits of five constructions: 1st, there is the downright *non-compos mentis,* that is the total abnegation of those functions which a sound mind ought, or should, or is expected to have. — 2nd, There is the *aberratio mentis;* that is the mind in the wandering state, — or occasional erratic tendencies a condition pertaining less or more to most men. 3rd, There is the *Lycanthropy;* this is properly speaking the wolf or dog madness, sometimes called the *rabies;* or species of *hydrophobia* peculiar to the genus *homo* of the species *snapatem.* Then again, 4thly, you have the *distractio-mentis* — that is the mind torn from itself, — driven about, drifted from its moorings — a species of lunacy derived from *Luna,* the moon.

MADAME NOHEART: *Interrupting.* That's it, Sir George, that's it. It all goes by the moon, the disease all goes by the moon, — it returns, eh, at the full o' the moon!

SIR G. MULISH: *Snappishly.* Hold your tongue, woman, hold your tongue, until I give the construction of the statute — and, 5thly and finally, There is the madness *furiosa,* — that is fierceness of madness, or *furor,* — or madness of anger or rage — which last appears to me to be the madness of the minister. But there are other cases in point, viz. that which occurs in 1326 and 1377, and of 1422 and 1455; and, lastly, that of 1788, all of which, you will perceive, have affinity to the case in point, and must be —

LADY MULISH: Have done, pray have done, Sir George, with your critical niceties and legal constructions.

SIR G. MULISH: Have done, woman! How can you form a legitimate judgment of the case, unless you have recourse to all the precedents, and carefully collate the law upon the subject?

LADY MULISH: Oh! You must know, Sir George, that we, women, love to come to our end by shorter means. We have resolved to hang the man — or, as Ecclesiastics say, suspend him. Find us the shortest way to come to that?

SIR G. MULISH: The shortest way is certainly a rope — three yards and a half of rope. But look you here, unless the thing be done legally and formally, and gravely and deliberately, and according to the statute, I shall have no finger in it. *Putting up his folios.* No Lynching for me.

LADY D. MOORESS: The rope, I vote for the rope. I shall subscribe a quarter, to procure the rope.

LADY MULISH: It will make him kick tremendous. He has kicked some of us too much already, — *casting a knowing look at Madame Noheart* — and then, too, what horrid names he'll call: were it not better to tie up his tongue?

MADAME NOHEART: Oh aye, that's the cure. I ken how to cure hams and tongues, and tie them, jest like the folk in Glesska.

MADAME WATERSON: Should not his feet be tied, too?

LADY D. MOORESS: I vote for the rope, tongue tying, feet tying, — all the three. We must catch him and corner him up. Mind what I tell you, — We'll never be secured from his madness till he be suspended, tongue cured, and foot bound. It is not woman's way to do these things by halves.

MADAME WATERSON: But won't we shave his head first? 'Twould look humane. And you know we must not forget our sex, or what would people say?

LADY MULISH: You Madame Waterson counsel wisely, and like a female Solomon; we must not overlook the tenderness which to our sex pertains, or we shall play a losing game. I, therefore, would recommend only the tongue tying and head shaving.

MADAME WATERSON: Oh! the feet, the feet, Lady Mulish, — the feet, too, must be bound over to keep the peace.

LADY MULISH: What is Madame Noheart's opinion of the feet? She is the most competent to speak upon that point.

MADAME NOHEART: O'd! I could like the feet bro'ht in, it would heighten the effec' upon the public mind. — Everybody would shudder, and shake their heads, and cry — *"He maun be an awfu' man"!*

LADY D. MOORESS: Feet and tongue, neck, head, and hands must all be fixed. Let all be put in one rope, even as Nero wished the Romans were. Mind, I tell you nothing else will do. Take my advice, *I know how to corner him up.*

LADY MULISH: But, my dear Lady Mooress, we must look to the effect upon the public mind. If we allow our *tender feelings* to outtravel that, we go too fast. — Although we sacrifice this victim we must not loose our hold on the affections of the people; we must cherish and maintain the Kirk; we must hold fast our power and patronage. All must seem to the good simple people to be done for the honour of the Kirk.

SIR G. MULISH: Yes, you'll make a fine Kirk and a mull of it.

LADY MULISH: We intend no less, sir, than to turn this Kirk into a mill, wherein this shaven Samson may grind for our amusement.

SIR G. MULISH: O, then, you'd better put out his eyes at once.

LADY MULISH: We'll leave that to others; our business is first to *shave* him. But who will be the barber? You can *shave,* Sir George.

SIR G. MULISH: I have often *shaved.* But I always did it on my own account, and not for others.

MADAME NOHEART: I have jeest been thinking that we maun bring in the childer tae. If we could only make him appear cruel to them, it would have a great effec' in this country. For without ill usage of them, folk will wonder for what he maltreated me. They'll be ap' to think there's something awfu' bad about me, when he was so kind to everybody else.

LADY MULISH: Very shrewdly bethought, dear Madame Noheart, — We'll try to place the children on the front of our attack. But, ladies, we must decide. What shall it be?

LADY D. MOORESS: The rope.

MADAME NOHEART: Let the tongue be cured, and the feet fettered first.

MADAME WATERSON: And the head shaved.

MADAME NOHEART: An' the bairns — O min' to bring in the bairns.

SEVERAL VOICES: All, all, — the head and feet, neck, tongue, and hands,
For he has dared dispute our dread commands.

The curtain descends, amidst a confused chorus of voices.

ACT II

SCENE I

The Consistory discovered in Session — Lady Mulish in the Chair.

LADY D. MOORESS: Ladies! I hold in my hand the draft of a petition to the
venerable Delectables, which, with your permission, I shall read.

LADY MULISH: Proceed.

LADY D. MOORESS: The Prayer of the Petition is to bring our rebellious subject
before the Court of Capables, to answer for his revolt against our time-honoured
jurisdiction.

MADAME WATERSON: Precisely what we desire.

MADAME NOHEART: But a' for the guid cause.

SEVERAL VOICES: That's it!

MADAME WATERSON: Let us hear.

LADY MULISH: Go on.

LADY D. MOORESS: *Reads.*
Unto the true Delectables,
The sneaks of snob respectables,
And members of the Club of Bathurst,
Who at our shepherds many a thrust
Have deftly dealt in days gone by,
When gossips raised the hue and cry.

'Tis still with gratitude remembered
That you this church well-nigh dismembered,
Upon a former great occasion,
Incited by our soft persuasion;
When Shepherd Hogg was nicely mangled,
We only wish he had been strangled.
But now we want our Shepherd Light
Hanged up at once, and choked outright,
He's grown so haughty and unruly.
He raves and rages like a bully,
Or like a Bedlamite in bed,
Who's got a crack across his head.
Our yoke, he says, he'll not submit to;
Against us flashes out his wit, too.
Yea, he proposes to preach down
The gossip of dear Darlingtown, —*
Denies that wisdom lies in talking,
(For which, we hope, you'll send him walking,)
Denounces idleness and prattle,
Condemns the most delightful tattle;
And says such things as can't be told,
Which make our very blood run cold.
Moreover, on inquiry, you'll find,
That is, if so you have a mind,
He uses many antic tricks,
With parasols, and cups, and kicks,
Within his house, both day and night,
And puts the inmates in a fright.
These charges all we'll prove to you,
By servants, *honest, faithful, true:*
And therefore, that you may amend him,
Be pleased directly to suspend him.
This is our motto and our prayer —
Corner him up, and do not spare!
And, with the dames of the Consistory,
You'll have a place in coming history.

We are at a loss to know whether this should be Darlingtown, or Snarlingtown. Antiquaries say the latter. — Printer (1856).

LADY MULISH: It appears to me, Lady Mooress, that the subject is much too grave to be treated of in so light a style. Now, although we dearly love to laugh at the Incapables — I mean the Capables — in secret, yet we must sink every other feeling and passion, to compass and secure his overthrow, who has so openly defied our dear authority.

MADAME NOHEART: 'Od, I would think they would be a' the better pleased wi' that; it sounds nice — it jingles fine to my lug.

LADY MULISH: You mean your ear, Madame Noheart.

MADAME NOHEART: Ear or lug — it's a' the same. You'll find them baith between the twa brods o' your dictionary.

MADAME WATERSON: Madame Noheart is quite right. And, though, I, too, like the arrangement in the draft, we cannot run the risk of letting our prey escape us. I, therefore, must support the *chair*.

LADY D. MOORESS: I must say, I did calculate, that they would treat our petition with more consideration and respect, expressed in measured language, than in common prose; and I could perceive no other way in which we could so well introduce that emphatical expression — "corner him up" — which, in my opinion, is the point in which the whole pith of the prosecution will lie.

LADY MULISH: I grant you, Lady Mooress, that "corner him up" is a most forcible expression, — a most womanly expression, — nay, altogether a lady-like expression, — moreover, a most telling phrase, — it tells us how the wind blows, — yea, also, it distinctly demonstrates the direction and strength of your mental energy in the good cause. But our object now is not so much to show our parts and rhetoric, as to enforce our authority and power, as an ecclesiastical Consistory. Nay, our strength lies in our weakness — in seeming as simple as St. Salvador's aborigines, and as demure as saints. Sink all considerations, say I, to crush the wretch who will not bow to our direction, and who dares refuse to put the keys of the Kirk into our hands.

LADY D. MOORESS: I do entirely concur in what you say; but still it's my opinion that this is the best form of petition that can be drawn. I shall, therefore, put it to the vote.

LADY MULISH: Very good, my lady, I shall put it. *Takes the vote.* The motion is *for* the draft, — the amendment *against*. What say you, Madame Waterson?

MADAME WATERSON: Against the draft.

LADY MULISH: Madame Noheart?

MADAME NOHEART: Can I vote baith for and against?

LADY MULISH: O no, you must vote for either the one or the other.

MADAME NOHEART: That's queer, na; for I would like to vote for them baith.

LADY MULISH: Explain yourself, Madame Noheart; tell us what you mean.

MADAME NOHEART: I would like to vote baith for his motion and amendment. Ye see, though they move him, if they dinna amend him, it'll a' come to naething.

LADY MULISH: *In a great puzzle.*   I surely do not hear very well!

MADAME WATERSON: O yes, I see it quite well. Madame Noheart is right again. She wishes a motion that may move him out of his propriety, and mend matters so far as to make her a person of consequence, at his expense. Is not that it, Madame Noheart?

MADAME NOHEART: Something o' that sort, I suppose.

LADY MULISH: But, dear Madame Noheart, you must enable us to facilitate business, by favouring us with your vote, at present, merely — For or Against.

MADAME NOHEART: O then, I say *for* the draft.

LADY MULISH: Miss Prim Proboscis, what say you?

MISS PROBOSCIS: Against!

LADY MULISH: Lady Dowager Mooress?

LADY D. MOORESS: For!

LADY MULISH: The votes are equal. I give my casting vote against.

LADY D. MOORESS: What now is to be done?

LADY MULISH: I see no other way than to get Sir George to file an information for us to the Court of Capables, against the culprit.

ALL: Agreed! Agreed!

LADY D. MOORESS: But will Sir George be brought to this?

MADAME WATERSON: Leave *him* to *her!*   *Pointing to the chair.*

LADY MULISH: I think I know where both his strength and weakness lie;
If I don't manage him, I'll know the reason why;
I've taught some Madames how to rule their lords before,
Think not that I shall fail in mine own especial lore!

The curtain drops, 'mid a great flourish of white handkerchiefs.

SCENE II

A public road. Enter Old Mulish.

OLD MULISH: Heigh, Sirs! things are turning serious noo. I doubt I'll need to look for ither lodgings. I'm ordered to leave the house, if I say anither guid word for the minister. All must be snubbed and snuffed out, and treated like dogs, that dare stand up for justice and fair play. They withdraw their nod frae this ane, and their custom frae that ane, and turn up their nose at every ane that dares enter the church door. And now they are plotting and counter-plotting, and training little servant-girls for the witness-box. They make them go through their parts just as if they were so many play-actors. Every ane has her story by note, just as the bairns got up their catechism in my young days. They get it up just as it's put in their mouth, like spoon-meat. If ye tak' them aff their track, they're completely bewildered and bamboozled. Preserve me! Some folk wud cut aff their nose to spite their face. They're gaun a fine length, and a' for the sake o' a woman without heart, without head, without hands, — discontented in her ain house, slandering in her neighbour's house, faithless to her husband, false to her children, deceitful to everybody — a walking epitime of imposture, as ignorant as a Hottentot, as forward as a dragoon, as vain as a peacock, as fierce as a pole-cat, and with a tongue like the tails o' Samson's foxes. But whare will a' this end? I doubt —

Enter Pedestrian, behind.

PEDESTRIAN or BEADLE: What do you doubt?

OLD MULISH: I doubt — you're no' the man I took ye for.

BEADLE: What do you mean?

OLD MULISH: I mean jeest what I said.

BEADLE: Who did you take me for?

OLD MULISH: I took ye for auld Nick.

BEADLE: And you were gladly disappointed, I guess?

OLD MULISH: Not greatly, — I took you for your faither — that's a'.

BEADLE: Good day, Mr. Mulish.

Exits.

OLD MULISH: Good day, good day. There goes a fine skinfu' o' bones. That's the Beadle o' the Consistory — the eaves dropping impertinence. Had he lived in the days o' the Pillory, he would have got his lang ears cropped, and his brazen nose slit, the impertinent loon! I hae nae charity for sic twirl thooms. To curry favour wi' the women o' the Consistory he'll insult and persecute the minister. I heard that he had been busy in their service already, cajoling witnesses, and trying to entice unprincipled servant-girls to swear that white's black.

But I must travel on, or I'll be late;
This thinking makes me travel like a coach in state.

Exits.

SCENE III

Parlour in Half-house Hall. Lady Mulish discovered. Enter Sir George.

SIR G. MULISH: The minister threatens to bring you before the session.

LADY MULISH: Me before the session?

SIR G. MULISH: Yes, you and Lady Mooress.

LADY MULISH: By all the blood of all the Stewarts, if he attempt such a thing, it will be the last session he will ever hold. Him, he! what is he? who brought him here? — what did we bring him here for? — was he not appointed to the place by our patronage? — does he not hold it by our sufferance? — could not a word of mine blast him, here, elsewhere, and forever? And, pray, what am I to be brought before the session for?

SIR G. MULISH: For slander and schism.

LADY MULISH: As for the slander, I shall cause the tongues of others so to blacken him, that my slander shall seem but as the shading to their colouring; and as to the schism, there shall be none: — the church, and every member in it, shall follow me, nor shall there be three left to acknowledge his authority. This shall be accomplished, if there is invention in my head, or blood in my body, or life in my heart!

SIR G. MULISH: Be calm, my Lady, be calm. Remember that, meantime, he is the head of the session.

LADY MULISH: Head! head! head! Him head? I would his head were in a sack, and rolling down the St. Lawrence, where his wife's mutilated rich satin dress was cast.

SIR G. MULISH: But how do you know the satin dress was cast there?

LADY MULISH: I know it was — I'm sure it was — I am positive it was — 'Tis said it was.

SIR G. MULISH: But did you see that it was?

LADY MULISH: See — I see — How could I see, when it was done in midnight darkness? I have not got cat's eyes.

SIR G. MULISH: *Aside* — Nor cat's wits either.   But how do you know that it was done?

LADY MULISH: There is no doubt that it was done. It must have been done.

SIR G. MULISH: But where did you make out the must?

LADY MULISH: O pray, don't tease me about that paltry dress.

SIR G. MULISH: Paltry? — but you said it was a rich satin dress.

LADY MULISH: I said, Sir, it was a dress — a dress — a mutilated dress — a black dress, if you will, — make it anything you like — a fine thing to make a work about.

SIR G. MULISH: Nay I don't want to make a work about, nor to make anything out of it.

LADY MULISH: I thought you wished to fish it up out of the river — to see all about it.

SIR G. MULISH: How you will distort my words. — I tell you I want to know how you know that the dress was cast into the St. Lawrence.

LADY MULISH: Dear me, Sir George, when will you leave the lawyer on the bench and learn to speak like an upright and honest man?

SIR G. MULISH: Tut! tut! will you —

LADY MULISH: Will you be silent? you have put me in a fever — me before the session? I'd sooner go into my winding sheet! Hark ye, Sir, bring me out of this predicament, or you shall get your house, and church, and children, and all to manage by yourself — from this day forward and for ever.

Exits.

SIR G. MULISH: I have gone too far. I see now I must follow suit. I must fall on some scheme to take her out of this most uncomfortable position. She'll go distracted, else she will incontinently leave me. I know her indomitable force of will. This wound is to her spirit what the demon was to him called *Legion,* — no man can bind it, no not with chains. The parson's fame, ay, and his children's staff of life must both be broken. Better they than that my peace be broken. But how to effect this, and yet preserve all legal forms, — this I must find out. The laws must be complied with, or seem to be; the forms must be preserved; as for the spirit, it is as flexible as a lawyer's conscience. Conscience! What is conscience but convenience? I never yet could feel wherein they differed; —

Most men find out that they are both akin;
But he who boasts the most, has mostly least within.

Exits.

SCENE IV

Nursery in Half-House-Hall. Enter Sally, singing.

SALLY: O! who can bear

This scanty fare,
Said a nursery maid at twenty,
While down below
The cook can stow
Her gab with every dainty?

Her sweethearts, too,
Come there to woo
For her pudding, cakes, and plenty,
While not a bit,
Nor spark to sit
With me comes up to twenty.

How long shall I
Sob here and cry
For the turkies, geese, and pudding,
Where ne'er a one
In shape of man,
Puts in his nose intruding?

Do you suppose
But for his nose —
Without your heart deluding —
He in would look
To see the Cook,
Or taste her cake and pudding?

I do declare
I'll have a share
Of every good thing that's going;
Both beaus and buns,
And all that runs
To kitchen pans, so knowing.

Sing hey for the pot, sing ho for the pan —
Sing hey for the pudding and cake man!

Enter Miss Prim Proboscis.

MISS PROBOSCIS: Your name is Sally Rubknocker?

SALLY: Yes ma'am.

MISS PROBOSCIS: You were in the minister's family for some time — were you not, Sally?

SALLY: Yes ma'am.

MISS PROBOSCIS: What can you tell about the Kickings, Knockings, and other things? But you must distinctly understand that no one tells you what to say.

SALLY: No ma'am.

MISS PROBOSCIS: Well, have you seen him kick his wife?

SALLY: No ma'am. But Lady Mooress says I must have seen it, — and so ma'am I suppose I must. She told me also, that modesty was the finest feather in a young woman's cap, and that there was no truer sign of modesty than to give up my memory and judgment to those of my superior. Her Ladyship's opinion must be right — and so I wish to say what's right.

MISS PROBOSCIS: Bless me, what a wise child you are. Lady Mooress has been your friend ever since you came to this country, I believe.

SALLY: She has, ma'am.

MISS PROBOSCIS: And a friend to your sister, has she not?

SALLY: She has, ma'am. My sister has been living out with Lady Mooress for the last seven years, and it was she who sent me to the minister's, to watch and report all that occurred in the house.

MISS PROBOSCIS: And you have fulfilled your mission well, Sally, I hope?

SALLY: I would like to do whatever she desires, ma'am.

MISS PROBOSCIS: O, Sally, you are a smart girl; you will do very well; you will get on in the world. Continue to do just as my Lady Dowager wishes you, and your fortune is made. But, remember, no one told you what to say.

SALLY: O no, ma'am.

MISS PROBOSCIS: Send up Ann Limper.

SALLY: Yes, ma'am.

Exits.

MISS PROBOSCIS: That one is pretty well drilled. She has been at the right school. O what an admirable disciplinarian the Lady Dowager Mooress is!   *Enter Ann Limper.*   Come hither, Ann. You were a servant in the minister's house for some time?

ANN LIMPER: Yes, ma'am.

MISS PROBOSCIS: Where are you now?

ANN LIMPER: No place, ma'am.

MISS PROBOSCIS: Have you been in no place since you left the minister's?

ANN LIMPER: O yes, ma'am. I was in Mr. Squashups.

MISS PROBOSCIS: Squashups? Squeezeup you mean.

ANN LIMPER: Squashup or Squeezeup, — I'm not sure that's the name.

MISS PROBOSCIS: Why did you leave him?

ANN LIMPER: Because they blamed me for taking the loan of things, and forgetting to put them back again.

MISS PROBOSCIS: That is certainly a very unfortunate habit, Ann. But where were you before you went to the minister's?

ANN LIMPER: I was in Mr. Sharp's, the ancient minister's.

MISS PROBOSCIS: And why did you leave him?

ANN LIMPER: Because — O, ma'am — it is rather a delicate question.

MISS PROBOSCIS: I believe you, Ann, to be a very modest, good girl. You will suit Lady Mulish very well. *Aside,* for a month, at least. Of course, you saw the minister kick his wife?

ANN LIMPER: No, ma'am.

MISS PROBOSCIS: Well, then, you are of no use to Lady Mulish. I thought you wanted a place?

ANN LIMPER: I do, very much, ma'am.

MISS PROBOSCIS: If you can say that you saw the minister kick his wife, you shall have a good place, Ann.

ANN LIMPER: O yes, ma'am, I can say it if you wish. *Aside,* I will say to her account — not my own.

MISS PROBOSCIS: And throw a cup of tea on her?

ANN LIMPER: O yes, ma'am — tea or coffee, or anything you wish.

MISS PROBOSCIS: And call her bad names?

ANN LIMPER: O yes, ma'am, bad names.

MISS PROBOSCIS: Horrible names, names such as no well disposed person would wish to hear or to utter?

ANN LIMPER: O yes, ma'am.

MISS PROBOSCIS: Very well, Ann. You may go down stairs: keep mind of all you have said and heard.

ANN LIMPER: O yes, ma'am. I'll say to his face what I would at his back.

MISS PROBOSCIS: That's a brave girl. Send up Marjory Crucklebuck.

ANN LIMPER: Yes, ma'am.

MISS PROBOSCIS: And, Ann, remember no one told you what to say.

ANN LIMPER: O no, ma'am.

Exits.

MISS PROBOSCIS: A very creditable witness! I am only afraid that Squeezeup's house-keeper will expose Ann's peccadilloes, and impair her evidence. But let me see — Sir George will manage that. The house-keeper, and Squeezeup, too, will cower under his frown and influential patronage. *Enter Marjory Crucklebuck.* You saw a very strange scene in the minister's house once, Marjory?

MARJORY: I did.

MISS PROBOSCIS: What was that, Marjory?

MARJORY: I saw the minister lying sick on the floor of a bedroom, in great agony, with a pillow under his head, when in slipped Madame Noheart, and kicked the pillow away.

MISS PROBOSCIS: Hush! hush! Marjory. You must not speak of that. Have you seen nothing else?

MARJORY: I have.

MISS PROBOSCIS: What else, Marjory?

MARJORY: I have seen Madame Noheart bathe her face with opium liniment, and wrap it up in a napkin, and tell me to say it was caused by the minister striking her.

MISS PROBOSCIS: But, Marjory, my dear girl, don't you think she was an ill used woman?

MARJORY: She was the most indulged woman I ever seen.

MISS PROBOSCIS: But don't you think her temper was often tried?

MARJORY: No, but I think his temper was tried more than ever a man's was. Indeed, I was sometimes afeerd that her conduct would drive him out of his mind.

MISS PROBOSCIS: O, Marjory, Marjory! you must not speak of these things. You know you must be careful of Madame Noheart's character. You know it is a christian duty, Marjory, not to injure our neighbours' good name.

MARJORY: I know that, ma'am, but when I am asked —

MISS PROBOSCIS: O yes. Marjory, you are a pious young woman. You belong to the Baptist persuasion, don't you?

MARJORY: I do.

MISS PROBOSCIS: Good people, they are all. But, dear Marjory, did you never see Madame Noheart have her face wrapped up with a napkin?

MARJORY: I have, many's the time.

MISS PROBOSCIS: And why, my dear Marjory, do you think had she her face wrapped up in that way?

MARJORY: Because, in cold frosty weather, she was very afflicted with the face ache, and as I have told you, used always to be bathing it with opium liniment.

MISS PROBOSCIS: But, Marjory, did you never see any mark on her face or head?

MARJORY: I never seen any thing more than a pimple on her face; as for her head, I never heerd her complain of that.

MISS PROBOSCIS: But, Marjory, Madame Noheart says she wrapped up her face to hide the blows.

MARJORY: What blows, ma'am?

MISS PROBOSCIS: The blows she got from somebody.

MARJORY: From whom, ma'am?

MISS PROBOSCIS: Well, Marjory, you should know that best.

MARJORY: I know no body except Mr. John Frost.

MISS PROBOSCIS: You are a shrewd girl, Marjory. But did you ever see Madame Noheart rub her face with opium liniment, except after a scolding?

MARJORY: Many's the time I've seen her rub it up when the minister was from home.

MISS PROBOSCIS: But where did she get the opium?

MARJORY: She got some from Lady Mulish, and sometimes I got it out of the apothecary's for her.

MISS PROBOSCIS: But, Marjory, do you think Madame Noheart would tell a lie?

MARJORY: I don't know, ma'am.

MISS PROBOSCIS: And do you think I would tell a lie?

MARJORY: I hope not, ma'am.

MISS PROBOSCIS: And do you think Lady Mulish would tell a lie?

MARJORY: O no, ma'am, every body believes her to be a saint — and you too, ma'am.

MISS PROBOSCIS: Well, then, you surely will not set up your opinion in opposition to our opinion. You know meekness is a great virtue — a christian virtue; you surely won't place your judgment above Lady Mulish's judgment, and above my judgment, and above the Consistory's judgment?

MARJORY: O no, ma'am. I should not like to do that.

MISS PROBOSCIS: No, my dear girl, I am sure you have too much humility to do that. A proud spirit is not a right spirit, Marjory, nor a self-sufficient spirit.

MARJORY: I know that, ma'am.

MISS PROBOSCIS: Well, then, you surely will admit that you may be wrong and we may be right.

MARJORY: Certainly, ma'am.

MISS PROBOSCIS: And when your testimony is called for, you must give Madame Noheart's version of everything. Here, Marjory, here is a small present for your mother, and all your expenses shall be handsomely paid to and from Toronto. It will be delightful, Marjory, to get a trip up and down the lake this fine weather. You are living with Judge Pritchard, in Toronto, are you not?

MARJORY: Yes, ma'am.

MISS PROBOSCIS: And your mother will be so glad to see you down. Good bye, Marjory, and remember to tell everything in the most telling way. You know what I mean? Think well, Marjory, think well before you speak. And remember the story about the broken parasol, and the buckram petticoat — the child's petticoat you know, and how it was cut, and shaken in her face.

MARJORY: But she was not present.

MISS PROBOSCIS: O well, she might have been present; that is a very trivial circumstance. And don't forget the morning he ordered you to get up to get hot water to bathe his feet. I suppose he came to you in his night-gown?

MARJORY: O no, ma'am.

MISS PROBOSCIS: Now, was it not long after bedtime?

MARJORY: Yes, ma'am, it was about two o'clock.

MISS PROBOSCIS: And how could he come to you at that hour, but in undress?

MARJORY: He had just come home from a journey, and the night was bitter cold, and he was sick, and wanted hot water to wash his feet, and Madame Noheart would not rise, and —

MISS PROBOSCIS: O Marjory, Marjory, that will never do; you had better see Madame Noheart, and compare notes with her; she will recall things to your memory as they ought to be stated. And now, Marjory, you may go. Remember every thing right. We depend much upon you. Lady Mulish will look after your mother and your little blind sister — poor dear girl. *Marjory going.* But stay, Marjory, did you speak of these things to anybody?

MARJORY: I told Mrs. Sharp, the furrier's wife, that I believed Madame Noheart would put the minister out of his mind yet, — or drive him insane, — or words to that effect; and I think I said the same to Mr. Mowatt, the moulder.

MISS PROBOSCIS: O Marjory, how unfortunate! *Aside,* But I must have recourse to Sir George Mulish to bring us out of this difficulty. He can twist the inside out of an eel. *To Marjory.* Be careful, Marjory; be careful for the future; and Lady Mulish will look to your mother and sister — the dear creatures. *Exit Marjory.* Marjory's mother and her poor blind sister — we will be kind to them. — Charity covereth a multitude of sins.

If there be any wrong in what I do,
T'will make amends to hand about a tract or two.

Exit.

SCENE V

Law Office. Sir George Mulish discovered writing.

SIR G. MULISH: *Reads.* I happened to be dispensing law — *Speaks.* — I should say justice. Law and justice are the same; in theory they are one, in practice they may differ; — the winner holds them to be the same, the loser thinks they differ. Yes, justice is the better word. *Resumes revisal of his letter.* I happened to be dispensing justice in our Court of Contra when your last communication reached me. I am glad that you have taken the initiative in this prosecution; all the Ladies of the Consistory will esteem and love you the more. They will continue to you your gowns — you that have them; and to those that are without, they will doubtless supply ones. The silk will be of the best corded, and the cut, the true Geneva. But the make and quality will, of course, as is to be expected, somewhat depend upon your diligence in carrying out the wishes of the Consistory. You ask my opinion of the flagellation and of the case in general. I cannot believe anything else than that the law allows a man to whip his wife — if he confine himself to reasonable limits, and do it from pure motives, and the *pater familias spirit.* But as to the case in general, my opinion is, that the minister is forever floored in Clatterville. I am, dear Sir, Yours with great affection, George Mulish.

Reads again.

To the Delectable Sandy Sly, Convener of the Committee Inquisitorial. *Speaks.* — This last sentence strikes the nail right on the head. It will be like Tallyho!

among the hunters. They will go at him like a pack of hounds, unleashed. I know their metal; at a signal from my forefinger, they are off — through mud and mire, cross creek and swamp. I've seen them chase a boar before, and they would have caught him, too, and cut him up, but for the ungracious rescue of the Notables of Montreal. Fie upon them for that untimed lenity. I love mercy well enough, but when others mar my sport with their mercy, it is not mercy to me — but cruelty and disappointment: it robs me of my lawful prey. I am tender-hearted, too, as other men — nay, I have a woman's heart. I shed tears like any girl in her teens, if I but see a piteous sight or hear the least pathetic tale. How often, oh! how often has a novel heroine wrung tears from my relentless eyes? Mercy is my failing — the weak point in my character. But I shall work this plot more warily. I'll lead the Capables, and all the while I shall seem to be dragged into it. But here comes Squire Waterson. *Enter Waterson.* Good morning to you, Squire.

WATERSON: Good morning, Sir George. I see you are busy. I shall call again.

SIR G. MULISH: Stay, stay. I've just to seal a letter. *Seals.* What think you of this intrigue of the Consistory? They wish to oust the minister.

WATERSON: To oust him?

SIR G. MULISH: Yes.

WATERSON: Do you tell me so?

SIR G. MULISH: I tell you for a fact.

WATERSON: *Aside,* The day of my deliverance draws nigh. *To Sir George.* That is the very subject for which I called to speak with you. Do you know he requires an account of my receipts and disbursements, whilst I was treasurer.

SIR G. MULISH: Well, I see no harm in that — you know there is a motion to that effect already upon the Session Record.

WATERSON: But you must know, Sir George, my cashbook is in rather an — an unbalanced state.

SIR G. MULISH: Yes, I suppose it lost its balance ever since that Bank affair? When a man draws too much in one direction, he is very apt to lose his balance.

WATERSON: No more of that, Sir George; no more of that.

SIR G. MULISH: I cannot object to your giving count and reckoning of the kirk funds, at least. When I was treasurer every penny was as accurately debited and credited as in a merchant's ledger.

WATERSON: But who can keep accounts with you, Sir George? Look how strongly the calculating faculty is developed in your capacious head! Your comparison and acquisitiveness would be quite a study for the phrenologist.

SIR G. MULISH: Yes, my memory is good. And I understand pounds, shillings, and pence pretty well.

WATERSON: But there I am at fault. My memory is extremely treacherous, especially in cash-books.

SIR G. MULISH: That is the very reason why your entries should all bear day and date.

WATERSON: But can you not be satisfied this time with a lump-sum statement?

SIR G. MULISH: I will neither make nor mar in such a matter.

WATERSON: But, Sir George, Lady Mulish says you must befriend me in this matter.

SIR G. MULISH: O that alters the case, if she says it.

WATERSON: Yes, Sir George, she positively says it.

SIR G. MULISH: Well, then, your best course to get out of the difficulty is to join the conspiracy. The Consistory alone can undermine the minister, — and nothing else will cover you.

WATERSON: I believe it, — and I shall give it my service with all my heart. I would give ten pounds to see him bundled up and shipped to the other side of the Atlantic. I shall kick the fellow out at the door, if he ever again cross my threshold.

SIR G. MULISH: But, my dear sir, you must be cautious — you must be cautious, or you will mar all.

WATERSON: I shall, Sir George, be guided entirely by your, and her Ladyship's suggestions.

SIR G. MULISH: Well, then, I shall let you into our councils. The first step is to devise some scheme that will cause him to clear out. This will be the easiest, and best, and shortest way to deliver us out of all our troubles.

WATERSON: You speak like an oracle!

SIR G. MULISH: Yes, my muttering goes as far as another man's roar. But listen, suppose we get Madame Noheart to run off with the children? The explosion will fall like a bomb, and scatter his wits to the four winds. He will then, I expect, take French leave.

WATERSON: You fill me with admiration!

SIR G. MULISH: O, leave him to me. My model of strategy is Fabius Maximus. If I don't dodge him, may I never draw another mortgage. But the plot must work naturally and spontaneously, you perceive?

WATERSON: I see it all. It will work sweetly, and no one seem to have a hand in it but Madame Noheart alone.

SIR G. MULISH: Precisely. But should it fail, we must be able, like a skilful general, to make a safe retreat. We must have something else to fall back upon.

WATERSON: What shall that be?

SIR G. MULISH: Why, apply to the Delectables to prosecute for maltreatment of one's wife.

WATERSON: Admirable! most admirable! But will the Delectables go into it?

SIR G. MULISH: Do you see this piece of red tape? I'll twist them round my thumbs as easily as I do this. A bow from Baron Mulish, of the Court of Contra, and Chief Kimbo of the Squatter Sessions, or a dinner cooked under the superintendence of Lady Mulish, or a seat at the table of Half-house Hall, will transmute them into so many walking-sticks.

WATERSON: With which, Sir George, you may belabour him just as you have a mind. But is there any precedent in Church Courts for such a charge? and then the proof?

SIR G. MULISH: Proof? The Consistory will manage that; and as to the matter of precedent, you know everything must have a beginning. His case will be a precedent in all similar cases, — in all time to come.

WATERSON: When I hear you speak, Sir George, the thought occurs to me (pardon me if I give it utterance), that Her Majesty has lost a very great prop of the empire in not having you in her Cabinet Councils. You would find a clue to every intricacy, and a solution to every problem. But especially in the financial department, your services would be inestimable.

SIR G. MULISH: I have long held that opinion myself. But it was only my own private opinion. I never could get it worked up into public opinion. You know that stupid, tyranical thing, public opinion, is often the ruin of many a great man. It has always been a drawback on me.

WATERSON: *Aside,* O, how the yeast works! you might flatter him to cut his wind-pipe. *To Sir George.* And on other great men, as you say, Sir George.

SIR G. MULISH: But now —
Be close in this that I have told you.
Let Chrysalis-like secrecy enfold you.
Exit Waterson.   Eliza is most unfortunate in her partialities. She always comes to the rescue of vagabonds. It was through her meddling that I was tricked out of seven hundred pounds by that rascal Saunderbundle. And here is another of her partialities, — *another of the same.*
But I suppose my wisdom is to bear;
Alas! the better horse is the grey mare.

Exits.

41

ACT III

SCENE I

Back-casement, top flat in Half-house Hall. Enter Lady Mulish.

LADY MULISH: Hush! hush! the carriage waits, and all's prepar'd
  To carry Noheart and the Children off.
  Oh! how I wish that they were gone. A day
  May pass before he knows that they are off,
  For not a whisper has he heard as yet;
  His study door is locked, and he within.
  It now is morning, and before the night
  They may have driven forty miles, or more; —
  'Tis only sixty miles to Cornwall.
  Next day they easily will reach the manse
  Of Parson Queerheart. There they'll stay
  Until our man of study quits his books and runs;
  For run he must: he cannot choose but run.
  For very shame he will be off, and hide
  His head among the Rocky Mountains, or
  The crowded streets of some great city.
  He will not bide the brunt of the exposure.
  How can he stay? I know that he will run;
  For Madame Noheart has declared to me,
  A thousand times, that he would run right off,
  The very moment that she quits the house.
  What would I give to see him when the truth
  Shall flash upon his mind: he'll stand as dumb;
  Then waver; wait; then think how he will face
  The public. No, it cannot be, he must
  Decamp. Oh! how I wish that lucky Wrong
  May manage right. I've sent her there to help
  Dear Madame Noheart to get the children out.
  But here comes Lady Dowager Mooress. What news?

Enter Lady Dowager Mooress.

LADY D. MOORESS: Deplorable! Our plot has failed.

LADY MULISH: How failed?

LADY D. MOORESS: That cunning man, Robert Peerthrough,
  Who takes delight in mischief, got his ears
  But touched with some quiet rumour of our plot;
  Then down he hurries to the Minister's,
  And in he comes just at the very time

42

That lucky Wrong had seized the eldest child
To hand it out to Madame Noheart, who
Was waiting in the archway, close at hand.
At once, he snatched the boy fast by the arm,
And cries, "No, no; I know your scheme; let go
The boy: it must not be." And straight way up
The stairs he limps, and gives him to his father;
Says "If you would wish to keep your children, keep
A good look out." This roused suspicion,
And now the sleepy, studious man is up,
And rampant like a lion, nor will he
Allow the children even cross the door.
Nay storms, and vows that none shall take them out
Except they take them over his dead body.
What will we do?

LADY MULISH: Oh dear! what can we do?
That fellow Peerthrough! Oh that Peerthrough! wretch!
I'll never set a foot within his store
Again.

LADY D. MOORESS: Nor I, nor any that I know,
If I can keep them out. What shall we do?

LADY MULISH: Cut Peerthrough! Cut him dead! No notice take
If he should meet you in the street and bow.
Officious man! If he would but attend
To his own private business, and leave
The public weal to us to manage, but
Especially the Church affairs, his *till*
Would fill the faster for it, I believe.

LADY D. MOORESS: I guess so, too. But now, what shall
We do?

LADY MULISH: What can we do? What can we do without
Sir George? 'Tis most perplexing to perceive
We can't get on without a man.

LADY D. MOORESS: 'Tis so.

LADY MULISH: We must assemble the Consistory,
Immediately to deliberate.

LADY D. MOORESS: I will go and tell the Beadle to give notice.

LADY MULISH: Ay, do, dear Lady Mooress. What trouble
Obstructs our path, before we can suspend
This man. Oh! if we had him once secured!
Confound all dilatory forms, say I.

LADY D. MOORESS: Amen! and thrice amen! is my reply.

LADY MULISH: Oh! would they but give us his ordeal.

LADY D. MOORESS: We would administer a cordial.

LADY MULISH: That would be balm unto our wounded hearts.

LADY D. MOORESS: And heal the rankling anger here, that smarts.

They exit, laying their hands on their hearts.

SCENE II

The Consistory in Session. Lady Mulish in the Chair.

LADY MULISH: You all have heard, dear friends, of our mishap;
This monster whom we hunt has foiled our toils;
Our net is broken through, and he's not caught.
What shall we do? Dear Madame Noheart now
Has not a home: she left it yesterday.
She has become an exile from her home —
A voluntary exile for our cause.
We must not cast her off, when she has done
Such signal service to the general weal.
What say you, Lady Dowager Mooress?

LADY D. MOORESS: I guess that Madame Noheart must abide
With me; until, at least, we get our prey
Right cornered up. I'll give her my best room:
There she may sleep at ease, and rise betimes.
There she needs fear no razors, nor the whip,
With which, she publicly avers, her life
Perpetually was haunted. Nor shall tea —
Except of very weak infusion —
For which you, Ladies, know my board is famed —
Be given to hurt her nerves, which must be braced
Up tight to meet her coming catechism,
Which soon, I hear, she must prepare to say.
The Capables have sat, and their Committee
Inquisitorial will soon be here,
To take her statement down in black and white.
I hear that those appointed to this work
Are three most trusty men, and notable;
Devoted to the cause. Their names are John
Morine, and Sandy Sly, and Billy Bone,
All champions of Matrimony; nay

The very Dons of Woman's rights supreme;
Who rather would upset the Church, and turn
A house right upside down: yea, drive a man
To beggary, than that a wife should not
Be lord and master in her own quiet house;
And rule, and turn her husband like a snipe, —
Just as the vane is by the changing wind.
When they have come, and catered up our tales,
Then we will screw him up, I guess. Meantime,
I wish to know, how stands the evidence?
Has Miss Prim Proboscis got that put right?

MISS PROBOSCIS: Permit me, Ladies, to report, that I
Have had the witnesses all precognosced.
I think they will acquit them well, and that
Without a blush. They hold their heads so nice,
And look so simple, that you would suppose
They never had an ill thought in their heads.
And, as for steadiness and drill, they would
Outface a regiment of dragoons. But still
I trust, Sir George will marshall them again,
And keep them under cover at the time,
And all the time they are in action.

MADAME WATERSON: I move that this report be now sustained;
And also that a vote of thanks be given
To dear Miss Prim Proboscis, for her care
And diligence in getting up the proof.

ALL: Agreed! agreed!

LADY MULISH: But here come visitors.   *Enter Sir George Mulish and Squire Waterson.*

SIR G. MULISH: Success, at last, is sure; — the Capables
Have served him with a libel. Now the whole
Depends on you, and your witnesses.

ALL: We thank you from the bottom of our hearts.

LADY MULISH: Be well assured, Sir George, we shall not fail;
We've drilled our damsels so, that, by your help,
We think they may be risked to testify
Against our proud and dexterous rebel.

LADY D. MOORESS: But you, Sir George, must play the guardian;
And, like a faithful watch-dog, bark and howl
Whenever you perceive the fox approach;
Our tender chickens else may flutter up,
And get their borrowed plumes a little ruffled.

SIR G. MULISH: Oh! I will watch him, if they only let
Me take my seat as member of the club.

WATERSON: *In great trepidation.*   But can there be a doubt of that, Sir George?

SIR G. MULISH: Some doubt. You see my membership expired
At the rising of the last great council.
If, therefore, I be not anew elected,
I have no legal title to a seat.

WATERSON: If you, Sir George, should be excluded, I
Tremble for the consequences.

SIR G. MULISH: *Aside,* And well you may.

MADAME WATERSON: Oh, dear Sir George, you must be there. You must.

SIR G. MULISH: I must and shall, if in my power; and yet
The practice in the Parent Church is clear;
Which practice, if they knew, would keep me out.
But here the council have no law specific
Upon this point. And if the doors are shut,
I think I may cajole the Capables
To gloss it over, and let me hold my seat.

WATERSON: I thought, Sir George, that your authority,
On points of law, would set aside all forms?

SIR G. MULISH: It will among the Capables, in civil law;
But then, their Ordinances Ecclesiastical
Are independent; as in their Records shown,
If only they had wit to look them up.
But most of them have got as much knowledge
Of their Church-laws as I have got of Greek.
Their ignorance allows me room to play
Upon their grave and pompous wisdomships.
But wherefore should you fear? You may depend
They have the will to screw him up as well
As you; and *where there is a will,* you know
There is a way.

WATERSON: Most true, Sir George, most true.

SIR G. MULISH: Already they have threatened, to his face,
"*We will take the majesty out of you.*"
Cheer up, they're all with us.

LADY MULISH: Oh it revolts
My very heart, the bare idea of being
Subjected to his cross-questioning.
I'll not endure it!

LADY D. MOORESS: Nor yet shall I.

MADAME WATERSON: Nor I.

SIR G. MULISH: Hush! hush! You must.

TRIO: We wont.

SIR G. MULISH: You must, I say,
  If you would have your victim pinioned up.
  Just listen here — *Enter Beadle.*

BEADLE: The Capables are come.

SIR G. MULISH: They are? Come now then, Ladies, fall to work;
  Screw up your courage; get all your forces
  Marshalled. Keep an eye upon the girls,⌢
  Have them ready at a moment's warning.
  Cheer up their spirits; — keep them close. Let none
  Have access to them, nor speak with them,
  Till I have got them snug beside my elbow,
  Before the Court of Capables.
  I'm off. *Exits.*

MADAME WATERSON: Oh, dear me, how my heart flutters.

LADY D. MOORESS: Mine leaps
  For joy! Now we shall have him cornered up.

WATERSON: Oh! Ladies, do your duty, like brave men;
  My peace, my safety, sanctity, and all,
  Is in your custody. Oh cast your *aegis.*
  Like Minerva, over me! *adieu! Exits.*

LADY MULISH: I must, dear friends, dissolve our meeting now.
  Keep secret, and keep cool. And let us vow
  By heart and hand, and as we hold our breath,
  We part, to meet in victory or death! *They exit.*

SCENE III

The Vestibule of Consistory Pavilion. Enter Old Mulish.

OLD MULISH: Oh! what a trial! Trial, did I say?
  It is a sham, the greatest sham that e'er
  Was played before the face of man, — a farce
  A solemn farce, — a mockery of justice;

47

A foul conspiracy to blast the name
And reputation of an upright man;
An envious machination of the Presters
To pull him down and cast him to the dust,
Because he is a brighter and a better man
Than they. Oh! it is the story of Joseph
And his brethren enacted once again.
The brethren from envy sell their brother.
Not that alone — they open wide the door
For every female Potipher to bring
A lying charge against his innocence;
And now, with all their suppleness and shams,
They see that they are likely to be foiled.
And so, at once, they cut the evidence
For the defence abruptly off, — adjourn to Perth,
Full forty miles from this, and advertise
Him, that if he would have his cause heard out,
He must produce his witnesses out there;
And failing that, they shall proceed to judgment.
Oh! bare-faced juggle! oh! wretched shift! Who
Can take a witness there? Not one will go!
There's no constraint — they are unpaid. A club
Of untamed savages had shown more mercy.
Nay, more discretion and more business-like
Procedure would be found among a tribe
Of Caffres. Fy! Oh fy! It will alight
Upon themselves — else God and justice sleep.
Preserve me from the mercies of such men,
And from the power of women in their rage.

Enter Lady Mulish.

LADY MULISH: Well, father, now you're satisfied, I hope?

OLD MULISH: I am satisfied.

LADY MULISH: I am glad to find
    That you have found your error out at last.

OLD MULISH: But stop! I'm satisfied that you have done
    What never can be undone; — what may cost
    You many a sigh and many a pang;
    Ay, and alas! your children too! Yes them!
    For this goes deeper than you think. You've struck
    The sceptre — the parental sceptre, from
    Your own frail grasp, and broke it in your rage,
    When you struck him who bore the moral rule.
    You've satisfied your rage — but at a cost
    For which you should not have brought the world,
    Had it been offered you at such a price.

LADY MULISH: Stop father, stop, — you over-rate the cost,
One minister is sacrificed — that's all.

OLD MULISH: That's all! That were enough, if that were all;
But that's not all — you'll find that you have sapped
The foundations of society itself:
I'm satisfied that you have brought yourselves
Much obloquy, and the church much damage.

LADY MULISH: Tush! tush! We soon will put the church to rights.
Give us a preacher to our mind, and then —

OLD MULISH: A preacher to your mind? was ever man
So great a favourite with you Ladies
As this man was, when first he came among you?

LADY MULISH: O that, indeed. But why should he be set
To rule the Church, who cannot rule his house?

OLD MULISH: A monstrous speech! He tries to rule his house,
And in you step, and cry out — No, oh, no,
He shall not rule his house, but as we please.
His very children must not be chastised
But as we shall prescribe the how and when:
Nay, we shall rule his house as well as rule
The church. And so you baffle his attempts
To rule. You say, "Here keep the waters in;"
And still you lift the sluice to let the waters out.
O wisdom most profound! O sophistry
Of subtlest essence! If a Man had uttered
Such a speech, he surely would have grown
Again, at once into a boy, — nonage;
Purility itself would be ashamed of it.

LADY MULISH: You take it, father, far too seriously.
How often have I heard you blame our sex
For fickleness. How should you think it strange
That we should be a little fickle in
Our preacher? But for once?

OLD MULISH: Nay — not for once,
My Lady! say for twice, thrice, ay four times.
Was not your cousin Comble glad to get
Away? Was Crookedlegs not jilted too?
And did you not attempt to bundle up
That good man Hogg, as if he were a bale
Of cotton, ay, and pack him right away
To Liverpool *via* New York? — And now
This is the fourth you send right face about.

LADY MULISH: *Aside* — I do declare he is a stubborn mule.

Why should I speak to him? It but provokes
And ruffles up my temper to hear him talk.

Enter Beadle with a letter.

BEADLE: A letter for my Lady Mulish.

LADY MULISH: From Perth?
Oh! this is news indeed — so soon? Welcome!
So! — they have made quick work with him at last.
Go, call together the Consistory.

Beadle Exits.

LADY MULISH: *Reads.* Dear Lady Mulish,
Permit me to lay my duties at your feet.

OLD MULISH: *Aside* — He would lay his head there to please her.

LADY MULISH: The man whom you hated with so good a cause —

OLD MULISH: *Aside* — without a cause —

LADY MULISH: — has now received a mortal wound, and is suspended, *Sine Die.*

OLD MULISH: *Aside* — A desperate sin.

LADY MULISH: He now will trouble you no more —

OLD MULISH: *Aside* — He'll haunt you while you live.

LADY MULISH: Your protege, Squire Waterson, is safe.

OLD MULISH: *Aside* — Not quite so safe as you think.

LADY MULISH: We have seized the Session Records —

OLD MULISH: *Aside* — To hide what? —

LADY MULISH: — and at our earliest opportunity will expunge the blots.

OLD MULISH: *Aside* — The blots will not come out; you'll only make them bigger.

LADY MULISH: Both you and Lady Dowager Mooress shall now escape exposure
before the Session —

OLD MULISH: *Aside* — But not before the world.

LADY MULISH: Pray remember our gowns —

OLD MULISH: *Aside.* Send him a petticoat.

LADY MULISH: — and we shall be forever bound to you.

OLD MULISH: *Aside.* Bound to her apron-strings.

LADY MULISH: Your children will reap the blessed fruits of this transaction.

OLD MULISH: *Aside.* Ay, that they will!

LADY MULISH: Rejoice, therefore, and be exceeding glad, for all will now be hushed.

OLD MULISH: *Aside.* A calm before the storm.

LADY MULISH: We deliver him up now to your tender mercies.

OLD MULISH: *Aside.* Then heaven have mercy on him!

LADY MULISH: His body you may dispose of as to you may seem most meet.

OLD MULISH: *Aside.* You may well give up the body, when you have destroyed his soul.

LADY MULISH: But we would recommend that you should deposit him, as soon as possible, in Coventry.

OLD MULISH: *Aside.* Which, like Westminster Abbey, holds the remains of many a good and great man.

LADY MULISH: Farewell.

OLD MULISH: *Aside.* So say I, too — Farewell —

Exits.

LADY MULISH: With best wishes for your welfare, I am, dear Lady Mulish, Yours, in bands and gown, Billy Bone, Clerk of the club of Bathurst.

Dear Bone! Oh, how this will rejoice the hearts
Of my dear sisters of the Consistory.
Their faces now will wear a sweeter smile,
Their limbs a more elastic step, their hearts
A lighter throb, their eyes a brighter glance,
Their brows a smoother aspect. Here they come!

They enter in solemn procession, carrying a litter, upon which is laid the body of the victim.

LADY D. MOORESS: Rejoice, dear friends, rejoice, and sing a song
Of triumph! Sing! for this day crowns our toils,
And well rewards our struggles in the cause
Of feminine intrigue and sweet revenge.

LADY MULISH: This is, indeed, a day of victory.
　　We meet to sing the requiem of a man
　　Whom once we loved, whom now we hate; whose voice
　　Has often sounded sweetly in our ear,
　　But never fell upon our heart. That's past.
　　Forget it all, nor more remember him;
　　Nor let his shadow haunt our waking thoughts
　　Or sleeping dreams. Our motto now is kill!
　　So perish all who dare resist our will.
　　Strike up the chant, and let our hearts rejoice.
　　His head is low, — and silent is his voice.

They sing the following chant.

THE CHANT TO PAEAN

　　Sing! mortals, sing! — the victim now is seized;
　　Hush! furies, hush! — your rage shall be appeased.
　　We've caught him, and him *cornered up,* —
　　We've hitched him, and him haltered up, —
　　Draw forth from your sheaths,
　　Strike him while he breathes!
　　We've bound him, and suspended him,
　　Spite of the hearts that defended him:
　　We thought it would have ended him,
　　But still he breathes!

　　Strike! females, strike! — his heart must now be crushed:
　　Pull it out, pull! — his tongue, too, must be hushed;
　　Nor word of defence must he speak.
　　Bind him down, like the dead, lest he squeak.
　　And pierce through our wiles,
　　Or denounce our guiles.
　　We have raised a famous *fama*-sound,
　　We have cast his honour to the ground;
　　We have him now forever bound, —
　　But still he smiles!

　　Up! women, up! — lay well about the brain:
　　Hoorah! dames, hwoor!* — the victim's now insane, —
　　Tis better this than he were slain, —
　　His blood on us will leave no stain.
　　But look how he laughs!
　　And the free air quaffs!
　　We've struck his head, we've struck his heart,
　　Expended all our female art,
　　But still his life will not depart, —
　　For see, — he laughs!

An interjection used by the North American Indians when scalping an enemy.

Cheer! matrons, cheer! — let him run if he will:
Slander, tongues! squirt! — slander him your fill!
Stands he yet this battery of tongues?
Alas! he is proof against our lungs!
Find some other hands
To do our commands:
For after all that we have done,
We find our work is but begun:
We thought, at least, he would have run;
But still he stands!

Help! Presters, help! — there's nothing now but to choke:
Hand here the rope! This would the saints provoke,
That we can't kill him as we wish to,
Without showing our fingers in the dish too:
Or our brazen beaks —
Or our crimson cheeks —
For, after many a horrid blow,
See signs of life still in him show:
He moves — he strikes — he kicks — looks — lo!
At last he speaks!

Here the mangled body of the victim rises and scatters the Consistory.

Finis.

Dolorsolatio

A Local Political Burlesque

By Sam Scribble

Montreal: John Lovell, Printer, St. Nicholas Street, 1865.

A PERTINENT QUESTION

MRS. BRITANNIA, "IS IT POSSIBLE, MY DEAR, THAT YOU HAVE EVER GIVEN YOUR COUSIN JONATHAN ANY ENCOURAGEMENT?"

MISS CANADA, "ENCOURAGEMENT! CERTAINLY NOT, MAMMA. I HAVE TOLD HIM WE CAN *NEVER* BE UNITED."

DRAMATIS PERSONAE

Grandpapa Canada	
Master East	*his son, a gentleman of French education*
Master West	*younger son of Canada, an overgrown boy*
Quebec	*"the fast," a specimen of Young Canada*
Kingston	*"the slow," a very old boy*
London	*a blighted being*
Mr. Abe North, Mr. Jefferson South	*Two noisy neighbours*
Santa Claus	*everybody's friend*
Montreal	*a fashionable young lady*
Toronto	*a young lady with a very good opinion of herself*
Ottawa	*a young lady scarcely "out"*

SCENE I

A Passage — Doors in flat, marked, left to right, Quebec, Montreal, Ottawa, Hamilton, Toronto, Kingston, London. A large stocking hanging from each door. Fireplace, R. Placards "Golden Bitters," etc. on Flat. Music. Enter Santa Claus, very stealthily from chimney, R. He carries a variety of toys.

SANTA CLAUS: Don't be alarm'd — I'm not a burglar, tho'
Appearance is against me, as I know,
And such an entrance is unique no doubt;
I'm like John A, — you *cannot* keep me out!
In fact I'd enter, for I make so free,
Uncle Tom's Cabin e'en without the key;
And yet unlike the usual thief you'll find me, —
I come and go, but leave 'the swag' behind me, —
Yearly I visit, with deserved impunity,
What the press calls the Juvenile Community —
But yet to leave such playthings here I'm loath,
For here are children of a larger growth,
Looking at names on doors, Placards etc.
Who'd scarcely be content with toys like these
If I may *argue* by *the premises!*
Rapid music, which continues till the end of scene. Santa Claus goes towards Quebec's door. Pulls toy Locomotive, labelled "International Railway" out of bag, and places it in stocking on Quebec's door.
First, here's the Railway, which, with Federation,
Will make you capital of this new nation!
Same business at Montreal's door — placing toy soldiers in Montreal's stocking.
And what for you, Montreal? ah! yes! of course

Here 'ud be a help towards your Active Force!
Same business at Ottawa's door placing bricks in Ottawa's stocking.
Miss Ottawa, you're *rayther* in a fix
With your new buildings, here's a *box of bricks!*
I hope you'll use them.
Going to Hamilton's door.
Ah! you've come to grief!
Poor boy! Well, here's "Municipal Relief."
Places bag labelled "Municipal Relief" into Hamilton's stocking. There is a large hole in stocking, bag falls through.
There's something rotten in the state — 'tis shocking
To see such carelessness!
Places bag in again — bag falls through as before. Santa Claus taking stocking from door and advancing.
Why, *darn* that stocking!
Showing stocking to audience.
It seems the constable he has out run,
And put his foot in it, — more ways than one.
Going to Toronto's door.
Toronto!
Feels in bag — Cock crows — Santa Claus starts melodramatically.
Ah! my senses feel a shock!
That summons from the early village C — *rooster!*
I'm a night bird, and so when once I hear
That matutinal *rooster's chant I clear!*
Chord. Santa Claus sinks down trap centre.

SCENE II

Interior of Grandpapa Canada's House. Grandpapa Canada discovered.

CANADA: Heigho! the time runs on, and yet I'm told
I'm better looking, now I'm growing old,
And hale and hearty, though I've lately found
My *constitution* is by no means sound —
And sure enough my troubles are unceasing,
When my small family keeps on increasing:
My sons are two fine boys, and yet I see
With sorrow that the lads don't quite agree,
The elder's all French polish, but the other
'Bosses' his Pa, and quarrels with his brother! —
And then, to add to all my cares and labours,
My rest is broken by two noisy neighbours,
Who over there make such a great to-do,
As if there was not room enough for two!

But, thank my stars! as the shop-keepers say
There's *"no connection with across the way!"*
But ah! here comes the child I love to spoil,
My western angel!
*Enter Master West, right, drawing Ottawa on sleigh. He leaves Ottawa at back,
who plays with bricks that were placed in stocking in Scene I.*
               Yes! I smell coal oil! —
My precious darling, how you have grown!
*They embrace — during the embrace enter Master East, left. — Tableau — East
looks at the others, à la Paul Pry.*

EAST: By Gar!
   Ve interrupt him!

WEST: How d'ye do, Papa!
   I'm pretty spry, I guess — but don't you think
   Common politeness would suggest a drink?

CANADA: *to East* Mon cher, you're rather late —

EAST: *C'est vrai* — you know
   Dat Grand Tronk Railway is so goddam slow —

CANADA: *Seeing Ottawa.*   And Ottawa? where is she? in disgrace? —

WEST: No — in the background — that's her proper place.

EAST: *Mon cher, vous avez,* what d'ye call it, reason: —

Enter Quebec, left, on a Toboggan.

QUEBEC: The compliments, dear governor, of the season —

CANADA: Gracious! you've made me jump!

QUEBEC: The fun's immense. I
   have just tobogganed down from Montmorenci!
   Our winters all the best of sport provide —
   All day I *skate,* —

WEST: And let your business *slide!*

QUEBEC: *Showing toy from stocking in Scene I.*
   Look what I've got, aint *the* a pretty toy!

WEST: It may do some day, but not yet, my boy!
   Talking of playthings, let my youngster show
   Her box of bricks.

Brings Ottawa down to centre, Ottawa tries to build, but the bricks always fall down.

QUEBEC: Well! here's a pretty go!
  Whoever thought a serious game like that
  Could be well understood by such a brat!
  Just let me try *my* hand —

Quebec advances — West interposes — and pushes Ottawa out right.

WEST: You'd like to bone
  Those buildings — never mind — she'll hold her own —

Lugubrious music. Enter Kingston, very feebly.

CANADA: And here comes Kingston — you look sad, what is it?

KINGSTON: I've not recovered yet the Prince's visit —
  I'm old, used up, and stupid, and in short
  I'm scarcely now, I may say, worth a thought.
  They call me slow.

WEST: And your appearance may
  Be held to justify what people say —

Sleigh bells outside.

CANADA: More visitors I guess — d'ye hear the bells?

Enter Montreal and Toronto, right.

QUEBEC: Toronto! and Montreal — and ar'nt they swells!

TORONTO: *To Canada.*   How well you look —

CANADA: My dears, and as for you,
  I scarcely know who's prettier of the two!

MONTREAL: Who Grandpapa, without of doubt a particle,
  I, Montreal, am *the* superior article!

TORONTO: You're well enough — in many ways you shine —
  But your appearance don't come up to mine —

MONTREAL: Appearance! yours! I laugh at such pretence —
  I've got the *Dollars!*

TORONTO: And I've got *the sense!*
  So I'll not quarrel.

WEST: That's well said, my dear;
  For even Politicians now appear
  To hit it off, and one don't know a bit
  Whether a man's Conservative or Grit!

59

CANADA: My boy, the moral to yourself apply,
And love your brother —

WEST: Love? that's all my eye!
I'll do as I darn please, because I choose —
I never could a-bear them *parlez-vous!*

EAST: *Getting angry. Dis donc, mon frère* —

WEST: Ding-dong! Say, no Sirree!
I won't be bullied — ain't this country free?
Your tight French cut no longer suits my figure,
For though you're older yet I'm much the bigger,
And growing still, although so stout of limb!
Look on this picture —

WEST: *Turning round and showing patches. He has out-grown his clothes to a
ridiculous extent — pointing to East, who is now very angry.*
And then look on him!
Look at my jacket — it would be a feat
If I could only make *the two ends meet* —
But yet extravagance is not my taste:
No one accuses me of any *waist.*
I thrive, whilst *he* remains in *statu quo* —
I'm sorry for him —

EAST: You take care, *mon gros* —
I knock you in de middle of next week! —

WEST: You will, by jingo! take that for your cheek!

*Boxes East's ears — they fight — the other characters form a ring, — Canada in great
agitation.*

CANADA: My goodness gracious! children, I observes
You've little thought for my paternal nerves!
My darling boys — *Fight renewed.*
But 'tis in vain I ask it —
East gets the worse of the fight.
Again he's got it in his dear bread basket!
Hit him! *Fight renewed.*
No! Stop them! I must not forget to!
East's teeth are knocked out.
There go his teeth! 'twas such a pretty *set too!*
Combatants are separated.

QUEBEC: There's no use fighting any more I see —
You've not yet fixed upon your Referee!

CANADA: My darlings, let's agree, for so we ought
Fighting at any rate is not our *forte!*

You silly boys let each concede a point: —
To East.   What matter if your nose *is* out of joint!

QUEBEC: Where's London? and that boy they call *th' Ambitious!*
Young Hamilton?

WEST: He's in a state most piteous —
And can't afford to leave the wretched place he has,
Although he's just escaped a *'fieri facias'* —
But London's coming, so he said, though he,
Poor *Forest City,* too, is *up a tree!*
And here he comes —   *Enter London.*

QUEBEC: He's seedy past belief —

LONDON: That's true for you — I've come to awful grief! —

KINGSTON: Cheer up! of kindness I will not be chary!
I'll lodge you in my Peniten*tiary!*

LONDON: Time was when I was happy by comparison,
But *now* what's life to me without my Garrison!
O for those happy days — when truth to tell,
I thought with reason that I was a swell,
Above all envy, and secure from doubt
That man of woman born could cut me out! —
But now, what Volunteers can e'er restore
The Military pride I've known of yore?
What care in collars now? what choice in suits?
What charm in waistcoats? or what pride in boots?
Old Rye's a mockery to soothe my grief,
Gin Cocktails even fail to bring relief,
And fevered thoughts come through me with a throb.
Can it be true they think that I'm a Snob? —

Noise of fighting at back.

TORONTO: Why, goodness! what's that most unseemly riot?

CANADA: It's our neighbours who will *not* keep quiet;
They're both big fellows, — tolerably strong, —
Don't hit much, but they keep it up too long, —

MONTREAL: Stop them.

CANADA: Of that indeed I've no intention,
They'd not appreciate my intervention! —

MONTREAL: A   wretched   state   of   things!   —   but   there's   no   doubt
There's nothing for them but to fight it out!

CANADA: What with their Telegrams and all the rest of it,
    One never knows who really has the best of it!
    For, when they seize each other's goods and chattels,
    One claims the Victories, t'other wins the Battles!
    And so the War grows fierce, their hatred double —
    Sometimes indeed I fear they'll give me trouble.
    So you, my children, must be smart as aiders
    In case we're troubled any more with *Raiders:*
    If Britain fails us then we come to grief —

WEST: Nonsense! you've Radway ready for Relief!
    But surely if our neighbours break the peace
    The Britishers won't grudge us their Police!

EAST: *Dis donc* — they'd better learn to curb their temper, or
    I'll be obliged to call in the French Emperor!

WEST: *That* to the States would be a perfect cure!
    Napoleon he would *bone a part,* that's sure! —

CANADA: My dears, take warning, as I hope you will —
    Think of their Taxes, — there's a *bitter Pill,*
    And hard to swallow —

WEST: Yes — such Pills give warning,
    There'll be a *Draft* most likely in the morning!

TORONTO: And all this row, I think I've hit the mark,
    Is 'bout the *Niggers.*

WEST: Keep that subject dark —
    What may turn out 'tis difficult to say,
    Although, I guess 'twill all come right some day —

CANADA: But of an end there seems no hope.

WEST: Not any,
    They're fighting like those two cats in Kilkenny!
    Their *late election* is as bad as may be,
    For still their *Alphabet* begins with A B!
    In vain of smartness now they raise the cry,
    There's *Lincoln green* too clearly in their eye!

Noise of fighting at back.

LONDON: Ah! there's a row! and so I vote for one,
    We're off at once, my boys, to see the fun!

CANADA: Agreed! but stay! I fear that this admission
    May pr'aps be construed into *Recognition!* —
    I'm strictly neutral! and my feelings smother!
    I hate one side! and can't a-bear the other!

I'll stay at home!

WEST: At home! what's that you say?
At any rate you're bound to see fair play!

Air: Billy Taylor.

LONDON: So off we go! There's a row I tell you!
Such a bully fight you will shortly see!
Come along, old cuss!

CANADA: Well! I will, young fellow!
Canada is the boy to enjoy a spree!

Repeat in chorus, and they all exit right dancing off in couples — Kingston by himself, in rear.

SCENE III

Gardens of Grandpapa Canada's House — Palings at back centre, villa left centre. Rapid music — enter all the characters, right, hurriedly — noise of fighting at back.

CANADA: Ah! here they are! by jingo! here's a tussle!
Stand back, you boys, and let them show their muscle!

Great noise of fighting outside — Enter centre, knocking down paling, Mr. A. North, and Mr. J. South, fighting down to front — Tableau.

LONDON: Bully for you!

QUEBEC: By jingo! ain't this prime?

TORONTO: I'll back the old 'un —

MONTREAL: I the young 'un —

CANADA: Time!

Combatants glare at each other fiercely, right centre and left centre — characters forming ring, Canada, centre.

CANADA: Not in my house! I won't have such marauders
Spoiling my garden, trampling on my borders!

Combatants glare at each other — they appear as if about to fight, but don't.

MR. SOUTH: I'll gouge him, that's a fact!

MR. NORTH: Snakes! there's a figure!

MR. SOUTH: You tarnal Yank!

MR. NORTH: You everlasting Nigger!

Same business, after which Mr. North and South skedaddle in opposite directions.

CANADA: I tell you what, this sort of thing won't do —
   We all must stick together —

KINGSTON: Yes, that's true —
   And get those palings mended —

CANADA: So I will.

WEST: And say, old cuss, you'd better learn your drill!

CANADA: But then this *soldiering* does so enlarge
   My bills —

WEST: Then you must learn *to stand the charge.*
   We're not so weak as every one supposes,
   Besides we now may count on the Blue Noses;
   We'll stand our ground, and laugh at ev'ry threat —
   The New York *Herald* never scared us yet.
   Now then let's liquor —

Santa Claus rises through trap, centre, as a quack doctor.

SANTA CLAUS: May I be allowed,
   Altho' a stranger here, to treat the crowd?

CANADA: And who are you?

SANTA CLAUS: Well, sir, first let me state,
   I've dined, and that I'm not a *Delegate!*
   I've heard with grief that you have long been ailing,
   In fact I'm told your *constitution's* failing —
   I'm the great Doctor, Santa Claus — *N.B.*
   Advice Is Gratis, — I'm above a fee —
   Giving his card.
   Here's Soothing Syrup, whose effect's immense!
   An instantaneous cure for fifteen cents!
   Offering bottle to West.
   Here's a Pain Killer, when the pain is crushing!
   And Pills to stop *involuntary blushing!*
   Offering Pills to Quebec.
   The Fragrant Sozodont! a nostrum new,
   And recommended to those gents what chew!

It gives new fragrance to the breath, I know!
Throw out your *plugs,* and try this *quid pro quo!*
Same business.
Ready Relief! I can with safety boast,
Which cures a stomach-ache, if sent by Post! —
Same business.
To all Dyspeptics quite a welcome treat!
And "Golden Bitters" I may add, *en suite!*

WEST: But all these things no more such puffing need —
Look at our palings — you may run and read,
When now each wall its pet prescription owns
A sanitary sermon in the stones —

SANTA CLAUS: True! these are trifles! you've been ill so long
I'd better try a med'cine far more strong!
Delays are dangerous! my advice is haste —
Showing a Demijohn labelled "Dolorsolatio."
DOLORSOLATIO! would you like to taste!
This remedy is new, but most expedient,
And "Federation" is the sole ingredient!
Takes out cork, and pulls out paper marked "Federation" — Tableau.
Take a long pull and you'll not fail to think
It is a most insinuating drink.
Gives bottle to Canada.

CANADA: A pleasant tipple! — and uncommon sound!   *Drinks.*

WEST: Drink fair, old cuss, and pass the bottle round.
Here's luck! gents all, and ladies!   *Drinks.*

MONTREAL: Yes, but stop:
You'll spare the ladies just a leetle drop?   *They all drink.*

ALL: We're all much better.

SANTA CLAUS: Then I need not stay.
There's nothing more for *me* to do — good day.

CANADA: One moment, pray don't let your favours cease,
You've stopped *our fighting;* now *conclude the piece!*

SANTA CLAUS: Nonsense! why you, since you're no longer weak,
Must for yourself henceforward learn to speak.

CANADA: D'you think I could? Well, really I must doubt it,
I've had such help, I now can't do without it —
I think, to save me from too great confusion!
Our friends had better draw their own *conclusion!*

Pause — Canada is pushed forward.
Kind friends, — for you're all friends that here I see;

WEST: Pitch it in strong, old Guv'nor, like McGee!

CANADA: *To Audience — advancing.*
You've seen how I've been cured, — to make me stand
Firm in my new resolve, give me *your hand!*
I see you will — then you approve — that's certain —
Thank you! now then, blue fire! and down the curtain!

Curtain half down — Music, piano: The Cure, then crescendo, Characters keeping time to symphony.

SANTA CLAUS: *Speaking through music.*   One moment —
Curtain up.
There's one duty yet before us!
We're bound, of course, to finish with a chorus!

Finale: The Cure

CANADA: To melody appropriate
(Though out of breath, I'm sure,)
Allow me once again to state,
I've found the perfect cure!
The Cure! the Cure! O yes! the Cure!
Then our success is sure!
If friends but say that our new play
Is the only perfect Cure!

Repeat in chorus — Dance by characters.

Curtain.

Santiago

A Drama in Five Acts

By Thomas Bush

Toronto: Published by Rollo & Adam, Publishers
Printed by Alex Lawson & Co., King Street, Hamilton, 1866.

DRAMATIS PERSONAE

Archbishop of Santiago	
The Pope's Nuncio	
Urangos, Costello, Fargo, Castanos	*Priests*
Vampries	*the Stranger*
Norman, Roland, Cloudon	*Foreign Residents in Santiago*
Mercedos, Cortez	*Chief Citizens*
Credulos	*a Spanish Traveller*
Diaz, Gorman	*Reporters*
Treacher, Avero, Gripos	*Robbers of the Cordilleros*
Sheeram	*a Jew*
Scran	*an Irish Tavern-keeper*
Crapo	*and other servants at the Arch Episcopal Palace*
Madam Mercedos	
Maria, Susannah	*her Daughters*
Sundry other persons, subordinates	

ACT I

SCENE I

A Shelf of Rock in the Andes. Snowy Peaks and a Volcano in the Distance. Enter Treacher and Credulos.

TREACHER: Look, senor, here it is — a chosen spot,
   To which I introduce the favoured few
   Deemed worthy th' indulgence.

CREDULOS: You've laid on me a thousand obligations.

TREACHER: Your honour's words have paid a thousand fold
   For leaving the highway. Lo! Senor's eye
   May take its fill at this clear font of vision.

CREDULOS: 'Tis truly wonderful!

TREACHER: Observe, betwixt those two white pyramids,
   The dark Pacific.

CREDULOS: Sancta Maria! Now I understand,

And share thy extacies, renowned Almagro.
Bravo! bravo! bravo!

TREACHER: And, look you, Don, to rest you in the shade
Nature provides a couch.

CREDULOS: A little hard, or so, for one's siesta.

TREACHER: Not to a hardy traveller.

They sit on the stone ledge.

CREDULOS: Guide, it strikes me you were never cradled
Among these mountains?

TREACHER: Not bear enough for that; no, senor, no;
My history is a melancholy one,
Yet most eventful — quite a wild romance.

CREDULOS: You make me burn to hear it.

TREACHER: Too long and too incredible for ears
Pricked to these prosey times.

CREDULOS: Sir guide, you're complimentary. Proceed.

TREACHER: Your pardon, Don; how easy to forget
A haughty scion of a noble house
Requires much cutting down before it takes
A humbler growth.

CREDULOS: How true! The apology is mine — accept,
My friend, a free acknowledgement.

TREACHER: Freely as given, senor.

CREDULOS: My faith, 'tis well there are no brigands here,
Or, by'r Lady, this grim solitude
To robbery and murder might betray
A chastened anchorite.

TREACHER: Nay, senor, suffer not unworthy fears
To over-reach your pleasure.

CREDULOS: Mistake me not, good fellow, if, too keenly,
I realize what your accustomed sense
Fails now to estimate; yes, on my soul,
That gaping black abyss which drinketh up
Those pale affrighted waters —
That devilish-looking condor on the crag,
Peering below — all preternatural things

In this weird sunlight; aye, the gusty wind
Seems peevish and dispiteful!

TREACHER: Think not too much of it; let homelike thoughts
And more familiar topics break this charm.

CREDULOS: By Jove! that's good advice. I'll cool myself;
Retone my spirits by a little rest.
Unbuckling his girdle and laying his weapons on the rock.
See here, fine fellow, this queer article
I purchased North — 'tis a Revolver — charged,
Gives you advantage 'gainst six enemies.
Treacher carelessly takes up the Pistol.
See, this, my trusty dagger; all the way
My true Toledo bears me company.
Inspect this bit of steel, while I refresh
My heated brow in yon dull Lethe — then
Your life romance comes next.
Exit Credulos.

TREACHER: 'Twere well for thee, poor trusting simpleton,
That stream could, from thy costive memory,
Purge of this surfeit of Heraldic pride —
Thus metamorphose thee without the noise
And ugly trick of killing.
Walking to and fro.
Practice, practice, practice and promptitude;
Abridge all useless dialogues; my part
I'd do in pantomime, but then, our client
Will say some stirring thing that moveth speech.
For tragedy I ever had a weakness;
I took it from the players; they, however,
At variance with true business principles,
Begin with tragedy, and finish up
With some egregious farce. Our farce is played;
And thus we mount the graduated climax
To our more sterling action. Ah! see,
Yon lamb runs bleating to the knife —
Poor silly lamb. Lo! here I drop the mask.
Re-enter Credulos.

CREDULOS: Ha! what has chanced to change your countenance?
Most Holy Trinity! am I betrayed?

TREACHER: A devotee, and not to recollect
One's infant prayer, which readeth — "Lead us not
Into temptation." Don, thou has tempted me;
I owe my burdened conscience this short shrift.
And now, with all convenient speed, *deliver*
Your personals, and mind, no cavilling.
Raising the Pistol.

CREDULOS: What, strip a stranger in this horrid place
And leave him pennyless?

TREACHER: Thou'll want but little there below.   *Pointing over the rocks.*

CREDULOS: For God's sake, spare my life, then, if you must
Take all.

TREACHER: *This* shall befriend you, for I hate long parleys;
Relieve yourself of all this worldly cumber —
Like a good palmer, take your peaceful way
Across this Christian land.

CREDULOS: Only bare life?

TREACHER: Only! This comes of mixing pleasantries
With serious business. Now, *instantly.*
Stamping his foot. He tenders his purse and other property.
That ring, sir.

CREDULOS: Ah! 'tis our ancient crest, and valuable,
But as a voucher of my noble birth —

TREACHER: Well, let me see it, Don.
Takes and regards it with a start; sighs as at some reminiscence.
Alas! I knew these hieroglyphics well;
Here, take and love it as an amulet
Which saved your life; also, I share with you
These fair contents of your well freighted purse,
Retaining but a moderate embargo.

CREDULOS: I'm bound to thank you.

TREACHER: That sounds a little churlish; come hither, now.
Going to the back part of the stage.
Muster your manhood — there, behold the path
Which hugs the breast of this hard precipice —
Safe only to the brave.

CREDULOS: Spare me a task so fearful! The sight of it
Dissolves my very soul!

TREACHER: The only road from hence that I dare trust thee.
Observe — once reached the river, follow it
To where it disembogues its weary waters
In the Pacific. Swear thou to leave that port
Three hundred leagues, or more.

CREDULOS: Most willingly I swear it. But —

TREACHER: The road? I've travelled it in safety often.
Come — time is pressing; let me plant your foot

Safe on that jutting rock; *that* firmly gained,
Most of the danger's passed; come nearer.
Timorously approaching, is pushed off; shrieking, descends.
Neatly disposed of — shaming Caesar's job
Of sanguine slaughter and most vulgar stabbing!
Mean, faded pattern of the old Castilian,
Pale, washed-out clout; how hard he took the dye
Of brave Pizzarro, idol of his worship;
And yet, by Jabus, 'tis a sorry joke
Above the wretch who hath his all divided
'Twixt me and death! — grim co-executor.
I see him grinning from the fatal rock.
How strange! I've often seen it — I'll turn me;
Bless me, it seems a fixture on these orbs
That won't rub out.
The ring, the ring! that timely ruse took well;
A seeming reverence for his worthless cypher
Bought back his confidence — yes, led the lamb,
Without a struggle to the fatal altar
Ere he could ope his mouth. As bargains go,
The terms were liberal; it needed not
To tell him of the secret pass that leads
From our sweet cave, fast by the Tarpean rock.
Ere long our vulture, Ghoulish Avero,
Shall overhaul the carrion.

Exits.

SCENE II

A Rocky Gorge. Enter Vampries, singing.

VAMPRIES: What a change! Lost spirit, tell,
Blotted out th' chastening day!
Faintly-hued, with shades of hell,
Where thy vanquished cohorts lay,
O Lucifer!

Like those chambers of remorse,
Where remorseless fiends are made;
Murderers, here, may hide their corse,
Grow familiar with their trade,
And blood prefer.
Stripes, the fallen, never mend;
Stains, indelible, remain;
So yon saffern waves descend —
Stagnate into filth again.
Foul Acheron!

73

Where, vain men, thy proud advance?
Vacant chasm, earthquake cleft;
Why not, here, the satyr dance,
Oread play! since all have left,
How drear and lone!

Ha! what is this? a mouldy skeleton?
No other! Poor, usurping prodigal,
To pierce these useless sepulchres of stone,
Only to hold possession with your bones!
Hold! perhaps no volunteer in this campaign.
It smells of murder! Bones — more bones;
Here's a Golgotha! Blasted trees are they;
Withered by famine; hacked by ravenous beast;
Hewn by fell murder; dead, and rotten? — less.
Once infinitely more than these, tall plants
Which interdict the sun; that sightless frame —
Once strung with organs, tender and artistic,
Responsive to the finger of wild passion,
Thrilling alternate interludes
'Twixt pain and pleasure — broken, unstrung.
And silent forever!
A deep groan.
Hist!
Exits.

Re-enter Vampries, with Credulos, limping, faint, and black with mud.

VAMPRIES: There, rest you, stranger, on this mossy stone
Until your wandering wits can tell me whence,
And wherefore here.

CREDULOS: If thou be human, and dost sympathize
With mortal wrongs, I can enlist your pity.

VAMPRIES: Wrongs? I pray thee, speak them.

CREDULOS: How long ago, I cannot now determine —
Such moments never end —
But, sometime since the blessed sun arose,
Whose beams seem here unknown, a treacherous knave
Betrayed me to yon over-arching brow, —
You see that patch of light, as 't were, i' th' clouds?

VAMPRIES: Distinctly; pray, go on.

CREDULOS: From thence that felon hand projected me,
Despoiled of my effects!

VAMPRIES: Most wonderful!

Laying a hand on his shoulder.

CREDULOS: Nay, question not the words of an Hidalgo.

VAMPRIES: Question! I felt but for your wings!

CREDULOS: Why jest ye with a man so near destruction.
I see not how I 'scaped yon perilous height,
Except through angels' ministry.

VAMPRIES: Angels! Ha! ha! ha! *Roaring to the echo.*
Come, render it in terms more rational.

CREDULOS: I own, the instant of my dreadful plunge,
My heart seemed split asunder.
And my senses wandered a little.
This hip striking against a jutting rock
Stung me to consciousness; thence, off I flew,
Grazing that stony death which stood beneath,
And settling deep in the soft stinking mire, —

VAMPRIES: From which I hauled you; these, your two bright angels —
I and the mud.

CREDULOS: Most singularly true.

VAMPRIES: I call myself "The Stranger"; pray, are you
A citizen?

CREDULOS: No, Creole senor; pure Castilian bred;
Only some weeks a denizon.

VAMPRIES: Indeed! Where landed you?

CREDULOS: At Valparaiso, having credit letters,
Besides, a special line to the Archbishop
Of Santiago;

VAMPRIES: Thunder! I, too, am thither bound.
I see you're speculating on the chance
Of this, my visit to a spot so dismal —
At such a crisis, too, in your affairs;
Call it an angel's visit.
Laughing sarcastically.

CREDULOS: Why should that phrase amuse you?

VAMPRIES: So innocent and quaint; but, time is pressing.
I have a secret fancy for such places,
So, landing from a coaster at the port
Which heads this stream, strolled hitherward.

CREDULOS: Why, can it be so near?

VAMPRIES: What near?

CREDULOS: The great Pacific!

VAMPRIES: I said not it was near — but, don't delay me,
Lest it should throw you back among the wolves.
Exploring, I chanced upon a canon,
Which cleaves this rocky wall transversely;
Narrow and dark, I entered, and pursued
The sinuous passage till th' increasing light
Told of its end; there human voices reached me;
But, mind, these ears can capture syllables —
Sure as the hawk, her unsuspecting quarry,
While far away. Those words elucidate
Your mystery; yea, add another act,
Not yet played out, to this weird drama.

CREDULOS: Your words wake new alarms; how may I leave
This place of murder?

VAMPRIES: I only can release you from their net
Laid so adroitly. Can you travel?

CREDULOS: Danger would spur a jaded beast to fly
From such a den of death — please, raise me up.

VAMPRIES: *Raising him.* You're on your feet; the only open way
Is by the stream; haste to the little haven;
I'll see you safely past that cut-throat alley
I told you of — mouth of their bloody trap —
Once past, you're safe; *then* wash away this filth,
And rest ere you proceed.

CREDULOS: Oh! stranger, thanks! Once at the port, what then?

VAMPRIES: Wait for me there. Hist! hist! I hear the vultures
Spreading their wings; now, now — they fly this way.

CREDULOS: Blessed virgin! help, help, help!

They exit. Vampries dragging him off.

SCENE III

Santiago. A Street. Enter Roland.

ROLAND: Mysterious sufferance! Mortifying strain

On the excruciating zealot's faith,
Impaled on sharp opinion. Savage Christian,
Who, Jonah like, his burden once delivered,
No thought of ruth, repentance or reprieve.
Yes, rather with a hectoring reproach
At heaven's forbearance, watching the event.
Call this a saint? A Nemesis, constructed
From the same guilty mass which heaven forbears
With charitable respite?
Enter Norman.
Most welcome, brother Norman; much I feared
You had construed amiss our late discourse.

NORMAN: No. I perceived the drift of your design —
To kiss your hand to Liberalism.
They're dangerous compromises. How would stand
Our Reformation with a silent protest?
And what seems worse, mute apathy of spirit
To these idolatries, so rife among us,
Which scandalize the age! Oh! can it be,
A mind informed of that most holy light —
So pure, so simple, and transparent —
Can tolerate these lying blasphemies
And pious frauds that worldly men do scoff at.

ROLAND: Stay — "worldly men?" Would you accommodate
Your faith to such? The Greek, much more devout,
Yet, stumbled at the cross; yea, deemed
This sign of our salvation foolishness;
Our crowning hope, the glorious resurrection,
To him an idle story, quite beyond
The grasp of his philosophy.
Alas, my friend, I own these things confound me;
Yet who, of men, erring and impotent,
Is equal, *here,* to stem this rage of custom
Urged by religious sanction? I leave it
With him who reads the heart and judgeth all.
These millions stand on common ground with us —
Convicted sinners 'fore heaven's diviner law —
A precient charity,
Too Catholic, for our contracted hearts
Yearns after all.

NORMAN: Ah! spare your charity, nor fling your alms
To pompous bedlamites, who mad vagaries
Might well excite a laugh, but for the pride
Which throws these scraps of pity in your face!
How, like those ranting fools of Ephesus!
These modern craftsmen use a worthier name;
They deify a holier chastity,
Yet for the same base ends; then stun your ears

And stop your mouth with this wild Slogan cry —
Infallibility.

ROLAND: Look — what comes here?

They exit. A procession of Priests and others cross the stage, bearing a large image of the Virgin in gay robes; candles, etc. Re-enter Roland and Norman with Cloudon.

CLOUDON: Bless you, my pious friends! Why don't you turn out, or *in,* rather? Come, fall in, with a candle apiece; so add another joint or two to the tail of this strange animal wagging along the street. Think of it — the pulpit duns you with the shortness and preciousness of time; and, here, this new religious fangle, which none but fools know or care anything about, stands up to claim one month out of twelve of this precious article! And how many more fasts and feasts, God knows.

ROLAND: Neighbour, I would not jest on such a subject;
A man, once recreant to those sacred instincts
Which bias him toward heaven, will scoff at all —
The false or true — to wrestle down his conscience,
Pleading for truth and God.
Religion is indigenous in man;
Yet often, o'er the landscape of the soul,
Rambles in wild luxuriance. Happy he,
Replete with scions from the tree of life,
Engrafted, on this blooming barrenness,
They bring forth sweet and seemly fruit.

CLOUDON: Good enough preaching, but a little too pointed. Shall we meet and settle it at the Old Company's Church on the eighth? The Virgin takes her special benefit. The Pope's man preaches and weeping Urangos, her postmaster, closes the play with a melting epilogue.

ROLAND: Doubtless, they'll give you room
And civil entertainment.

They exit.

SCENE IV

A pass in the mountains. A caravan — mules, Indians and travellers cross the stage; When they have passed, a door opens stealthily in the rock. Enter Gripos and Avero.

AVERO: I surely saw him ere that devil's dragon
Went wriggling past.

GRIPOS: Why, then, the eyes of our old basilisk
Have got the blinks.

AVERO: Lord, pity us! That devilish caravan
    Has licked him up; but heark'ee, comrade,
    I fear he'll prove a hornet in our nets;
    He looks as fierce and lithe as a wild cat!

GRIPOS: Thou ugly spider, trembling on thy toils —
    Well may your coward heart mistrust a craft
    Unbacked of courage. Don thy feather togs
    And kite a little. Repeat it, basilisk —
    Didst search each rock and cranny?

AVERO: Scoured every nook, I tell ye, till I found
    A stinking muckhole in that horrid Styx,
    As if all hell had bolted through it.

GRIPOS: This comes of the white feather practice;
    He cast him off alive.

AVERO: Surely he'd bleed him first.

GRIPOS: And what delays him now, I'd like to know?

AVERO: Bolted, as like as not. That Don bled well,
    I'm very sure; he's got the lion's share,
    And bolted with it.

GRIPOS: Damned croaker! Cease thy jaw — I know him better.

AVERO: Glad of it; on a spree, belike.

GRIPOS: Hist! get on thy feathers — quick.

They exit, closing the door. Enter Vampries, singing.

VAMPRIES: Gentle Hylas! Mysia's heir —
    Tell me Dryades, tell me where
    Youthful Hylas dips his urn —
    Why from me so coldly turn?
    Echo answers — Coldly turn.

    Wicked Nymphs! I see them smile;
    Did you, then, the youth beguile?
    Here, I track him through the glade —
    Doubtless ye my friend betrayed!
    Echo answers — Friend betrayed.

    Fled! derided and deceived;
    Of my youthful charge bereaved;
    Onward, my companion's gone —
    Here a wanderer, left alone!
    Echo answers — Left alone.

Gorgeous vision, truly! elaborate shadows,
Ephemeral as the frost work of the North,
Built on its liquid blue. Nay, these
On more capricious fires. Say to what end,
Dread architect, upshooting to the skies,
These barren pinnacles, which rise and fade
Before the eye eternal like a dream?
Oh! thou mysterious circumstance of Being,
From the inert, through all its graded functions —
Matter inspired — clay moulded into life!
Now, ask the topmost Emperor of this realm
Of life, what is it? Cloudy, dismal day,
Some few stray glimpses of the sun of joy
To sheen the draperies of this masquerade;
A whirl of aspirations unrequited.
Success itself is but a dangerous glacier
Where bold adventurers climb the slippery steep
To stand on tiptoe, clutching at the air,
Till crowded over to the yawning gulf —
Base lumber of oblivion! Ha!
Avero appearing on the rocks above, attired as an Indian.
Methinks those gaudy trappings of the Jay
Sit ill upon that Hawk. But why this ruse?
Girdled and cinctured brow — how picturesque,
And primitive, as when Columbus first
Broke into this new world.
Enter Gripos.
Ha! whence your ghostship? Do ye live and breathe
A proper man?

GRIPOS: Yes; such are my pretensions.

VAMPRIES: And ready, perhaps, to earn an honest fee?

GRIPOS: If it should lie within my calling — yes.

VAMPRIES: Thy speech is prompt; I like thee none the worse
   For ready bluntness.

GRIPOS: Mention the service you would have of me?

VAMPRIES: I travel North, and want assistance
   To cross these mountains.

GRIPOS: That's just my following, sir.

VAMPRIES: Name your charges.

GRIPOS: According to the trouble you occasion.

VAMPRIES: Trouble — how?

GRIPOS: Some travellers must loiter on the way
To view the scenery.

VAMPRIES: Aye! now I understand; I must be free
To visit ought worth seeing.

GRIPOS: I'll leave the wages till the work is done,
And charge accordingly — you being willing.

VAMPRIES: Well spoken; then, proceed.

They exit.

SCENE V

The Robbers' cave. Enter Avero, with a large Bloodhound.

AVERO: Boser, you rascal, hain't we had some fun
And many a spree together — Boser, eh?
Wagging his tail.
That dog knows all I say. I sometimes think
If that dumb animal should come to speech
Suddenly, what then? Why, when he 'peaches,
Leave me outside the door. And would ye split
On your old croney, Boser?

BOSER: Bow, wow, wow!

AVERO: What — tell the wicked works we've done together, eh?

BOSER: Bow, wow, wow!

AVERO: And tell them what fat monks, and other meat,
You've ta'en a liking to?

BOSER: Bow, wowe!

Leaping on his master.

AVERO: Down! blast your bloody eyes. I see you'd do it.
You'd eat me up alive — you would.
Down! or I'll —
Drawing a pistol. The dog cowers in a corner.
A dangerous thing it is for animals
To taste of human blood; why, e'en a wolf,
Trained young, will make the best of dogs; but, then,
Keep 'em from Christian blood! I knew a man —

He'd a pet wolf which followed him about;
Never did creature look more innocent;
One day his master stumbled on a rock,
Grazing his leg — it bled, and pained him;
Far from home, he tried the beggar's doctor —
Set the dog to lick it: the wolf I mean.
From that same day a change came o'er him;
That foolish man regarded not the signs;
What then? A few days afterwards the wolf
Was found — how? Just eating up his master,
Fallen, but yet alive! The creature slunk away,
Becoming a terror to all that country.
Boser! ye thief, come hither; those eyes,
I like them not; I see a bloody language in 'em!
Nor am I sure if dogs ain't evil spirits!
I've seen such devilish cunning lately in him,
It troubles my sleep. Boser — sport on hand;
To the trap, Boser.

Dog leaping about, greatly excited. They exit.

SCENE VI

The ledge of rocks. Enter Vampries, gazing eagerly about, followed by Gripos.

VAMPRIES: And call you this attractive?

GRIPOS: No: but some are mad on novelties;
   Others, affecting love for ugliness,
   Would court an ogress.

VAMPRIES: Yes: as you said, I see the great Pacific;
   From this great altitude, a sight worth seeing.

GRIPOS: And those, whose heads will countenance the feat,
   Let them look down from hence.

VAMPRIES: *Walking carelessly to the edge and looking over.*
   Yes: this is something too; how many fathoms
   Down to yonder mud-hole?

GRIPOS: That's quite beyond my reckoning.

VAMPRIES: And there is something like a skeleton;
   Dost know if't is?
   Suddenly looking Gripos in the face.

GRIPOS: Never look down, sir; I durst not do it.

VAMPRIES: Wait here awhile; I'll take a little stroll
Around the cataract.

Exits. Vampries visible in the distance.

GRIPOS: This fellow bothers me! That falcon eye
And wolfish tread of his take me aback.
See! there he goes across the slippery rocks,
Where e'en the waters seem hysterical
At looking over. Cleared it like a panther.
He scarce looks human-like; it staggers me.
Devil! he came so temptingly and bold
Before me on the precipice — I could
No doubt, have done it, but that dreadful eye
Came like a fiery dart across his shoulder
And paralized me. But two chances more —
To pistol him; its tell-tale replications,
So near the road, might bring us into fear.
Come — rusty blade.
Drawing his knife and feeling the point.
What if it should not enter? perhaps go through
That wizard body, aye, and leave no hurt?
By Jove, I'll try it! Never shall 't be said
Stout Grip has missed his man. Something mutters,
Mutters, mutters, "This fellow's dangerous!"
Assault? A kitten to a catamount!
I fight with yon tall, wiry devil? No.
Strike i' the rear, i' the rear, i' the rear!
Lord — he's coming!
Sheathes his knife. Re-enter Vampries.

VAMPRIES: Ghastly spot! It surely is the navel
Of this storm-ridden realm, round which
Convolve its stoney entrails; let us leave.
Turning to go.
Ha! fell assassin, is it thus ye strike?
Smiting down his arm and clutching his throat.

GRIPOS: My arm is broken — powerless — at your mercy.

VAMPRIES: Wretch! knows you that word? Th' unbranded Cain
Crying to all thou meet'st for public vengeance.
Felon! know this arm doth ne'er relinquish,
Nor this heart relent. Body and soul are mine.
Ha! start ye? Body and soul, I said!

GRIPOS: Lord — has it come to this?
Trembling, sinks on his knees.

VAMPRIES: Mercy is it, villain? Yes, such as thou'st shown.
I'll treat thee to a sight which, doubtless, thou
Hast oft bestowed on others; come on, then.
Thrusting him to the precipice.
Look there! — what, sick? I'll soon restore thee.
Holding him by the hair over the gulf.
Poor craven wretch — to shriek so dastardly!
I did but act the jibbet.
Laying him back on the rock. Walking to and fro.
Another sentence of this dismal story
Comes to a rueful stop. Such paragraphs
And periods illustrate the page
Of this dull book of life. See: he revives;
Just one more glance.
Turning his face over the edge.
Look down — thou seest those pointed rocks?
Right down among the shadows, and near by
A skeleton? Pleasant remembrancer;
Well, think now of thy journey through the air —
Then what a smash these cracking bones and thews —
This quivering flesh — will make on yon hard bed;
All to wind up in Hell. Ha, ha, ha!

GRIPOS: My God! my God!! my God!!!

VAMPRIES: *Swinging him to and fro over the abyss.*
Thy prayers are profanation. Heaven is dumb.
Go, taste of retribution.
Casting him off, amid shrieks of terror.
Body and bones! I saw the felon strike;
And I'll go wash this business off my fingers,
And wait on other issues.

Exits. Enter Treacher — Peering on the ground.

TREACHER: No blood, but other signs of trouble.
Lo! here the moss has been rubbed off the rocks;
And *here* has been a struggle — deadly — recent.
Methinks the very stone seems dark and wet
With some poor wretch's agony! Gripos
Has had some custom in my absence. Ha!
Who's that I see out yonder?
Why looks he down below so earnestly?
He sees me, and approaches.

Enter Vampries.

VAMPRIES: Ha! stranger, have you lost your way?

TREACHER: Well may you ask that question, senor, here;
Perhaps you're in that predicament?

84

VAMPRIES: No, no. I'm much too old a traveller
To lose myself.

TREACHER: Indeed! I once was here before, and thought
It so remarkable, if ere I came this way,
I'd visit it again.

VAMPRIES: It's a suspicious place!

TREACHER: And, yet, it seems to court admirers, senor.

VAMPRIES: Some travellers have strange caprices.

TREACHER: Yes: very true; and some strong prejudices.

VAMPRIES: Listen, stranger, to its weary burden: —
Murder! that doleful stream articulates,
Those cynic rocks have set themselves to mock,
Appeals for mercy; and that awful gulf —
Black, deep and wide — stands by with open mouth
To swallow up the victim!

TREACHER: Most truly, senor, your imagination
Would populate a chaos.

VAMPRIES: All fancy, is it? Come up, hither, stranger.

Leaping to the edge.

TREACHER: Senor, I'll be excused; my head won't bear it.

VAMPRIES: I see beneath a wandering beam of light
Crossing a skeleton; know'st how it came there?

TREACHER: Strange question, senor; pray, how should I know it?
Greatly embarrassed.

VAMPRIES: I have my warrant for it.
Hold! I've missed a jewel from my person;
I must recover it.

Exits.

TREACHER: This surely is the devil turned policeman!
At first I thought him game that one might fly at —
Lord help me for a simpleton!
If I aright can read, he'd overreach
Great Lucifer! and there's that precious jewel
For which he hunts so diligently yonder —
Some trap for me? By Jabus! I'll withdraw —
Should my long tried discretion serve the end
Of my deliverance.

Treacher exits. Re-enter Vampries.

VAMPRIES: Ah, he's gone, 'tis best, my talisman
　　Detected him, but gave no valid power
　　Without the overt act; a crafty knave,
　　Convolved in serpent folds no counter craft
　　Or cunning can uncoil, no prick of passion
　　Rouse to untimely action. Well he's gone
　　Not much enamoured, as I take it
　　Of his acquaintance. Thus in these mountains
　　My mission ends.

ACT II

SCENE I

A street near the sea. Enter Vampries.

VAMPRIES: Dumb and besotted this dull haven lies,
　　As in a doze upon the lazy breast
　　Of old Pacific. Say, what minds this odd
　　Melange of vermin, mud and rottenness,
　　Of pagan Inca, or of Christian King,
　　Still less of rude, starklimbed Democracy,
　　Which promises so much and pays so little.
　　Here like an undressed clown in stupid wonder
　　'Twas seen these pageants pass. Each left her yet
　　An unkempt slattern out of all regard
　　Of changing Dynasties — ha —
　　Enter Credulos.
　　　　　　　　　　　　　My most revered,
　　My venerable chum! though all in black
　　I left you, now you're out of mourning —
　　How's your nerves?

CREDULOS: Thank you, senor, the sea has set me up.

VAMPRIES: A pleasant contrast then, I found you down,
　　And low enough.

CREDULOS: Most truly, Don, but tell me your adventures.

VAMPRIES: I never stoop to such formalities.

CREDULOS: Pardon me, senor, I too much presume
　　On my most wonderful deliverance.

VAMPRIES: Some passages in my experience
Belong to you, and those I render.

CREDULOS: T'were rank impertinence to ask for more.

VAMPRIES: Your enemy still lives, yet I've enforced
A heavy penance on th'assassin's club,
For your disaster.

CREDULOS: Oh, senor, you indulge me.

VAMPRIES: I lured the bird from his familiar brake,
Into that very bush already limed
Up in the mountains —

CREDULOS: Where I was caught?

VAMPRIES: The same.

CREDULOS: Santa Maria! go on.

VAMPRIES: Instead of your smooth plausible assailant,
One blunt of phrase and dogged in resolve
Confronted me. I need not tell you how
This bear was baited — When discomfitted,
How hugged his heavy chain of guiltiness
Not yielding even one remorseful roar,
Till mildly hinting at his sure damnation,
Then he broke down.

CREDULOS: And you reprieved him, senor?

VAMPRIES: Dismissed him with his life on the grand tour.
Which counts so high in your accomplishments.

CREDULOS: Explain this riddle, senor?

VAMPRIES: Just sent him o'er the rocks.

CREDULOS: Lord help the wretch!

VAMPRIES: I gave him ghostly shrift, I warrant ye.

Enter a Sea Captain.

CAPTAIN: Which o' yu tu gentlemen's going to Valprasa?

VAMPRIES: Both, sir.

CAPTAIN: Both, eh?

VAMPRIES: You're the captain?

CAPTAIN: I guess so.

VAMPRIES: Not a native?

CAPTAIN: No, sirree! I'm a full blooded yankee right up and down straight, cap and boots; where was you raised, if it's a fair question?

VAMPRIES: Saligoola.

CAPTAIN: Bless me — name o' my ship — as near as aint no matter Sally Goodall, odd that, chalks out of my latitude I guess.

CREDULOS: When do you sail, Captain?

CAPTAIN: To-morrow, bright and early, jist as quick as I twist up anchor, wind serving, so I reckon gents you'd better bring yer plunder aboard to-night and fix up the fare.

They exit.

VAMPRIES: What barbarous idioms shock the mortal ear
  . Around this Babbling earth!

SCENE II

The Robber's Cave. Enter Avero with Bloodhound. In great terror.

AVERO: I had a mortal dread of it — to see
That elfish staring face! perhaps not quite dead —
Such creatures never die — like grizzly bears,
They'll carry pounds o' lead and kill at dying.
O Lord o' mercy! think of it — instead
Of that queer varmint there lay our own Grip.
And such a picture eyes ne'er looked on —
He seemed as he had caught a sight infernal
Fixing his eyes, so scared — not minding ought
The havoc of his body, fearful heap —
Topped with that frightful face. O Treacher, come.
Nor leave these eyeballs ridden of that spectre
To meet the darkness. Then, what if he come?
Informed of what has happened — crafty Treacher
Would keep the plunder of the Don and clear!
No; I've more gumption — Lord save us!
Enter Treacher.
My Treacher! never in the honey-moon

Did husband trouble for an absent wife,
As I for thee. Tell me good news
Sweetheart, and raise my courage.

TREACHER: Put bowels in a stone! Craven, look here.
Shaking a bag of gold.

AVERO: Aye, aye, good Treacher, gibe and welcome, man,
Only bring in the gilt — Doubloons! hail Mary!
Sweet comrade, let me count em.

TREACHER: Sordid wretch! hast thou no curious inkling
To hear how these were won?
Putting them back under his cloak.

AVERO: Lord, how techey! did not the Romans thus —
Preface their exploits with the splendid spoils?
So thou — twice edified, the *prize* and *triumph.*

TREACHER: You saw the senor pass?

AVERO: Yes, from the cave — not having on the gear
Of Indian hunter, I kept close.

TREACHER: Poor Don!
Enamoured of Pezzaro's gallant deeds
Had come thus far to set his tiny feet
On the broad footprints of the conqueror.
Much as a wren might track an elephant!

AVERO: Ha, ha, ha — but you're a trump.

TREACHER: I soon succeeded in his confidence
Thence all was easy — as his *faithful* guide
Soon compassed him. So, skipping details,
My moiety I took, thou, trusty vulture
Made legatee for the remainder —
Thou found it in the devil's bank all right?
Say! what ails thee, gosshawk?

AVERO: And that my share o' the swag, eh?

TREACHER: A good 'en too for such a skulking knave.
Who dares not face the dangers of his calling.

AVERO: Might have been so before a pair of legs
Walked off with it.

TREACHER: Wings, man, wings — nought else could do it.

AVERO: Whichever way, t'as left my freehold

Among the clouds with only air to rest on.

TREACHER: Gramary! where's Grip?

AVERO: Ah, there is something that I want to tell ye
But don't know how — where's *Grip,* indeed!

TREACHER: Speak, Jackass!

AVERO: Wish I was with plenty of sweet provender
Honestly gained.

TREACHER: Speak, or by Jabus, I'll kill ye.

Knocking him down, dog growling fiercely.

AVERO: *Rising.* Down Boser, down.
Hard conditions Treacher, — if I must, I must.
There came a stranger that unlucky day
Of lofty stature, rakish swing and bearing;
Humming a tune. His voice was terrible
As some great barrel organ underground —

TREACHER: Less prolix, if you please — I feel impatient.

AVERO: Grip, in his easy way soon had his lasso
About the fiery beast. They lead off north,
So in due time I visited the trap —
Fancy the shock — instead of Belzebub —
There lay — all in a mash upon the rocks,
Our comrade — dead! oh! such a spectacle —
I shudder to think on't.

TREACHER: No, never Grip, such a dead hand as he —
I can't believe it! changes come in death,
And death like that; it must have been the Don.

AVERO: The Don! mistake that scowling figurehead
Dark, haught and scornful as the king of hell!

TREACHER: Belay that rigmarole — if it be so,
No time to spout, to criminate or cocker,
The hawks may soon be on us — lend your ears —
I met this angel in our upland bower,
Of which you speak, there's mischief in him.

AVERO: Ha! did you though? oh! oh!

TREACHER: I'd like to question more about the Spaniard
Not now, nor here, delays are dangerous.

AVERO: Prepare we then to vacate?

TREACHER: Most instantly — here's five gold pieces for thee —
Handing over the gold.
Paid for the absconding Don.

AVERO: Bad luck to the defaulter! This property?

TREACHER: Give me my arms, of all the rest
Take the fee-simple — I'm off.

AVERO: Nay, give me just ten minutes grace
I'll set my chattels in such durance
As midnight witch would baffle.

TREACHER: Follow me South, or part here — as you will.

Exit.

AVERO: Gone! oh wicked generation — follow him.
What can I else? Too miserable to bear
My own acquaintanceship.

Exit Avero loaded with sundries.

SCENE III

Santiago. A room in Mercedos' house. Enter Mercedos and Cortez.

MERCEDOS: Betwixt ourselves, these shows of mother Church,
Cheapen her credit in the public eye:
And for these frauds, to which the Holy Virgin
Is made a principal, tis sacrilege! rank sacrilege!
Such pious forgeries, away with them.

CORTEZ: Good senor, why should your severity
O'ershade a glorious pastime?

MERCEDOS: My dear young friend, 'tis not compatible
To Faith and its religious services,
To put this strain upon them. Think you now
This postal trick of that o'erzealous priest
Is no disparagement to both our Church
And these solemnities?

CORTEZ: I am not heedful of these church disputes,
But find repose in her substantial rule —

Unerring and infallible. To me
Her long experience in the ways and want
Of changeful man may justify her course:
These relaxations tone the appetite
For doctrines recondite and orthodox.
And if the line be curved a thought to reach
Some laudable design which countervails
The damage? Witness the British Isles
Where wave o'er-rideth wave of novelties.
A roaring sea, no voice to say "be still" —
The dogged round-head stubborn Covenanter
Puritanic zealot: each conventicle
Deals out the truth in its peculiar measure,
Through which there falls a dark residium —
Bigotry, intolerance, *Fatalism* —
Its milder name — predestination — leaving
One half the race to perish.
Enter Maria and Susannah.
Ladies, your most devoted — I call to say —
To-morrow I propose a day of leisure —
At your service, being the last day
Of our grand festival.

MARIA: Sir, how very kind of you!

SUSANNAH: With such protection we will out betimes,
And make the most of it.

MERCEDOS: I would my girls had come a little sooner,
To hear our Jesuit preach; but I will spare him.

CORTEZ: Truly this comes of leaving one's vocation —
Your words reprove me, senor.

MARIA: I fear, dear father, age and earthly cares,
Have chilled religious fervor in you.

SUSANNAH: *Aside.*   Hush, hush Marie, don't prolong this subject.

MARIA: Well child, it may be so, alas it may:
As in the spring time of the changing year
The beam that feeds and opens out the bud,
A few weeks later wilts and withers up,
The exhausted flower; so too young ardent faith
Comes warm and glowing, spiritual impressions —
Fancies — to Faith more sober — less robust
Which rather weaken than confirm their grasp
On pure substantial truth.

Enter Madam Mercedos.

CORTEZ: Madam, my service, timely have you come
To introduce some matronly apothegm,
And check this controversy.

MADAM: Oh sir, I'm use to them; its most distressing —

MERCEDOS: Now, Madam, make not this our light discourse
Most solemnly ridiculous!

MADAM: Ah, that's the way — always the way.

MARIA: Dear mother, hear me — will you not be glad —
This gentleman has most politely tendered
His company to-morrow, our Chaperone
Am I right, good sir?

CORTEZ: Precisely, Madam.

MADAM: How good of him! mind in the evening,
I further shall impose myself upon him.

CORTEZ: 'Twill be a pleasure Madam — to-morrow
I'll wait upon you ladies. Fare you well.

MERCEDOS: Cortez, I'll walk with you.

Mercedos and Cortez exit.

MADAM: What a fine young man, Maria darling —
But mind your p's and q's, and he is yours.

SUSANNAH: Mother, how commonplace!

MADAM: Betwixt ourselves, you know, what matters it?

MARIA: Do you so much admire him, mother dear?

MADAM: Just my choice dear, had I to make it now.

SUSANNAH: Well, what a pity?

MADAM: Child, you're always taking me up.

MARIA: Dear mother, do not mind her, only say,
If I secure him you will intercede
With father for him?

MADAM: Intercede! your father would be proud of him.

SUSANNAH: Mary. The course is clear. Your bird is salted,
Now only take your bow, Dan Cupid's arrow,

Sped wittingly, will bring him over!

MADAM: Hark at her again! Susan, you're envious!

SUSANNAH: Mother, the game is yet uncaught, why envious?
I would it were not an uncertainty.

MARIA: I know it, loving sister; far too much
Am I beholden to your prudent counsel
To harbor a mistrust.

MADAM: Well, you're good loving children, Pythean
And Damon over again.

SUSANNAH: Saving the pantaloons.

MARIA: Susan — for shame!

MADAM: What can she mean?

They exit laughing.

SCENE IV

A room in the Archbishop's Palace. Enter Archbishop, Credulos and Vampries.

ARCHBISHOP: It grieves me, senor, you a friendly stranger
Should fare so hardly in a Christian land.
This gentleman was made the instrument
Of your deliverance.

CREDULOS: Your grace, it is most true; I owe my life
And freedom from the crafty toils of villains,
All to him.

ARCHBISHOP: Yes, under Providence, 'tis clearly so,
And for this deed I have commended him
To our Urangos, and the brotherhood,
For Christian countenance.

VAMPRIES: I thank your excellence, my stay is brief,
Nor shall I draw too heavy on the debt
This liberal Don has written down to me.

CREDULOS: We'll trench no more upon your Grace's leisure
At such a time.

ARCHBISHOP: Thank you, gentlemen, adieu.
They exit.
"Stranger," an alias? has he then no name?
If so, I caught it not — a mystery —
Stamp and bearing — all a deep enigma.
Proud as Lucifer! Methinks I never saw
The fitness of this epithet before.
That eye and countenance can never fade
From my remembrance.
Enter the Nuncio.
Ah, met your Excellency a cavalier,
Tall, of a princely bearing, yet withall
An aspect sinister — most hard to fathom?

NUNCIO: Yes, I met him with a Spaniard
Exchanging with them common courtesies —
Why ask your Grace?

ARCHBISHOP: Simply to learn if this strange man's appearance
At all impresses you.

NUNCIO: Ha, by the by, I saw him with Urangos,
His skill in pyrotechnics, as I take it,
Being brought in requisition by the priest.

ARCHBISHOP: Ah, say you so? in sooth that bronzen image
Is more suggestive of the Salamander,
Than one that breathes the air.

NUNCIO: Thus, just the man to help our zealous brother
In the vast struggle to eclipse the shows
Of our metropolis.

ARCHBISHOP: I hear you take his pulpit on the eighth.

NUNCIO: Yes, at his strenuous instance, I agree
To lend my aid to close the festival.

ARCHBISHOP: What thinks your eminence of Europe now?

NUNCIO: Nay — add the world, and in a few brief words
I'll show you my opinion.

ARCHBISHOP: Fain would I hear it brother.

NUNCIO: Despite dark warnings overthrows, rebukes;
Ambition takes no heed; persistent still;
These godless *juntos* labor to reform
Vast cumbrous circles round a central power;
For why? for what? while man is what he is,
And hath been ever — engines of oppression,

Under whatever name. God left his protest
On the first Babel 'gainst these coalitions
And registered his fiat in the tongues —
Those landmarks of our nationalities,
The terrible crystal of eternal truth
Hath smitten the old image of oppression,
And woe to those who touch the accursed fragments
To reconstruct. That's my opinion.

ARCHBISHOP: Most reverend brother, did the time allow,
'Twould be a pleasant subject to pursue
Through all its leadings.

NUNCIO: We'll take your Grace's hint and waive it
Till further leisure. Good-day.

Exits. Re-enter Credulos.

ARCHBISHOP: My son, what brought you back so soon? and yet
I'm glad of it. To say the truth, I feel
Uneasy apprehensions of this stranger.

CREDULOS: I thought you did, therefore returned to ease
Your Grace's mind thereon, if possible.

ARCHBISHOP: Your meeting, and escape, down to the port
I know, now briefly tell me what you saw
Of him while on your voyage here!

CREDULOS: Truly like all the rest, 'tis marvelous,
But not suspicious.

ARCHBISHOP: Proceed, and let me judge of it.

CREDULOS: By day he found at times, an unctuous pleasure
In one rough skipper's slang, and northern phrase —
To me an uncouth jargon. Suddenly,
He'd break away — in wild abstraction walk,
Like an inspired colossus, to and fro
Dirging a tune; but when the freshening gale
Swept o'er the deck, and curled the rising wave,
He seemed the avant courier of the Gods
With agitated plumes alighted down
For rest or recreation on our decks,
Again about to fly.

ARCHBISHOP: There, there — and then at night?

CREDULOS: When night came on, 'twas then in truth appeared
His force of character — mounting the bulworks,
Tripping round the bows — out on the bowsprit —

Standing with folded arms above the surge,
On easy balance like the resting gull,
Calm on the rocking sea. The sight of him
Embarassed much one's breathing — yes, while he
A ranting Triton trumpeted our march
Across the ocean swell —

ARCHBISHOP: When did he retire?

CREDULOS: When or where, none ever knew, your Reverence.

ARCHBISHOP: Had he then no berth?

CREDULOS: Your Grace, he never used one.

ARCHBISHOP: What thought your Captain of him?

CREDULOS: Sire, all I ever learn't of his opinion,
Was rendered thus: "a darned queer critter this,
And no mistake!"

ARCHBISHOP: How did the seamen treat him?

CREDULOS: From reverance or fear, always avoided him:
One day I overheard them in discourse
Assert his features like a glowing coal
Glared in the darkness; so awe-struck were they.

ARCHBISHOP: My son, I must dismiss you with my mind
More puzzled than before. Peace be with you.

They exit.

SCENE V

The Sacristy of the Compania. Enter Fargo and Castanos.

FARGO: Castanos, why so dumb? You seem to move
Hither and thither in a reverie.

CASTANOS: Not without reason, brother.

FARGO: Reason — what can have happened then,
Whereof I may not know.

CASTANOS: Take you much note of dreams, Good Fargo?

FARGO: Sometimes; when did you dream?

CASTANOS: Last night.

FARGO: Perhaps something doleful, was it?
    Pray tell it me — speak low.

CASTANOS: I will, and yet I fear to bring it back.
    To my affrighted mind — I seemed
    Bewildered on a wide and blighted plain;
    'Twas night and apprehension on the rack.
    Awaiting something dreadful! all at once
    A glare of horrid light burst through the darkness,
    So blasting to the sight I could not tell
    At first from whence it issued. Soon appeared
    A roaring cordon of volcanic cones
    Erupting fire!

FARGO: Terrible indeed, but not uncommon here.

CASTANOS: Ah, hear me out, the hideous smoke assumed
    Appalling shapes, like devils shot from guns;
    The roar broke into howling; from the flames
    Red snakes vermiculated down the hills,
    And lost themselves in one vast sea of fire
    Devouring all the plain! the trembling earth,
    Dissolving round me, broke away and rose
    In wild tumultuous waves.

FARGO: Good heavens, that would be dreadful!

CASTANOS: Ah, brother, think of it, that spot of earth
    I stood on, loosened from the main,
    Rolled like a water-logged, dismantled hulk
    Among the fiery spray — listen good Fargo
    Those livid billows leaping up around me
    Were crested with known faces, hideous
    With pain, and each successive wave
    Discharged wild shrieks of anguish!
    Now mark — to crown these complicated horrors;
    There issued from that writhing, roaring deluge
    A dreadful shape, borne up on dragon wings,
    Armed with a flaming trident! such a yell
    Burst from the fiend — it swallowed every cry —
    Here I awoke — List Fargo — that dread spirit
    Was this same stranger!

FARGO: Most horrible — yet all a dream.

CASTANOS: Hush! — here he comes.

Enter Urangos and Vampries.

URANGOS: True, as you say, Saint Peter's blaze of splendor
Owes to this dangerous agent its success.

VAMPRIES: None doubts the fact — the essential spirit
Of quick and active fire dwells in these fluids
But then remember tongues of living flame
Announced at Pentecost the coming in
Of this great dispensation! wherefore then
This dubious dread of heaven's selected sign?
It were enough to implicate your faith!

FARGO: Most fairly rendered, and my mind's consent
Goes with this cogent reason.

URANGOS: Then no more parley with pale shrinking fear;
Time cites to instant action.

VAMPRIES: Now ye speak like men!

URANGOS: Fargo, I challenge now your ready zeal,
Go urge this business, up and add more strength
Where our ingredients wane. Castanos, thou
Shake off this lukewarm sloth, and play the man.

They exit.

ACT III

SCENE I

A room in a hotel. Enter Gorman and Diaz reading a letter.

GORMAN: What news from Valparaiso?

DIAZ: News! expectation stands on tiptoe *there*
Stretching her neck for news from Santiago.

GORMAN: God speed the press say I, a glorious following!
Widening the circles of its proud domain
With every missile of contention thrown
Athwart the popular wave.
Potters, glaziers, and quack doctors thrive
On accidents and human miseries,

Which leave their fractured vessels beyond cure:
But see how we can override this line
Of drivelling practice, we their trumpetors
From draught or pill of artful empiric
Extract our wind. A fair precipitate
Of scandal, accidents and litigations
Our daily gatherings, with politics
Our stalking horse for beef.

DIAZ: Hold, Gorman, hold lest thou fulfill the adage —
"Foul is the bird that soils his homely nest,
Where he was nurtured."

GORMAN: Let me illustrate — the other day,
Forage being scarce, sensation paragraphs
Grown stale, I pitched into old Capulet,
A piece played off before against the house
Of rival Montague — one prick behind
Brought up the starch hidalgo with a bounce!
I hooked my fish and kept him well in play,
Till other game was started.

DIAZ: Most dangerous game I'm thinking.

GORMAN: Not for your Nimrod bred among the bears
In northern Gotham, where *I* learned the craft.
No game too high to strike — men, families,
Or nations; judge, priest, or president,
Matron or maid — for your almighty hunter
Lawful prey! *There,* boy, our sway is potent
As the rescriptions of an Emperor.
Tell me, dearest Di, your favourite dodges.

DIAZ: Far less ambitious, bred in tamer school;
My speculations take a humbler range —
Sensation paragraphs, and politics
Sur highest flight.

GORMAN: O with paper agonies, blue fluid battles,
Murders, "devouring elements," and broken bones
Your humble engine groans — he?

DIAZ: I own to this impeachment.

GORMAN: Well, not so bad for your laborious tug,
A local drudge to ply around the port,
Or coast a little; not the craft for me.
Your roaring steamer launched upon the waves
Of human agitations, in her hold
A thousand horses, snorting at the touch
Of aggravating fires! on her approach

Lightnings await to thrill the iron nerves
Of a vast continent!
That's *my* jewel, there's the berth for *me!*
But tell me, Diaz, know you anything
Of that queer devil yclept "the stranger?"

DIAZ: But little — Yes, I've seen him in the church
Prompting the priest Urangos.

GORMAN: To me that fellow's an infernal riddle,
As such I patronize him — mysteries
Intrigues and plots, my life sustaining breath;
Their charm attracts me like an evil eye.
I asked him hither, should he come, I pray
Be not afraid — Ha! *Aside.*   Talk of the devil
When, lo, he appears!
Enter Vampries.
Welcome, most reverend seignior!
What of the night, my friend?

VAMPRIES: The watch is newly set, her sentinels
Wink round the peak of Tupuagato.
Commend me to your friend, here.

GORMAN: Diaz, — my friend, "The Stranger," — your *nom de guerre?*

VAMPRIES: Exactly, at your pleasure.

GORMAN: Be seated, sir, — Rumour assigns to you
Good senor, a new Pelides?

VAMPRIES: Sir — explain?

GORMAN: Pardon, if I offend, yet it is patent
How you are touching up for our Urangos
His grand illustrations.

VAMPRIES: They'll doubtless be imposing.

GORMAN: Fame gives you credit for the better part
Of these arrangements.

VAMPRIES: Bare *credit* yet, cashed only by success;
Till then an unpaid bill.

GORMAN: Surely you see no omens of a flare
Beyond your stipulations?

VAMPRIES: Omens! earth, air — and yon significant stars
Are full of omens.

GORMAN: To your deep practiced eyes. I'd fain take lessons
In this quaint science of astrology.

VAMPRIES: Nay — mock not! Think you I am one to deal
In obsolete absurdity? Adieu.
Exit Vampries.

GORMAN: That look struck me clean dumb! I've let him go
Ununctioned by apology! Diaz,
Thou seems distraught, what ponderest thou?

DIAZ: I would not have that man my enemy —

GORMAN: Nor I, if lowly suit can soften him —
Come with me, let us follow him.

DIAZ: Excuse me, I much fear him.

GORMAN: And thou a man? a friend? come on
We'll laugh it off in jest.

DIAZ: Inflaming thus his pride to fiery wrath,
And your perdition!

GORMAN: Come friend, and rescue me by your discretion.

They exit.

SCENE II

An open place near Santiago. Enter Treacher and Avero.

TREACHER: Now tell me Basilisk, what hast thou learn't?

AVERO: Nay, treat me civily; I'll answer to my name.
Remember we are in a Christian city,
And stand on equal terms.

TREACHER: O that's your cue now all the gilt is gone,
Well then, I'll humour thee — proceed.

AVERO: By way of preface, as the night was falling
I saw the Don or else his apparition.

TREACHER: By Jabus — no!

AVERO: No other I assure you.

TREACHER: What next, great Avero — did he see you?

AVERO: No, no! I minded that.

TREACHER: Lucky! we'll blot out our identity,
If our poor means will serve — go on.

AVERO: I found a kennel in a ruinous suburb,
Where we can stretch our limbs.

TREACHER: What is it like my gentle Avero?

AVERO: A tavern kept by an Hibernian
Of easy conscience and a facile wit.

TREACHER: His company, no doubt, select?

AVERO: Swell negroes, drovers, muleteers, Indian
Hunters from the hills. This ragged regiment
Officered by faded gentlemen.

TREACHER: Well beggars have little choice. Say Avero
Where you acquired such language?

AVERO: Strange question, *now,* why ask it?

TREACHER: Oddly timed, no doubt — I often mark you,
Like a small Samson rise and shake yourself
As just awake from some Delilah's shears.

AVERO: Cutting simile! it minds me of the years
I've ground in prison — sport for my companions!
Your wretched Troglodite, once honoured, trusted —
Walked off with their exchequer — hence his fall!
Never probe me more.   *Shedding tears.*

TREACHER: Nay man, I would not trouble you —
What learnt you of mine host, and what among
The illustrious constituencies?

AVERO: 'Mong other items that tomorrow night
Comes off the grand finale of the long feast
Of the Immacculate.

TREACHER: Well, what is that to us with empty pockets?

AVERO: A time and place to fill 'em.

TREACHER: Explain?

AVERO: There is a church called 'The Compania'
They hold a grand illumination there.
A crowd will congregate — of ladies chiefly.
Daughters of Mary! bless 'em — in their best —
Jeweled to match; let us but gain admission;
Once in the crowd, 'twere sheer stupidity
Not to admire — you know!

TREACHER: I understand; your scheme seems feasible.

AVERO: I'm sure our winking host will not object
To take a *sleeping* partnership — hark!
That voice — it comes this way —

TREACHER: I know it, quick — steal to that copse.

They exit. Enter Vampries.

VAMPRIES: I've watched the shadow creeping up the hills
Like apprehension at the heels of hope —
Winning its way till all is left in darkness.
I saw the beam across those mighty peaks
In even balance. Fatal counterpoise!
Symbolical of that tyrannous power
Weighing those mountains. Stolid nature bend!
Why should each day repeat her homilies?
And lecture still this unresisting slave
Of grim necessity? It might suffice —
Go witness, thou relentless demon, go,
As I have done of late, the tombs of kings
Those ghastly fragments of departed power!
I stood in Luxor; in the exhumed palace
Of proud Senachrib. Looking back I saw,
Through all the silent past, the dream revive
Sesostris in shadowy pomp lead out
His conquering fyles to subjugate a world!
The Assyrian Jackall, glutted with the blood
Of worried nations, leaves the vulgar offal
To feed the crows. And think ye to escape
Ye spiritual hierarchies the common doom?
What, make your structures timeproof with cement
Of mouldy superstitions? pointing up.
This moral rotteness with weak concrete
Y'cleped "Emaculate"! 'Tis but to hang
A new encumbrance on a tottering base!
'Tis thus, O fate, revolving centuries whirl
In idle dust, the pomp and state of man!
And yet — from these fantastic ashes springs
This germ of Hope the living to sustain
Across the gulf of life. Not so the damned!
His ixion wheel bears on the essential body

Undesolved — fit horologue of hell —
To point and tongue its dreadful revolutions
Never to pause! *Enter Roland.*
Sir, a citizen! I dare avouch it
Since none from home so peaceful and subdued.

ROLAND: You judge me rightly, sir — a resident.

VAMPRIES: Sweetly yon snow-clad giants icy breath
Tempers the evening air.

ROLAND: Yes, 'tis the mildest of their attributes,
Surcharged with earthquake, avalanche and fire!
Might I presume — a recent visitor?

VAMPRIES: Ten days ago I reached these southern shores
From the antipodes.

ROLAND: A bound from Cancer down to Capricorn
Is a most desperate leap!

VAMPRIES: How oddly your December summer contrasts
With chilly Kurdistan.

ROLAND: *Terra incognita,* to our good Chileans,
To me, a land of special interest.

VAMPRIES: You know it, then?

ROLAND: Only from history — sacred and profane —
We claim the Ararat as sacred ground.

VAMPRIES: And why?

ROLAND: Because the Ark there rested, and 'tis deemed
The scene of the temptation.

VAMPRIES: Mere idle legends, pray excuse the term
I know its shaggy top, from long acquaintance.

ROLAND: Indeed! I thought it inaccessible?

VAMPRIES: To *common* tourists only — pray excuse me, sir,
My time is up. Good evening.   *Exits.*

ROLAND: Strange person this, and that sardonic sneer!
Tells nothing in his favour. A stranger
Therefore no hard construction shall he have
From one who bore a stranger's lonesome heart
Once o'er this very ground!   *Exits.*

SCENE III

A room in the Archepiscopal Palace. Enter Crapo and Tabatha.

CRAPO: Tabby, dear, don't you think his reverence looked a little down as he left the palace today?

TABATHA: I did not observe it, sir, why should he, I wonder?

CRAPO: Goodness knows, for I warrant you he and the grand Roman will be the biggest guns let off tomorrow; I shall go to see the church, get a letter from the Virgin's post-office, and see the dignitaries in their robes — Three birds killed with one stone! Ha, ha, ha.

TABATHA: Oh, Mr. Crapo, I should so like a letter from the Virgin Mary!

CRAPO: Well Tabby, I've put in for one — maybe I can do something for you with the priest; the father is very accommodating. You see I'm always in with the clergy — hand me your money, *that* you know always works wonders. *Winking.*

TABATHA: Good, Mr. Crapo, you was always a kind man, here is the money. *Handing it over.*

CRAPO: Say nothing about it to old Dorcas; she'll go mad with envy, now I must seek Gormuz. *Exits.*

TABATHA: If I should be so lucky! I wonder what the Virgin will say — something very very nice — how very wonderful to think on. *Enter Dorcas.*

DORCAS: You, Tabby, here? the day gone and nothing done! that old cady's tongue will ruin *you* like all the rest that enter these doors! once out of my sight, and nothing going on but idle talk. Come huzzy — come away; the house in disorder at such a time as this! *They exit. Re-enter Crapo.*

CRAPO: It's enough to make a saint give in! what I have taken from that woman, to be sure! I thought she would have knocked me off the stairs, or bitten the nose off my face! No more of Tabby tonight I fear. At her about the letters, and the money — the old infidel; she must have listened, or done worse, dealt with a familiar spirit! yes, wicked enough for *that,* and in a religious house too, shocking to think on! *Enter Gormuz.* Oh Gormuz — how did you slip past?

GORMUZ: I just dodged about till the course was clear.

CRAPO: Depend upon it, the old sinner would like a letter as well as anybody.

GORMUZ: Aye, I know, she's too fond of her money, bless you.

CRAPO: And too old and ugly for one of the *Daughters.*

GORMUZ: Aye, that's it — I knowed 'twere like Eve and the apples — her mouth was a'watering all the time. *Re-enter Tabatha.* Golly, thought the old un was coming! Tabby, are we safe?

TABATHA: She's gone to her room.

GORMUZ: Didn't yer perceive, wench, when she said in that scornful way, "the letters are none of hern," it was all spite?

TABATHA: And you think, Mr. Crapo, the letters are not *forgeries* as she calls them!

CRAPO: Make yourself easy, Tabatha, I have no patience to think of it.

GORMUZ: Why, it's wicked to doubt em Tabby.

CRAPO: Ah, talk of wickedness — I'll tell you what brought me to my senses on such things — the great earthquake of 1822. I was just come to the country, and put up at a cafe in Valparaiso. There was a many rough seafaring men, and others still worse in the house; such swearing as there was on that particular night! The bar was full of noise and blasphemy at ten or a little after I was on the stairs going to bed when the awful crash came! the stairs seemed to straighten up before me; before I could stretch out my hand to anything I was flat on my back, my mouth the extinguisher, and those blasphemers rushing over me to the door, some calling on the Virgin, others with half spoken oaths, others dumb with terror. As I struggled to my feet I heard groans deep down under like the bowels of the earth in distress — heaving too like great sea waves, everything above ground creaking, cracking, bowing and falling, where nothing could fall, the ground seemed trying to swallow you up — stone walls, roofs, churches — swaying about like trees in a tempest; people rushing wildly about, into the danger they sought to escape, it made one's heart stop to see it! falling houses alive with dreadful cries, struggling forms, screams, groans, prayers! dust, crash — fire glaring among frightful rents of houses ready to fall on the persons within, unable to open the doors. Now the sea rose like a boiling pan of milk, and the troubled earth — think of it — the solid ground worse than the deck of a ship in a storm, such sounds too, far away and near, as if the big mountains had tumbled over and smashed the face of the earth. To finish up, the sea rose like a great roaring monster ready to swallow up the whole country.

GORMUZ: My! that was a fix — what did you think would become on yer?

CRAPO: At one time I gave up all hope. Flying away from everything that could fall. To look down the streets was dreadful! The moon and stars, calm and bright as if nothing had happened — this, and red glowing fires which broke out gave a dismal light; poor creatures crushed and bleeding, limping past a bowing wall, their tread bringing it down on them! Oh Gorman — to see them escaped from one death walk into another, and no power to help or warn them, made me mad with distress, so I fled away to the open country.

TABATHA: Oh dear Mr. Crapo! please don't tell any more about them earthquakes; I saw the last and it makes me tremble all over again! oh dear.

CRAPO: No Tabby, I have no wish to frighten you, I only wish to show you such calamities sharpen our faith, and drive us to the Virgin for protection.

GORMUZ: Well Crapo, at a time like that, I should think more of the son nor the mother. You see she makes a fine image and writes beautiful letters — beautiful! but I think t'other has rather most power.

CRAPO: Excuse me, Gorman — you're from the north, its quite excusable, they are not so enlightened among the heretics.

GORMUZ: Golly — listen, I hear the olden about agin! let's clear. *They exit.*

SCENE VI

The Sacristy. Enter Costello.

COSTELLO: Oh God forgive me! Is it wavering Faith?
How much I see so hard to understand
Or tolerate. I fear, an hypocrite
Walks forth concealed behind this priestly stole —
I hate an hypocrite! Lo, solemn vows
Are on me; while I live upon the altar
Which I serve! what then ensues? Deceiver —
Heretic! and other hornets may escape
Pandora's box which plague the ear, yea worse
That sting the conscience. I hate to think on't.
Enter Castanor. You're seeking me?

CASTANOR: Yes, so was I commanded.

COSTELLO: By whom?

CASTANOR: Urangos.

COSTELLO: For what especial end?

CASTANOR: That all absorbing one if I judge rightly,
The illumination.

COSTELLO: I shall not hurry since it is to serve
No sasardotal call.

CASTANOR: I've given you due notice brother,
So you must answer it.

COSTELLO: Most certainly, but to confess my views —
These garish shows I hate.

CASTANOR: Strong language, brother — I'm not your confessor.

COSTELLO: I cannot help it, for besides the danger,
It seems a profanation.

CASTANOR: At what particular breast point ye these strictures?

COSTELLO: That lying fraud, the Post Office, and this
Extravagant and dangerous flare.

CASTANOR: I thought we had renounced all private judgment?

COSTELLO: Surely not all!

CASTANOR: Good Costello — time, place and circumstance,
Make indiscreet, perhaps dangerous,
This contraband discourse.

COSTELLO: Faith! let me take it as a just rebuke;
This sample of a true and constant heart
To holy mother church — admire.

CASTANOR: Nay flatter not, nor feel unmeant rebuke
My moods are now ungentle — hark, they call.

Voices from the Church. They exit.

SCENE V

A Street. Enter Norman and Clouden.

NORMAN: Know ye the man we met?

CLOUDEN: Know him? As soon admit the Devil himself
To my acquaintance.

NORMAN: I fear me this Urangos' fiery science,
Comes through this salamanda.

CLOUDEN: Could I believe those bug-bears of your faith,
I'd judge that walking smoke, jack nothing less
Than goblin from below.

NORMAN: Thank heaven, my creed from all these fooleries
Which flourish here, hath long been swept. Most true
This stranger seems a dangerous mystery. *Enter Roland.*

CLOUDEN: Give me your hand good Roland, hence our tongues
    Shall run in sweet accord: but did *thee* know
    I have turned quaker? Hence to *thou* and *thee*
    My father or a king — for conscience sake!

ROLAND: Ah friend these arrows heedlessly let fly
    At sect so harmless, have a larger range —
    There levelled at the heart of all devotion.

CLOUDEN: Well, an' t'will please you, let me doff the broad brim —
    Swap Ephraim's bell-pulls fur a shaver crown
    Turn out, a walking candlestick i' th' street,
    Will that square any better?

ROLAND: Trifle not — if thou be more than beast,
    With that high faculty which apprehends
    A God; and yields to him a ready homage —
    Such worship as shall satisfy thy soul,
    With all the light around thee; being sincere
    'Twill be accepted. *Through the atonement.*
    There's surely room betwixt these two extremes
    At which you stumble? Meaning no offence,
    My charity regards with far less blame
    Those overt actions of an ardent faith
    Than the cold opposite — no faith at all.

NORMAN: A Protestant and thus accommodating?
    Such casuistries paliate all rites;
    Unscriptural and extravagant.

ROLAND: Yes, paliate I would, but not commend,
    Ought that my rule, and conscience disapprove.
    When I remember how this hierarchy
    Did battle with the world's idolatries
    Of ancient times, and for a thousand more
    Great memories, I feel we owe too much
    To wish her aught but health, *regeneration*
    And God's speed!
    Frail human nature stands before her Lord
    Like the adulteress covered with shame.
    Let hands whose conscience must convict of sin
    Forbear to cast a stone. With God alone
    These heavier judgments rest.

NORMAN: Abate your mild behests "Those heavier judgments"
    Sound like prophetic words.

CLOUDEN: Farewell, sweet honied charity.   *They exit.*

ACT IV

SCENE I

A room in a tavern. Music — A dance of the motley company — Negroes, Indians, Gamblers, Muleteers, etc. Song — By a gentleman of colour.

Dis chile him so almighty smart,
Becase ob dis high breedin;
De book — I had him all by hart
Widout the trouble readin.

When I wos born I members well —
De queer dark place Ise born in;
I rub my eyes, sez I — "Ole gal —
How long before it's mornin?"

Whares I wos raised em know it well —
Dare gineral remark is —
"Dis sarcumstance is why de call
Dese coloured people "Darkies".

Up norte em say 'de washed out white'
Some darkey blood am needin;
Dem waitin till hab don dare fight
Den take dem all for breedin!

Uproarious applause. They exit.

SCENE II

A private room in the tavern. Enter Scran and Sheeram.

SCRAN: I sent for you misther, Sheeram, to speak wid you ov the two gintlemen staying in my house, that I mentioned afore in discourse wid you.

SHEERAM: Your nation ish very polite, but use de time with many vords. I am Eli — you are Pat — dare den, vill dat do?

SCRAN: Aye, faith will it, ant ye say so.

SHEERAM: Time ish de meat, monish de gravey;
Ven de meat ish vell done
De gravy vil run! dat ish my own remark.

SCRAN: Bedad Eli an its fine pothery.
Dese shentleman's in your house ish dem rascals.

111

SCRAN: How know you that?

SHEERAM: My leetle bird tell me. Now, vat they vant!

SCRAN: Nothing — gist nothing.

SHEERAM: Very vell — Patrick Swan vas always a sensible man;
He knows de vays of goot buisnish — tell me vot
Your friends vant vithout more vords.

SCRAN: Faith an they wants to attend festival this evening in clothes fit to stand
among the ladies wearing the fine jewelry — that's what's they want.

SHEERAM: Vel, you shall see de Jew vill lend his raiment for good Christian
shentleman's to worship te Virgin! Say, dat ish liberal.

SCRAN: I'll send them in to you. *Exits.*

SHEERAM: Mr. Swan ish a very goot man! *Enter Treacher and Avero.* So you
are de goot pious men vantin garments for ta temple, to vate upon de virgin and her
holy daughters — say is dat de ting?

TREACHER: Well, something like it.

SHEERAM: An your fren, so dumb and vise — vat does he say of dese tings?

AVERO: Oh! we row in the same boat; where he steers I follow.

SHEERAM: Vara goot — I sal bring you my vara best suits of raiments, and for my
clos you vill pay four dollors de suit, dat vil please you?

TREACHER: Pretty good pay for a night's wear.

AVERO: Golly! is it not?

SHEERAM: Vell, you sall do better, I am content — hear me to de end — and if I or
you find anything in de pocket — come in by accident, you understand? I vill pay
de fallest price — dare now!

TREACHER: Well, bring em on.

SHEERAM: And you sar?

AVERO: I'm content, bring me a smart suit.

SHEERAM: Smart day sal he — goot and smart — dat is in de new style vate one
small moment. *Exit Jew.*

TREACHER: Avero, we are in luck, for think'st thou not
We've skill enough to give this fox the slip?

AVERO: Or else our practice is to little purpose.

TREACHER: For such a service they'll be sober black,
With a white choker; add some odd trimmings, and
We might commence the trade of wandering friars,
Hedge priests or Acolytes, just as the turn
Might serve — what is your mind upon it?

AVERO: Once grab the stock, our tact may surely serve
For something short of coarse and brutal murder!

TREACHER: Hush e-e. *Enter Scran.*

SCRAN: Well boys, hev ye secured the togs?

TREACHER: The Jew has gone for them.

SCRAN: Onst in his liveries — bedad, look out! he'll hev
His eye upon ye till safely back with payment.

TREACHER: Those who intend no wrong have none to fear, I trust?

SCRAN: None in the least, my friend, only keep on the squares wid the old fellow,
and ye'll hev the length of his foot. *Re-enter Sheeram.* Be the powers! here he is
true as a trojan.

SHEERAM: Vas you tink different — tell me, vas you?

SCRAN: The very soul of honor — I know't.

SHEERAM: Here ish de clos, goodly as te garment of Babylon.
Which Achan did hide in hish tent, *and lost ish life!*
Looking gravely at them.
Give us de private apartments, Patrick, ve
Vil fit em to de body's — come away.

They exit. Re-enter Scran and Sheeram.

SHEERAM: You brought avay the key?

SCRAN: Faith, but I hev, the birds are safe.

SHEERAM: Did you give dem de hint?

SCRAN: I did, they dare not bolt — I'll sware it.

SHEERAM: Dat ish goot — you loos, I loos, both alike in dis
Cave of Adullam with de scape grace.

SCRAN: Thrue for you, Misther Eli.

113

SHEERAM: Now da vil be into de clos, you vill vate to see.

SCRAN: Sure I will, here is the kay.   *Exit Jew.*
Be the holy pope! but it will be a tough piece of confession, will this some day —
whenever I come to make a clane breast of it! Niver can I face the Virgin — this
night and year of our Lord, after plotting for her daughter's jewels! be the powers
it's a ugly business.   *Walking to and fro, groaning. Re-enter Sheeram, Treacher
and Avero.*
Misther Eli, yez made perfect gintlemen ov poor
Vagabones! saving yer presence, frinds.

SHEERAM: Vel, dat ish all right — de fit ish illigant.   *Turning them about.*   You
are free and welcome to go over de house, but let me advise for your goot — do not
go about te street. Keep close till ye go off fresh and genteel to de temple — take my
goot advice — dat is all.   *Treacher and Avero exit.*
Tish done so much, Misther Swan must keep vatch
I vill keep vatch — my people sall keep vatch.   *They exit.*

SCENE III

A Street. Enter Vampries and Credulos.

VAMPRIES: Indeed, the very ruffian — he who cast
So ruthlessly that body o'er the rocks —
His pal and he are here!

CREDULOS: Nay — is it so? 'tis terrible to think on!
What brings them hither?

VAMPRIES: Plunder.

CREDULOS: Pray God it's nothing worse; assassination
Stalks on behind me like an armed ghost
Waiting to strike. Good Lord, preserve me!
Greatly excited.

VAMPRIES: Dismiss these fears; They're in the greater peril.

CREDULOS: Alas, I carry about their bloody writ
But fear the risk to nail it to the scaffold
Would I were rid of it.

VAMPRIES: Patience man — there is a secret spirit
Who goes in circuit holding regular court
Throughout the moral world. Now, mark me senor —
His officer is after them!

CREDULOS: Once valiant faith! 'Twas equal at all points;
 Has ta'en such damage in his bouts with men
 'Tis hard to rally — who is this justice?

VAMPRIES: Retribution.

CREDULOS: I might have guess'd it, but my mind is dulled
 With terror and mistrust.

VAMPRIES: Whip up your courage, man — twist out the wheel
 From this deep muddy rut. I have my eye
 On your sly enemies — the toils are round them
 E'en now they're being played off 'gainst other pieces,
 In a fresh game. They deign you no regard!

CREDULOS: I'll bless the holy Virgin for this thing —
 I'm proud of their contempt!

VAMPRIES: I could, with ease have compassed their destruction,
 Why not? to catch these most voracious pike
 My gudgeon must have suffered, he, alas,
 To limp already!

CREDULOS: Safe — I can afford your jest.

VAMPRIES: Now Don, attend to me! no time to waste;
 I have for once, a curious regard
 For one thrown on my hands as you have been —
 Let me advise — eschew the dangerous *crush.*
 Tonight at the "Compania" — Farewell. *Exits.*

CREDULOS: My eyes seem strangely opening — but to what?
 For who can understand this airy compound
 Of insolence and pride? Yet tempered so
 With fitful kindness — kindness is it? no,
 I fear me not — mere whim and patronage.
 I've rent of him, but never saw before
 Guy Fawkes in effigy till this last scene!
 What can I do? Why, warned about a danger,
 I'll ponder on it, being so bound to him;
 'Twere sheer ingratitude to carp and strain
 At hard constructions. *Exits.*

SCENE IV

Front of the "Compania." View of the Interior, Post Office etc. Enter Urangos.

URANGOS: Yes, I had well forejudged this correspondence
        Twixt holy mother and her lively daughters,
        No sinecure; but then it brings in wealth
        While giving harmless pleasure — what is more
        Poor feeble staggering faith puts out its hand
        To something tangible. Its trembling steps
        Must be sustained, and do require at times
        Some virtuous deception: what of it?
        A river turbid at its hidden source
        Filters away its pristine feculence
        Among the stones and sedges in its race;
        So the red runnel grows into a stream
        Of limpid living water.
        Exit Urangos to the Post Office. Enter Marie.
                                Daughter, 'tis well;
        Our Lady deigns to you her special favors —
        See — here's a letter, radiant with her grace
        Directed —   *Reads.*   "Maria, my beloved!"

MARIA: Oh Father, give it me.   *Kissing it, greatly excited.*
        And if I may acquit a debt so high
        With golden dross — take this.

Exits. Enter a bevy of ladies, taking letters, talking — great excitement. Re-enter Maria, urging in Susannah.

MARIA: Sister dear, you know I have no secrets,
        But which your faithful bosom share with me;
        Here is my letter — how it smells of heaven!
        And think you not, sweet Sue, a heavenly lustre
        Starts from this caligraph?   *Kissing it.*

SUSANNAH: Open it child.

MARIA: Ah! I see it moves my cooler sister
        Almost to impatience; yet, how dares one
        Break or mutilate this sacred seal?

SUSANNAH: Here, give it me.   *Opening she reads.*
        Daughter beloved,
        I well knew what passion moved your gentle heart before the written appeals; and
        next to your vows, and the claims of heaven, I hold a kindly interest in these
        affairs of the heart. Know daughter, when I favor its aspirations, I give effectual
        aid. Carry yourself before him with modesty and discretion, and Cortez shall be
        yours.
        Beloved, Faithfully Yours, Mary.

MARIA: *Hands and eyes raised in a rapture — repeats:*   Hail Mary etc.   *Enter
        Cortez.*

CORTEZ: Ladies, so fortunate, to meet again!

SUSANNAH: Most timely — here's my sister with good news,
Fresh from the Virgin.

CORTEZ: Indeed! permit me to congratulate her then —
Dear Mary —

SUSANNAH: Nay, heed her not, her mind is discomposed
By the celestial missive. Come with me;
You also are a candidate, I see,
For Mary's favours — follow us sister.

CORTEZ: *Crossing to the Post Office.*
Father Urangos — ho! letters, letters.

URANGOS: *At slide door.*   My son, and you, my daughter;
For each of you a letter.

CORTEZ: And here good father, take your postage.

URANGOS: My blessing — and adieu.   *They exit. Enter Vampries.*
Ah stranger, we have practised with your light —
Surpassing all in power; 'tis wonderful!
A sunbeam to the cold and pallid ray
Of our nocturnal lamp — but harkee, friend,
Thinks thou there's danger? Speak it low.

VAMPRIES: Danger? where is the pathway ever trod
By mortal feet, but hides a lurking death?
Boldness shall pass unscathed where craven fear
Invites the ambushed foe to rise and strike.

URANGOS: Fairly I stand committee to this trial —
In one short hour the fiery ordeal comes!

VAMPRIES: Truly yes, the auspicious time draws on
The grand climaster of your gala day
Which shall be memorable!

URANGOS: Verily, does thou think so?

VAMPRIES: Assuredly.   *Calls at the Post Office. Exit Urangos.*
Poor dupe — an ordeal truly which shall make
The bleeding hearts of hundreds dirge their loss
Through many dolorous octaves. Poor Urangos,
Illustrious candidate for high renown —
Eclipsing Herostratus!   *Exits. Enter Crapo.*

CRAPO: Yes, truly — from the Virgin! God bless her!
To think this comes all the way from heaven, and
To a poor serving man like me — wonderful!
Kissing it and weeping for joy. It will surprise 'em at the palace. Gormuz shall read it to me, my eyes fail so of late — how condescending to be sure of our holy mother to take such trouble for her unworthy son. I thought that gentleman in the dark complexion looked envious as I took my letter — well he might — perhaps disappointed of one himself. I'll hurry home. *Exits. Post Office still thronged by "Daughters of Mary," and others.*

SCENE V

A room in the Palace. Enter Archbishop and Costello.

ARCHBISHOP: Urangos strains beyond all bounds, I fear,
The license of the Church.

COSTELLO: Your grace, so others think.

ARCHBISHOP: This festival, thus far, hath been to us
A pleasant interlude 'mid common cares;
Why should we sully, on this closing eve,
Our sacred dignity — turn our sublime
To rank absurdity?

COSTELLO: With these just views, why not your reverence come
And interfere?

ARCHBISHOP: Costello, 'tis too late! I've held the reins
With much too light a hand; confusion *now* —
Perhaps secret schism, would alone ensue
At such untimely check.

COSTELLO: Another matter in this night's proceedings,
Has brought me to your grace.

ARCHBISHOP: Speak it.

COSTELLO: We fear Urangos, since his eminence
Hath pricked his emulation with the spur
Of Rome's unrivalled splendours, has become
Most reckless to excell: I need not tell
Your grace the danger of excess in using
This fiery element.

ARCHBISHOP: Jesu, Maria, save us! the legate
Did but jest.

COSTELLO: Then what shall be our course?

ARCHBISHOP: Watch with a careful eye, and over all —
Pray God avert calamity! *Exit Costello.*
Mary and all the saints befriend us!
To suffer this rash man to play fanatic —
That not enough, lo, now to push his follies
Hard on the frightful verge, at least,
Of dire catastrophy — again to start
The howling wolves that hover round the fold,
And — *Enter Fargo.*
Most opportune — good brother, tell me all
You know of the Compania?

FARGO: I'm proud to tell your grace it far outrivals
Ought seen before in Santiago!

ARCHBISHOP: My heart misgives me and foreshadows grief —
Some great approaching trouble.

FARGO: I fear Costello's nervous apprehension
Has wrought upon your grace.

ARCHBISHOP: Pray, have you seen him lately?

FARGO: Just met him on the street.

ARCHBISHOP: Spake ye together of this?

FARGO: Little of ought save street civilities.

ARCHBISHOP: How seemed he?

FARGO: Hurried and anxious, like a poor confessor
Who has outlived his Faith.

ARCHBISHOP: Hum. Say what hath brought you hither?

FARGO: To pray your grace before the night comes on,
Would with His Eminence of Rome vouchsafe
A visit; thus giving our endeavours
Your gracious sanction.

ARCHBISHOP: Good Fargo, there are things I scarce approve;
How can I sanction them?

FARGO: Your grace confounds me; would you condescend
Some explanation?

ARCHBISHOP: 'Tis inexpedient *now:* On second thoughts,
I think it best to visit you.

FARGO: Thanks to your grace — we lack but this to crown
Our labour and success — THE NUNCIO IS AGREED. *Exit Fargo.*

ARCHBISHOP: Great Shepherd — what a charge! how shall I render
Due satisfaction to these varied claims
So full of contradictions?
'Mong weak unstable men, who is sufficient
For these things? As saith the Apostle — *Enter Nuncio.*
Ah, good my Lord! an adventitious visit.

NUNCIO: Wherefore, good brother?

ARCHBISHOP: Fargo, from the Compania — just dismissed,
Solicits us to visit there, ere night,
What say you — will you go?

NUNCIO: I have agreed, and wait upon your grace
In that regard — to say I'm at your service.
But why — may I presume, look you thus careful?

ARCHBISHOP: Most reverend brother — an odd calendar
Of small vexations, much too numerous,
Too motly and ridiculous to meet
Your serene eye.

NUNCIO: Adroit circumlocution, giving point
To the sage proverb — "Every heart
Knows its own bitterness as well as joy,
With which the stranger intermedleth not."
Excuse me brother.

ARCHBISHOP: Excuse, nay thanks for your solicitude;
But time grows truant to our task.

NUNCIO: We meet then at the vestry. *They exit.*

SCENE VI

A room in the house of Mercedos. Enter Mercedos and Madam.

MERCEDOS: I tell you, Madam, more than cause of scandal,
Dwells in this licence. Think you the same priest,
Could play these tricks on sober-thoughted men?
And why on gentle feminine trusting Faith
So lovely, rightly led and not abused.

MADAM: I know not dear — things often puzzle me;

Yet if one cannot trust one's confessor,
Who may we trust — you know?

MERCEDOS: Dear simple spouse, we may not disregard
The plainest dictates of our common sense;
How'ere sublime the mysteries of our faith
They harmonise, so far as understood,
With our more humble judgment.

MADAM: Ah, it's hard to judge betwixt you, husband,
This one cries out against your "worldliness
Your secular sharpness, and hard grasping ways,
On which proud Reason mounts as sentry
In specious mask to hide the hideous face
Of Infidelity!" Now there, love, answer that!

MERCEDOS: Your spiritual advisers might have added
Falsehood, deception, and these shallow tricks —
Too gross as agents of these worldly men,
With any shade of honour; still find credit
In the church — find sanctuary there,
Though banned by general execration!

MADAM: Fine talk indeed, but yet it seem to me,
These things can never alter.

MERCEDOS: And why, good spouse? Because these crafty men
Enter our houses with seducing words;
Thus ready captives lead our silly women!

MADAM: Nay — those are cruel words —   *Weeping. Enter Susannah and Maria.*

MARIA: Dear mother — why those tears?

MADAM: It's nothing, darling, — nothing.

MARIA: Holy Virgin! at such a time, too!

SUSANNAH: Father, you'll bear us company?

MERCEDOS: No, child, I cannot go.

MARIA: Come, mother dear, if we delay much longer,
The eager crowd will leave us in the street
Gazing at the blank walls.

MADAM: Come with me darling, help me to prepare.

Maria and Madam exit.

SUSANNAH: I feel a strange reluctance, dearest father,

To leave you here alone — a sinister shade
Hangs lowering on my vision — so portentous!
And a voice, so mournful, seems within me
Like a dying wind — "Farewell!"
Oh, father, let me stay with you; rather
Will you not go? parted this night — *perhaps*
We meet no more on earth!   *Oh, think of that!*

Sobbing hysterically.

MERCEDOS: This my Susan — my strong-minded daughter?
My girl, I may not pander to these freaks
Of tyrant superstition. We've enough.
Already canonized, I would no more.
Go help your mother, think no more of this.
Exit Susannah. Enter Cortez.
Good evening, friend, you'd pass the church?

CORTEZ: Yes, senor, passed the hoary temple.

MERCEDOS: One brief hour hence and every greedy eye
May sate itself with Mary's vestal charms.
What signs saw you of gathering?

CORTEZ: The street was filling fast, but guarded doors
Staid back the public till the appointed hour.
Shall we be honoured with your company,
Good senor?

MERCEDOS: Faith, no — the time has past when I could gaze
Delighted on an image.
Still, those who have no image on the mind,
The outer sense must serve.

CORTEZ: Most true, and yet the young and plastic heart
May take from obvious things divine impressions.

MERCEDOS: Yes, from the works of God.   *Enter a servant.*   Is the carriage at
the door?

SERVANT: Yes, senor, and the ladies are all ready.   *Exit servant.*

MERCEDOS: I'll see you started, Cortez,
And speak *adieu.   They exit. Re-enter Mercedos, pacing to and fro.*

MERCEDOS: Oh man! poor Janus with these several faces!
What aspect represents thy proper self?
Surely the stoic most of all the shams
Of cold philosophy, belies thy nature!
Dwarfs down the true proportions of his being,
As earth-bred fogs denude the mounting sun

Of His celestial beams — they swell his form,
But minish his full glory, — thus it is,
Our worldly wisdom's finely maximed veil,
Cuts off the rays of heaven's deviner light —
Too often leaves him sphered a joyless lump,
Inflated but obscured in selfish pride.
Ah fluttering thought! poor bird beneath the spell
Of keen-eyed conscience. How that strange "farewell"
Steals in upon me — left along in silence!
Their faith — how beautiful! the impressible heart
Upbraids me as a truant from the school
Of this mysterious lore! Error can mix,
Yet fundamental truth may still remain —
The resting place of souls — poor birds of passage
O'er this wild main. What if her boding words,
So roughly challenged, prove stern prophecies?
And I, to curb my pride, must be bereaved?
How hard to face this vagrant speculation —
Good heavens! If once a *fact?*
How would those words, like echoes in the mountains,
Range through my empty heart.   *Exits.*

SCENE VII

Front of the church. Enter Legate, Archbishop and Clergy in their robes, Urangos meets them at the church door.

LEGATE: Brother Urangos, we are here to pay
Due hommage to these brilliant endeavours
Not quite eclipsing Rome!

URANGOS: Your eminence may condescend to think
The outer spheres of our celestial system
Can in their borrowed lustre ne'er eclipse
Our central sun!

ARCHBISHOP: Well timed, Urangos, let us pass on.   *The magnates and train pass into the church.*

URANGOS: O cursed Ambition! how he fools his slaves.
Here I have ventured like the ancient Titan —
Prometheus-like to snatch ethereal fire,
Nay, almost scaled the glowing gates of hell
To rob that dire dominion of its glare —
Still Rome's proud legate sneers! old Vulcan willing,
I'll glass him in a blaze transcendant — such
As earth has seldom seen.   *Exits. Enter Cortez, Madam, Maria and Susannah.*

CORTEZ: 'Tis early yet, I think too soon to enter
That heated atmosphere

MARIA: Oh, think you so? It looks so much like heaven
I fain would enter in.

MADAM: Wonderful! how wonderful! see how she smiles!
Most blessed Virgin!

SUSANNAH: Better, good sir, to keep the open air
To the last moment.

MARIA: So let it be, dear sister, we'll walk the square
Awhile. *They exit. Enter Gorman and Diaz.*

GORMAN: By special privilege lo we have seen
The astounding elephant! Now I propose
We scape the early crush and to our notes,
Bottle what we have tapp'd while full of spirit;
And as the night decays coast round to gather
Wrecks of the sermon — what say you, Di?

DIAZ: Excellent counsel, for to speak my mind
The place is much too hot for comfort.

GORMAN: Then come away.

ACT V

SCENE I

A room in the tavern. Enter Treacher and Avero.

TREACHER: Fine feathers make find birds. Now tell me, Avero,
How sits this geer upon you?

AVERO: Queer for a time, now getting naturalized,
Yea these vile harpies make them smell unwholesome.

TREACHER: Abide your time, we'll shake them off, I warrant,
Or I'll foresware my practice.

AVERO: Old Eli minds me of a falconer
Flying his hawks.

TREACHER: Yes, we are hooded yet. *Enter Sheeram and Scran.*

SHEERAM: Shentleman's, tish time for your devotions!
De temple ish lighted up and te goot peoples
Ish going in.

TREACHER: Well, comrade, are you ready?

AVERO: Ready.

SHEERAM: It ish in my vay, I vill follow.
Too fine to valk with old Jew — all too smart.
You, Mister Scran, vill go before, *only*
to show de place — go your vays.

SCRAN: Faith, an it's a fine arrangement for all the parties.

TREACHER: Very. *Enter a Dutchman, smoking, and two Negroes.*

1 NEGRO: Don't tell dis chile no more. I'll die wid laughing, ho, ho, ho, he — Go on.

2 NEGRO: By dis time old Abe's men smell me out, I guess.

1 NEGRO: How was it Bambo?

2 NEGRO: I hab tole Mas Pine t'officer how I smoke out our people, fire de place,
kill missus, abuse daughters an all dat — good! serve 'em right, dam rebels, says
Mas Pine t'officer. Gib your name! Bambo sar — we want just sich men, you'll take
t'bounty and fight for t'Union? No sar, can't do dat ting, no how. How so? berry big
family in de bush; can neber leabe 'em to starve! Bambo, him said, I like you better,
if I gib you te bounty; can't I trust you take 'em to Vixburg — say? Sar, you berry
kind, fore I takes bounty, will see wat ole woman say. So I was away possumin' two
days, den was back wid full consent; golly him bite sharp, pay de money, off I cut
like to wind.

DUTCHMAN: Mine Got!

1 NEGRO: Ho, ho, ho, he.

2 NEGRO: Stop dat, you jingo ole hoss; you 'sturb my discourse — long time back
dar cum dam Yankee pedlar sellin notions: lookin' in my face at dese great freks
and spots: "Ugly as sin! a spoilt nigger!" says dis old rascal, cum I'll sell ye a die to
make a 'spectable darkey ob ye; roarin' mad, I bot dis stuff to spite dis face, put it
away safe till dese troubles cum, when I 'members dis dye, tried it, — by Jeff, I was
converted to rale African. In dis face I put te dodge on Mas Pine. Dis done, I tink,
loss my wife and family; must go out ob mourning — den I wash and scrub, scrub
and wash, till all dese beauty spots cum out new —

1 NEGRO: Ho, ho, ho, he —

2 NEGRO: Wait one bit, I hab forgot myself — don't know Bambo, no more at all,
neither will Mas Pine, I'll try dat same. I go to Master Pine — Sar, my brudder,
gone to Vixburg wish me say, you look for him in few days — de devil! say him, I

guess some white feller play tricks wid yer mudder, he? Don't know about dat ere, dat what he tole me tell Mas Pine — good day, sar — stop you, will ye list? Don't know about dat; you had better, you'll be fine company — we like brudders; hab you a family? yes sar, come make up your mind, I'll put you in the same company, what name? Jingo, Jingo it is, here's your bounty, take your family after your brudder, and come on, yes sar. Good mornin', Capen Pine.

DUTCHMAN: Mine Got! dat vas one grate gobe!

1 NEGRO: I say *two,* ho, ho, ho, he, well done ole fellar, I'se nebber beat dat same, — which way did ye cum?

2 NEGRO: Froo Texas, like a streke to Metamoras.   *They exit.*

SCENE II

A Room in a Hotel. Enter Gorman.

GORMAN: Thus far — I've opened the first bulletin!
This gorgeous vision, like the monarch's dream
Has too its head of gold — the glowing Mary!
Why not those blazing lamps, the lines and breast
Of polished shining silver: the populace
Most aptly type the belly and thighs of brass;
Legs, feet and toes, — Urangos and his fellows?
By Jupiter! I have it.   *Enter Diaz.*

Ah Di, I've had a vision — much too rapt
To break on common ears. How goes it, boy
With your tall manuscript?

DIAZ: I've written my exordium, and wait
For new developments.

GORMAN: I tell you that great image is a poser:
But our degraded planet for her footstool —
How hangs this symbol?

DIAZ: The woman of the Apocalypse no doubt
Clothed with the sun, the moon beneath her feet.

GORMAN: Being so, this figure has a two-fold aspect —
The Virgin and the church. Ha, by the by,
What of our quandam friend?

DIAZ: Who mean you?

126

GORMAN: Knight of the sable plume or tall sombrero
As you like it best, *A knocking without.*
Spirits of darkness! should this be the man,
I'll write him *man* no more; it scares me Di —
Come in! *Enter Vampries.*
Ah senor — quite a stranger!

VAMPRIES: My unpretending title and estate
In your grand city.

GORMAN: What news predominates?

VAMPRIES: The all-absorbing topic is your feast,
To honour the Emaculate: the night
The gala final.

GORMAN: Yes, senor, yes. How read the heavens upon it?

VAMPRIES: Smiling. As Mary's face to sottish woo'er;
To the instructed ominous enough,
I saw a fiery meteor sweep the. air,
And burst above the temple —
That chosen symbol of your lusty Faith,
The Southern cross hath a portentous look;
Disastrous comments give these babbling stars —
Impune this feast and menace its conclusion.

DIAZ: 'Tis well this freedom of your licenced tongue
Falls upon liberal ears.

VAMPRIES: So, little man, thou's made a desperate sally!
Look! am I, think you, made of stuff to scare?
Starting back in a rage. Exit Diaz in great terror.
To me *laughing hideously* earth's puny terrors are a farce!
Add heaven's loud thunders — roar profoundest hell —
I've breasted all! Ha, ha! to cower at last
Before the shade of a departed power
Which lingers yet on sufferance! What offends
The nostrils of high heaven? This fulsome reek
Of creature incense — conjuring on the stage
Another agency more native to its air.
I tell you there awaits your waning faith,
A stunning blow which old expediency
Shall stagger under! Good — spread out your sheets
Quick! polish up your pens, and — mark my words —
E're yon blue gnomen *pointing to the clock* travels o'er a third
Of one brief hour, your harvest will be ripe —
I give you joy of it — Farewell. *Exits.*

GORMAN: Diaz! *Re-enter Diaz.*
Smell you not brimstone?

DIAZ: Nay, jest not o'er so dark a prophecy.

GORMAN: Jest! I'd rather gnash my teeth and weep.
It makes my blood congeal, only to guess
Upon these dreadful issues!
Why sit we here confounded like the lepers
By the beleaguered city, famishing
For news? let's venture to the camp —
See if our enemy has struck his tent.

DIAZ: I feel indeed confounded — almost guilty —
As an accomplice, so poisoned is my ear
With this dread secret.

GORMAN: What would ye do? too late, I fear, to warn;
Bethink ye too — our warning who'd believe
Based on such premises? yet 'twere a sin
To linger with this secret on our souls.   *They exit.*

SCENE III

A Square. Background — the Church — a crowd before the door. Enter Sheeram and Scran.

SHEERAM: I vash looking just now.

SCRAN: Did yiz see the min?

SHEERAM: No! — I'm fear de sons of Belial vill run avay in my goot clos; der vill make off — o dare!
See   *a bright flash from the Church*   Great I Am!
Vat ish dat?   *A piercing cry.*
Fire, fire, fire!

They exit. Great commotion in the crowd, bells strike up tolling an alarm. Cries, shrieks and commotion. Crowds hurrying up — Police, etc. The glare of fire seen on everything — cries, shrieks and groans increasing — great confusion at the doors. Flames issuing over the heads of the people. Bells, like tongues of doom, keep beating on greatly adding to the terror. Enter Police.

1 POLICE: Verily, comrade, then you saw begin
This dire calamity?

2 POLICE: I did — my duty held me near the door
I heard a smothered cry — so looking in,
Flame, like a spirit flew from the high altar,
Ah — just as 'twere a wicked angel!
Enter Gorman and Diaz in great consternation.

GORMAN: Police, do tell us what has happened?

2 POLICE: Read it senor on these glowing walls,
You hear it in those groans — the church on fire!
The doors so jammed, escape seems hopeless
To the huge burning mass.

GORMAN: Let us to it friend   *to Diaz*   something may yet be done.   *They exit.*
Enter Norman.

NORMAN: My help may serve a turn.   *Exits. Re-enter Gorman.*

GORMAN: Jesu, Maria! never sight like this
E're blasted mortal vision!
One glance across that sea of liquid flame
Full of its writhing victims — all banked in
By flashing reef and roaring breakers —
Must be burnt in forever. Where's my friend,
O surely not sucked in by that dread vortex?

Exit. Bells dismally tolling still. Enter Roland and Cloudon, bringing in a rescued body.

ROLAND: Poor suffering clay! This life that trembles still
On even balance. Cruel charity
To wish the tenant back to its sad ruin.

CLOUDON: What comes of all this fooling?

ROLAND: Hush! — surely none, no, not an enemy
Dare mutter a reproach! If the eternal
Mysteriously let slip his kind restraint
O'er latent death, remember those on whom
Siloam's tower fell, were not therefore
The greatest sinners.   *They exit carrying off the body. Enter Mercedos, and two men bearing in Cortez.*

1 MAN: I fear it's all up with him.

2 MAN: Never seed anybody fight for life after that fashion before, niver — why, he mounted the pile at the great door, a lady under each arm and one hanging on behind, all on'em in a blaze.

MERCEDOS: Oh God! Oh God, what fits me but to follow,
Take thou this worthless life, let me die, let me die!

1 MAN: Aye, here's my hands all burnt; I ketched hold of his collar, off it cum.

2 MAN: Then we got him be t'arms — the look he gen us at lettin' go the wimmin, was awful!

129

MERCEDOS: All gone to feed the fire! is there a God?
Looks he on such a scene — can he behold
And not rebuke these fierce devouring flames!

1 MAN: What's next to be done, senor?

MERCEDOS: Oh bear him on dear friends; I'll go and seek
Some further help and shelter. *They exit with the body. Enter Fargo and
Castanos carrying the image of the Virgin.*

FARGO: Here rest awhile. Oh Christo! is this all?
This tattered remnant of that glorious image?
See rags her garments — all the incense turned
To filthy odours!

CASTANOS: What wonder after twenty pails of water
To put her out. I'm sick, let us move on.

FARGO: Hold — hark! I hear sweet music in the air —
Cadence divine! it comes like falling waters
To palliate these flames — there — heard thou not?

CASTANOS: O yes! they are the spirits of the dead,
New chastened martyrs mounting into life!

FARGO: Most happy explication! doubtless 'tis so —
Those holy souls have burst their mortal bonds
And travelled into liberty — brother proceed.

*They exit. Priests and others hurrying across the stage, with church property. Enter
Norman, greatly excited.*

NORMAN: Two thousand victims more to Popery
At one fell swoop! O surely never more
Can Rome erect her head before the nations!   *Enter Urangos.*

URANGOS: Ah bitter enemy! at such a time exultant?
Bethink thee of the latest faggots piled
In Christendom — not Rome's, but Puritan
Intolerance. *This* is a dire accident
Most cruel murder *that* of poor old women!
Of ignorant superstition branded — witches!   *Enter Cloudon.*

CLOUDON: Aye, aye; I heard it — six o' one it is
And half a dozen o' t'other, I tell ye, Norman
It's one great humbug!   *Enter Gormuz. A loud crash and general cry.*

GORMUZ: There goes the roof! the gallant ship on fire,
The hatches closed upon the passengers.

CLOUDON: Stranger, you see this tragedy?

GORMUZ: Yes, verily, and not yet acted out
To its most bitter end. *Groups still rushing over the stage — some carrying bodies.*

CLOUDON: My God! will no able pen take it up —
None strike a blow for liberty among these
Priest-ridden slaves? Poor devils, a libel
On human nature!

GORMUZ: *Aside.* Good — Butter for once out of this currish throat
To grease my reputation.   *They exit. Enter Crapo.*

CRAPO: Save us, Mary and all the saints! all this dreadful work since I was here — merciful Jesu! It's just like walking out of heaven into hell — as I should say such a word, with the souls of all those blessed martyrs present. Awful! what can I do — what *can* I do? poor groaning creatures there, calling for help, and here I stand! *Rushing out distracted. Enter Roland, Citizens, and a Doctor, with a body on a shutter, bleeding.*

1 CITIZEN: Ha, whence is this? here's blood!

ROLAND: More trouble, see Doctor, see this arm!

DOCTOR: It's dislocated — ha, Good God! far worse —
Torn from the clavicle — see all exposed
The started ligaments and quivering muscles
Lower extremities all charred — still breathing!

ROLAND: A heavy sorrow truly, at such risk
We try to save the twentieth of a tithe
From this entangled death.

2 CITIZEN: Now, Doctor, lead the way, we may not tarry.   *They exit. Enter two men bringing in a body.*

1 MAN: Some people appear to run into danger for no end in life but to make trouble. Here stood this poor old creature stretching his neck into the mouth of this furnace — everybody else rushing away, down he went, everybody treading the life out of him.

2 MAN: That's so. Is he dead? turn up his face — who of all else in creation? Old Sheeram, the Jew!

1 MAN: Save us! what could have brought *him* here?

2 MAN: What to do with him is the next thing.   *Enter Scran.*   Just the man we wanted.

SCRAN: Faith, an what's the trouble?

2 MAN: Here is your friend Eli, trod to death in the doorway.

131

SCRAN: By Saint Patrick — and so 'tis!

1 MAN: Mate, here's no time to waste on this ere old coon — what's the word?

2 MAN: Take him to Scran's, he?

SCRAN: Well min do so, I'll make em pay for salvage. *They exit. Enter Gorman.*

GORMAN: Is't not a dream? oh, my incredulous soul,
Can it be true? A grim astounding fact,
Mocking the boldest fiction. Who dare waste,
However prodigal of scenic honour's
Treasure's so vast of life's most cherished prime
To zest a wild romance? Fastidious taste
Would loathe the sacrifice, and turn away
Disgusted, what? two thousand souls or more
Rushed out affrighted from those smoking heaps
Erst redolent with joy. Prodigious moments,
Intensed by passions' terrible extremes
To a long life's emotions!
A sickening task, my appetite for once
Is palled with horrors, what can ere absterge
That fiery vision o'er the sweltering ridge
Locked in the grasp of Death?
Anon one struggled from the heaving wreck —
Plunged through the fiery sea, suspiring flame —
Maddened with pain, a hell it seemed, the flames
Pursuing demons! Another rose to pray —
It's hard to tell it — how red angry snakes
Leaped at the gate of life and snatched the prayer
From her hot, bubbling lips — oh God — what then?
Poor creature! flinging up her arms — one shriek
That drowned the rest, left her an hideous corpse!
One full of lusty life, with scorched extremes,
Drew out his head and, starting to his feet,
Received upon his stark disordered hair
A burning baptism — out flashed the fiend,
To goad him round and round to his destruction,
One moment those scorched eyeballs rolled reproach
Against high heaven — madly he whirled about,
The pivot of a vortex, till the spirit
Wrestled him down. *Enter Diaz.*
                    Oh, Diaz, is it thou?
On this malicious night a face familiar,
Creeps on one like the storm affrighted moon
Out of a thunder cloud, where hast thou been?

DIAZ: I cannot answer thee — lost half the night —
Heaved up and down within the dreadful arms
Of this dire hurricane, let us away. *They exit.*

SCENE IV

Precincts near the Sacristy. Enter Vampries.

VAMPRIES: The play is ended, dying out the glare,
    Which makes of this a memorable night,
    For luckless Chile. Stirring little scene
    In earth's great drama, this! Gentle Mary;
    'Twas queer to deal to her assembled daughters
    Favours so hot — yea in her proper person —
    That image did the business! dangerous footstool,
    Offended Hecate claimed for expiation
    This delicate offering. Now what next?
    Urangos, equal to the occasion, tells
    The sorrowing relics of the Virgin's household
    How enviable those blessed martyrs state,
    Call'd up so early to a martyr's heaven!
    Enter Urangos, scowling at the "stranger."
    Nay, must that frown enforce me to recall,
    The just panegyric my lips have spoken?
    Sure testimony of a lofty soul,
    Its courage in misfortune!

URANGOS: Avaunt thou fiend.

VAMPRIES: What! Spurn away your humble artist thus?
    I claim for hire these few last parting words:
    Two things, remember, are most dangerous,
    Fireworks in churches, and the manufacture
    Of bogus deities. I've been *accoucher*
    At the most critical apotheosis!
    These goddesses are ever troublesome —
    Witness the advent of our warlike Pallas —
    Rough-handed Vulcan, with his brazen axe,
    Clave her a passage from the head of Jove!
    See! out she leaps in her resplendent arms!
    Alas for our *miscarriage!*

URANGOS: Thou impious, mocking fiend, avoid!

VAMPRIES: Ah, quite implacable? Divine Urangos —
    No insult from this steadfast heart of mine
    Can alienate my friends; especially
    A friendship sealed like this,
    Tonight, then, fare thee well. — Ha, ha, ha.

URANGOS: Nay, were it possible? The Devil himself
    Could not appear more wicked; doubtless he
    Some wandering misanthrope, which envious Fate
    Hath drifted hither with his forked tongue
    To snake my pride; would I could charge it on him!

No; what can palliate or disabuse
This stricken conscience? Hark!
Cries without, "bring out the treacherous priest."
These, my late worshippers, pursuing hounds
Hotly they catch the scent and mouth their prey.
Come, friendly darkness, swallow me. *Exits. Enter mob, yelling.*

1 MAN: I saw a shadow o' somat black.

VOICES: Where, where, where?

1 MAN: A creepin' round hereabouts.

2 MAN: What like wor it.

1 MAN: Black like a evil spirit — there might be two.

VOICES: The priest and the devil, the priest and the devil.
There they go, there they go, avast, boys, avast.

SCENE V

A Room in the Hotel. Enter Gorman and Diaz.

GORMAN: Smell you the horrid odour that prevails
Through atmosphere entire of street and closet?

DIAZ: It's horrible. I dread asphixia this night,
Or rueful nightmare.

GORMAN: One essential of our painful duty,
I fear, escaped us both.

DIAZ: What is it?

GORMAN: The number probable of those who perished.

DIAZ: And of the rescued.

GORMAN: Exactly.

DIAZ: I am restless and will take another turn.   *Exits.*

GORMAN: Most willing, fellow; now I'll stretch my legs
And furbish up my thoughts till he return.   *Enter Vampries.*

VAMPRIES: Nay, I'm suddenly become a terror

To startle one with whom familiar speech
I held so lately?

GORMAN: Ah, stranger, in that direful interim,
Assuredly this big, round world of ours —

VAMPRIES: As usual, has miscarried?

GORMAN: But that it is no time to bandy words,
I should have said, gone mad.

VAMPRIES: Mad! Wean not that the mortal agonies
Of thousands perishing, can ever move
The order of the spheres. Hard, tireless Fate
Like hireling slave, delivered of one load
Buckles his belt and hurries on his barrow
Up to the unwasted pile. Wrecks of today
Which call the astonished natives to the strand
In groups tumultuous, charged with tears of commerce;
A few days hence, the passing stranger sees
These wrecks cleared off, the little harvest gathered,
Life cradled back into its old repose
By a few platitudes.

GORMAN: Nay, spare me stranger, quench those awful eyes
Lest they rekindle tophet!

VAMPRIES: Badly compared, and personal withal,
A spiteful stone rebounding from a rock,
Harmless but to its caster. Let it pass.
Rare chance for one ambitious as thou art
To fill the public ear.

GORMAN: Yet ne'er to know the trumpeter — 'tis hard
To crack one's cheeks for naught.

VAMPRIES: An accident of not unusual hap —
Absurd aspirant he who pins his name
Upon the breezey back of every post
With his despatches. Bare reticent power
To stand behind the scenes a stern magician,
Moving the world's great heart!
Re-enter Diaz. Looking alarmed at the stranger.
But here's your friend with most courageous aspect
Burdened with later news.

GORMAN: Speak, Diaz, from the fire?

DIAZ: No, from a black tartarus full of stench
And images of terror, outraging hell! *Exit Vampries.*

I've touched the talisman — did you observe it?
My citing hell has sent the devil packing!

GORMAN: No, Di, a brilliant mad enthusiast,
At war with heaven and earth.

DIAZ: Therefore to be avoided. The enraged mob
Rave round the city for the noxious priest
And his "familiar" — here they come, by Jove
What shall we do?

GORMAN: Give 'em our room for company. *They exit the back way. Loud knocking without. Enter Mine Host.*

HOST: Why this disturbance here? *Opening the door. Enter Mob.*

1 MAN: Has old Nick been here?

MANY VOICES: The priest's man who fired the church?

HOST: No such person visits my house, what think you friends, would it not be better to go home and pray for the souls of those poor creatures lying dead in the church?

1 MAN: That's just what we're after, first settle the score with these devils about their murdered bodies, then pray for their souls, eh Mister? *Cheers from the mob.*

HOST: It seems very shocking — the city drowned in grief and you — *Loud cries, there he goes, there he goes! Tullio boys. Exit Mob. Re-enter Gorman.* The person I have seen with you, senor, it appears, besides his ill favour, has an ill name, now for the credit and safety of my house and all in it, he must for the present discontinue his visits.

GORMAN: Most reasonable, I'll rid me of this man
Or leave your house.

They exit.

Curtain.

THE FAIR GRIT;

OR,

THE ADVANTAGES OF COALITION.

A FARCE.

BY

NICHOLAS FLOOD DAVIN.

TORONTO:
BELFORD BROS., PUBLISHERS,
11 COLBORNE STREET,
1876.

DRAMATIS PERSONAE

Alexander McPeterson — *a Grit and a Senator*

Brownson Banbury St. Clair — *a relic of the Family Compact*

George St. Clair — *his son, educated abroad*

Ronald — *a friend of George, and a cynic given to express himself strongly*

Supple — *a Grit candidate*

Snapper — *a Tory candidate*

Editor of *Smasher*, Editor of *Dasher* — *various editors*

Angelina McPeterson

Mrs. McPeterson

Servant

Policeman

Sheriff

Ladies, Citizens, etc.

SCENE I

A hall giving on a ballroom. George St. Clair and Angelina McPeterson promenading.

GEORGE: I hope, Miss McPeterson, you are going to the Cheapleys' next week.

ANGELINA: No: we don't know the Cheapleys.

GEORGE: But there can be no difficulty in your being invited. Shall I get Mrs. Cheapley, who is a particular friend of ours, to send you an invitation?

ANGELINA: It would be of no use. Papa would not let me visit them, and you would find the task you propose more difficult than you think. It's only on occasions like the present that you and I can ever meet. The Cheapleys are Tories. The Jews have no dealings with the Samaritans, nor the McPetersons with the Cheapleys.

GEORGE: The Tories are not so terrible as you think. I'm a Tory *With a smile* or at least my father is. *With a touch of anxiety.*

ANGELINA: Although born in it you do not know the country. You have lived too much abroad.

GEORGE: But, surely, politics do not embitter social intercourse.

ANGELINA: They pervade all life. We carry the war along the whole line. If a member of our party "jibs" in the least, my father gets word from headquarters to frown, and he tells us all to frown, and we do our best to send the offender to Coventry. A hungry Tory would not touch a joint cooked on Grit principles. The very look of a pudding made according to a receipt furnished by one of your party would disagree with the strongest member of ours to such an extent, he would fail to recognize the value of a five dollar bill. We have Tory delf and Grit ware; we eat off party plate and wash our hands in basins of faction. *They change sides.*

GEORGE: If this be so, then I fear our opportunities of dancing together will be few, now that the season is so far advanced. But I hope we shall meet.

ANGELINA: I fear not: my father would be very angry if he knew I had this long *tete-a-tete* with a member of the opposite —

GEORGE: Sex. Is he so particular? *Laughing.*

ANGELINA: No, no. *Laughing.* I was about to say "opposite party". Here comes my partner.

GEORGE: That gigantic gentleman — "pride in his port, defiance —"

ANGELINA: Hush! That is the Speaker of the Imperial Bund.

GEORGE: God bless me!

Exit Angelina with the Speaker of the Imperial Bund. She smiles at George St. Clair as she goes away. St. Clair remains for a moment in a brown study, whence he is awakened by a tap on his shoulder from Ronald.

RONALD: Why, St. Clair, what is the matter with you? Are you in love? Have the starry eyes of the fair Grit cast their spell athwart your heart? Has your soul been captured by that smile which breaks like sunshine from the purple cloudlets of her lips, and glories each dimpled rosebud, and wreathes her snowy chin with subtle charms? Ha! ha! ha! Say — Have the darts of Dan Cupid pierced the joints of your worship's harness? Ha! ha! ha!

GEORGE: Come, Ronald. No chaff. Good Heavens! what a beautiful girl! How she dances! What a lithe figure! Her little feet! I could take both within my hand. And her eyes! And that columned neck on which the head rests in lovely praise!

RONALD: Yes: the neck of a swan and the eye of a Basilisk. I see you're hit hard. But there's no use; she's a Grit.

GEORGE: She told me that herself. But what matter? I suppose mine is the oldest family in the country.

RONALD: Barring the Indians.

GEORGE: I'm well off; or shall be.

RONALD: Of good appearance — go on. .

GEORGE: Come, don't chaff.

RONALD: Well, then, your father would cut you off to a penny if you were to mingle the aristocratic blood of an earlier with the plebeian blood of a later emigrant, and a Grit too — fair though she be.

GEORGE: Are there indeed such great causes of division between the two parties?

ROLAND: You are as ignorant of our politics as the latest-arrived Englishman, who thinks he does us an honour if he comes to earn his bread in what he calls our "blarsted country", and fears he is about to be charged by a bull from the prairies when the driver of a sleigh who has been waiting for rugs, cries: "Here come the buffaloes." Great causes of division? Sir, they are like infinity — you cannot grasp them. Do you know the cry with which the Grits intend to go to the country at the next election?

GEORGE: How should I know?

RONALD: "Loyalty and Condy's Fluid". They say they found this invaluable mixture most useful for purifying, deodorising, and disinfecting the Government apartments in Ottawa after the death of the late Government, and that it is very appropriate for the "Party of Purity". But the Tories will be even with them, for they mean to inscribe on their banner "Our Ancient Institutions and Chloride of Lime". The chasm that gapes between chloride of lime and Condy's Fluid is a measure in its way of the great differences between the two parties.

GEORGE: But why will the Tories cry "Chloride of Lime?"

RONALD: Because they contend that the present Government has become vicious at a bound, and not by the ordinary process of deterioration, and that they have out-Heroded Herod in practising the corrupt arts of their predecessors. Hence the great need of chloride of lime at Ottawa just now.

GEORGE: Surely our politics cannot be such as you describe them. We have not fallen so low.

RONALD: Yes, but we have. It is a rivalry in indecent hypocrisy in which practice and profession are more than usually apart. They out-vie each other first in professions of purity, and then out-do each other, as far as it is possible, in acts of corruption. It is a buncombe struggle — a battle of quacks. Each has his sham *nostrum,* his delusive specific, and the poor country is the patient whom the betraying drug of the blatant and brawling Pharmacopola leaves worse than he was. In Opposition all is virtue; in power all the reverse.

GEORGE: Horrible.

RONALD: Horrible indeed. Aye, Sir, horrible hypocrisy. Fancy a polecat crying out for *eau-de-cologne* at the approach of a fox and you have an idea of some of our statesmen. Next election decency will be outraged, characters stained, reputations ruined, life's life lied away, in a battle between rival corruptionists, fighting over the respective merits of Condy's Fluid and chloride of lime, while our local Government will be the Boss Tavern Keeper of the Province.

GEORGE: What a picture!

RONALD: Say, rather, what a picture it would be were there an artist capable of drawing the deformed reality in its proper lines, and painting it in its veritable colours. It is not even the quackery of incompetent or time-serving allopaths who go in for homoeopathy; ours is in part the quackery of utter ignorance. We have ministers talking like children about political economy — a science they never studied, and if they had, they couldn't have mastered it. We have persons who don't know its rudiments thoroughly, dogmatizing about free trade, as if any man of mark ever held that free trade was applicable to the condition of every country. We talk about constitutionalism. But we are at present ruled by a personage responsible to no one. If taxation without representation is tyranny, still more is power without responsibility.

GEORGE: You have attracted attention by the earnestness of your manner.

RONALD: The manner is as out of place here as earnestness itself is elsewhere. I suppose you are thinking of the fair Grit.

GEORGE: *Taking hold of Ronald's arm, and leading him to the door.* Look how she dances. She moves like a goddess. The motion of the wave is not more graceful in its curves. She has the sweep of the swallow and the poise of the sea-gull. If Grits look like her I shall love them all; and every bit of Grit in her I love.

RONALD: What an enemy Cupid is of policy, and yet he is the best of diplomats.

GEORGE: She is the fairest figure in that fair scene.

RONALD: That fair scene — pshaw! It's a mass of vulgarity. Gilded hollowness! Jewelled meanness; gems, and panniers, and skirts, and lace in many instances borrowed; poverty and pride, haughtiness and vulgarity, confidence and ignorance go hand in hand; and all powdered like — but I won't proceed. Are these young ladies? Why, they dance like Bacchantes and like barmaids leer. George, let us here in Canada make no mistake; to have a real society, that shall have good form, you must have a real head of society, and that head should find his or her inspiration not in the brackish waters and moral poverty of imitation, but at the springs and fountains of principle and nature, and in elevating companionship with the ideal heights of human character, round which blow for ever more the breezes which keep the heart fresh, and the bloom on the cheek of the soul. But these mendicants of fashion, these social Lazzaroni —

GEORGE: I see you're a cynic.

RONALD: So much so that I advise you to drive love from your heart.

GEORGE: Never.

RONALD: Tush.

GEORGE: I mean it.

RONALD: You want to marry her?

GEORGE: I tell you without her, life is worthless; it is the setting without the gem.

RONALD: Or the Irish stew without the mutton. Ha! ha! ha!

GEORGE: You are profane.

RONALD: No; rational.

GEORGE: Ronald, pray do not talk in this way. I love her, and you must help me to get her — if all the parties under heaven stood in my way.

RONALD: Why, really, your case is hopeless. Come, 'tis nearly time to go. We will talk this matter over as we drive home. I will not say it is quite so bad as that the Tory who would be mated with the Grit must die for love — but it is very nearly.

They exit.

SCENE II

A Hustings erected on one side, on the other stands the House of McPeterson. Enter St. Clair and Ronald.

RONALD: Good day St. Clair; sharp frost — though summer ought to be at hand. Has it cooled the ardour of your affections?

GEORGE: If you brought the bulks of ice, which make the pole sacred from man's spade and keel and placed them round my heart, they would not chill the great pulse of love which beats for Miss McPeterson. This is the gulf-stream of my existence. I saw her father the other day; such a jaw and such manners. They say there is no rose without a thorn, but my rose blooms amid a whole hedgerow of prickles.

RONALD: Thistles you mean. You say you are well off. But even "another ten thousand" would not enable you to pluck that rose. If a marriage between you and Miss McPeterson is ever to "come off" you must make a "big push" and a "grand stand"; and you may not then win her. You have come here for the nomination, or for the chance of seeing your goddess?

GEORGE: I thought I might see her.

RONALD: Be sure you look as romantic as possible. All Grits are romantic. Their great leader, steeped in tenderest hues of poetry — you understand — and if you

143

are to win Angelina you must approach her from the romantic side. Mind that side is not her pocket. But here they come. *Enter Supple and Snapper, the Grit and Tory Candidates — McPeterson and Brownson Banbury St. Clair (father of George). People before the hustings.* While the preliminaries are going forward let us chat more over this question of your marriage. But, see, McPeterson is speaking already.

MCPETERSON: *Comes forward, and is greeted with loud cries of "Bravo Sandie".* My friends, I don't think it shows much good manners on your part to call a man of my dignity 'Sandie'. I am a Dominion Senator, and even when I say my prayers I always ask the Lord to bless not 'Sandie' but the Honourable Alexander McPeterson, Senator of the Dominion of Canada, and the Lord feels honoured by being addressed by a person of my dignity. *Cheers and cries of "So he ought!" with a voice of mockery in the distance: "San-die!" which is greeted with laughter.* My wife never speaks of herself but as the Hon. Mrs. Senator McP. And the motto of our family has always been for six months or more — "Let us be dignified or die". I should be overwhelmed in addressing such a meeting did I not call to mind the great principles of Gritism — those principles which sustain the canopy of freedom — *Cheers and a voice, "Sandie", and laughter.* those principles for which Chatham thundered and Sidney bled. *Cheers and confusion.*

1ST CITIZEN: I thought only Tories bled well.

2ND CITIZEN: Yes, Sidney was a Grit; he took money from the King of France; he was in foreign pay; he was a Grit.

1ST CITIZEN: Then it was the King of France bled. The King of France then was a Tory.

MCPETERSON: A base hound who has got amongst you *Confusion.* some miserable Tory scoundrel, some traitorous villain, some insufferable blackguard, has dared to interrupt me — me, a Senator of the Dominion of Canada *Sensation.* and I would denounce him as he deserves but that it is contrary alike to my political and religious principles to use any but the gentlest words. *Cries of "That's so".* Believing that my friend Mr. Supple will support our respected leader, and knowing him not to be over-burdened with education, which is the great foe of sound statesmanship, I ask you to elect him. *Cheers.*

MR. BROWNSON BANBURY ST. CLAIR: Gentlemen, I am a Tory of the old school. Gentlemen, in an ancient country like this, with our venerable institutions to conserve, who would not be a Tory? Gentlemen, will you support an ugly old Grit like this Supple? Gentlemen, the Grits are not a bit better or more refined than we are in the use of nice delicate language.

ALL: Hear, hear.

BROWNSON: I'd scorn to stoop to personalities; nor will I say a word against Supple but that he has the face of a villain, and the walk of a sneak. *The crowd applaud. The orator wipes his head with his pocket handkerchief.* Gentlemen, my father was a member of the Family Compact, and did great things for Canada.

A VOICE: And for himself. *Laughter.*

1ST CITIZEN: I love dearly classicality.

2ND CITIZEN: He is too gentle with those Grits who brought in hard times and the potato-bug.

1ST CITIZEN: And is the potato-bug a Grit?

2ND CITIZEN: Yes, potato-bugs have been Grits from time immemorial.

1ST CITIZEN: That can't be, for then it would follow that all Grits are potato-bugs. I am something of a Grit; do you mean to say I am anything of a potato-bug? *Makes as if he'd fight.*

2ND CITIZEN: Now, hear me patiently, and I'll give you reasons. A bug is a bug.

1ST CITIZEN: True.

2ND CITIZEN: A Grit is a Grit.

1ST CITIZEN: True.

2ND CITIZEN: Now, mark me. All potato-bugs are Grits; therefore, all Grits are potato-bugs.

1ST CITIZEN: A striking conclusion, and deserves a blow. *Hits him; both are removed fighting.*

BROWNSON: See what fellows those Grits are. I know the two just removed for the direst members of that unholy fraternity. Gentlemen, I abhor making charges against private character; but to my knowledge, or rather to the knowledge of a friend of mine, Mr. Supple in his youth stole a pair of gaiters, and he and his wife get drunk every morning before breakfast, and finish up at night just before they say their prayers. *Cheering and confusion.*

ONE CITIZEN: The country is going to the dogs.

ANOTHER CITIZEN: We must have prohibition.

BROWNSON: *Continues.* I ask you to support Snapper. *Here two drunken men, smeared all over with filth stagger on to the stage and fall side by side.*

POLICEMAN: *Bending over one.* What party are you?

1ST DRUNKEN MAN: *Holding up his soiled hands.* I'm the party of purity.

POLICEMAN: *To the other.* And what party are you?

2ND MAN: I'm another. *They are led off the stage.*

BROWNSON: *Proceeds.* I say I ask you to vote for my friend — my consistent and honourable friend, Mr. Snapper, who with our worthy leader will fight the beasts at Ephesus. *Cheers.* Mr. Snapper is a cheese manufacturer, but he could sell a charter as easily as a cheese, and pocket the money with a conscience that would give him no more trouble than one of his own mites. *Renewed cheers. Then all sensibly agree that the Returning Officer shall put the question. There are conflicting cries. A poll is demanded. The Election day is fixed for the following Monday. The crowd disperses.*

RONALD: Well, what are your chances now?

GEORGE: I know not. How dreadful!

RONALD: What?

GEORGE: McPeterson called my father a forger and a murderer, a robber and a thief.

RONALD: That's nothing. Do you know what your father called him?

GEORGE: Good Heavens! I heard him call him a brigand.

RONALD: Worse; He said he was a hypocrite.

GEORGE: And do you call that worse?

RONALD: Yes, for 'twas true. Will you still insist on having Miss McPeterson?

GEORGE: The current of my thoughts are set that way, and shall know no retiring ebb. True love gives strength to purpose and breath to character; its food is hope and sweet imaginings; its instinct, effort; its rapture, worship. It will outwatch the stars to catch a glimpse of the beloved's eyes, and scorn sleep to know itself near the unconscious angel of its thoughts and vows. If I cannot marry her —

RONALD: You'll do something desperate. Oh! I know. Ha! ha! ha! I see your case is a bad one. Come on, and let us see if we cannot help you. Perhaps the Government would subsidize a little railway for you from your own to the fair Grit's house.

They exit.

SCENE III

The same. Night. Light burning in one of the bedroom windows of McPeterson's house. Enter St. Clair with a fiddle and a ladder of ropes.

GEORGE: Ah! that is her room. O, dearest one! *He kisses his hand towards the window.* To sit beside you and see your wealth of golden hair shower its largess of glory round your peerless form! To watch your pensive beauty in a pleasing sadness, it would be mine to dispel! To hear your laughter gurgle like a stream of music through the pearls and corals! Oh! — *Enter Ronald.*

RONALD: *Touching his shoulder.* Oh! —

GEORGE: Ah, Ronald, it is so good of you to come.

RONALD: Yes, I have come to play love's lackey and to act the A.D.C. to a madman. I hope I won't prove myself a nincompoop, like other A.D.C.'s. I see you have got the fiddle. Now play a little in order to attract her attention, and let it be as sweetly, as sentimentally cadent as the "mee-yow" of a hungry kitten.

GEORGE: Ronald, how can you?

RONALD: And then when she comes to the window sing the song I composed for you in a thoroughly feeling manner. *St. Clair plays, and after a little Miss McPeterson lifts up the window and listens.*

GEORGE: The difficulty about your song is I have no boat.

RONALD: An an Irishman would say your guitar is a fiddle. However, it is all the better. Lying and loving have gone hand in hand from the creation.

GEORGE: *Sings.*

Our summer nights are fleeting,
My boat is in the bay;
Our summer nights are fleeting,
My boat is anchored near.
Pale as the ghost of ill-starred love,
The moon her course doth take,
And sad and sweet as hopeless thought,
Her light rests on the lake.

Our summer nights are fleeting,
And youth is fleeting too;
Our summer nights are fleeting
And rapid joy's decline;
Unveil thy beauty to the night,
And I'll fetch my guitar;
The moon is waiting for your song,
And waiting, every star.

Our summer nights are fleeting,
Sweet the honied-lapping wave;
Our summer nights are fleeting,
With their silver-shadow'd walls;
Whose echoes of soul-born song,
Wake ghosts of happier years.

And faint far o'er the shimmering deep,
And die among the spheres.

MISS MCPETERSON: *Aside.* I do believe it is Mr. St. Clair. Who is that?

GEORGE: *Aside.* Ronald, hide. *To Miss McPeterson.* 'Tis I.

MISS MCPETERSON: Mr. St. Clair?

GEORGE: Yes, dearest Angelina.

MISS MCPETERSON: If papa were to hear you, I don't know what he wouldn't do.

RONALD: *Aside.* Make a Grit of him perhaps, but *you* could do that better.

GEORGE: I brought a ladder of ropes.

ANGELINA: *Aside.* Enchanting. It makes me quite a heroine. Hush, Mr. St. Clair. *Here old McPeterson comes on the stage unseen by the rest.*

MCPETERSON: *Aside.* As I live, serenading my daughter. Who ever heard of such a thing as a respectable lady Grit being serenaded, and by a Tory, too!

GEORGE: Will you come down, dearest, and walk? We can slip into the garden. At your approach the flowers will open to a dawn more lovely than the sun ever steeped our planet in. They will diffuse their fragrance in homage to a fairer Flora. Oh, come down.

MCPETERSON: *Aside.* How I hate such stuff. I hates poetry like pisen.

ANGELINA: *Closing the window.* I'll come down in a few moments.

GEORGE: Ronald, all goes prosperously.

RONALD: You did it well. If you should ever become impoverished you'll be able to earn an honest livelihood as a Christy minstrel. But you forgot to offer her the ladder of ropes. Look where she comes. *Miss McPeterson here enters on the stage, but just as George is about to greet her, her father steps between.*

SCENE IV

Room in McPeterson's house. McPeterson, Mrs. McPeterson and Angelina arranging for a garden party.

MRS. MCPETERSON: Really, Mac, these big affairs don't suit me at all — though it is pleasant to be so grand as we are — and to be able to send out invitations on enamelled cards; it is a delirious thing.

ANGELINA: You mean delicious, mamma.

MCPETERSON: Of course she means delicious. But she must suit herself to her station. I'm a Senator of the Dominion, and I'm rich, and therefore I'm a great aristocrat. We are grand people. What matter who we are, provided we're rich; and what matter whether I'm ignorant of political science or not, so long as I'm a Senator? Hang all aristocracy, say I, except our own aristocracy. And what I say is this — what's the good of being in a high station if we don't shine? Your European aristocracies be hanged — having their family tree, indeed. Though I do like to be seen in the street with a lord, whenever one comes this way: and doesn't Angelina feel the better of dancing with a lord? Nevertheless and notwithstanding, as Mr. Blake so elegantly says in his orations, give me the aristocratic plant that has its roots in the gutter, surrounded by dead rats and decaying cats, and with the sap of a fine, fat, purse-pride — or to change the figure — you see I have been studying the orators — an aristocracy which is like a pimple on the hide of a deranged society — an angry self-assertive thing as full of pus as of pride.

MRS. MCPETERSON: Shall we invite young St. Clair?

MCPETERSON: No! No Tories for me.

MRS. MCPETERSON: You are too bitter. I think Liny would like to have him invited. He wouldn't be a bad match, and he'd introduce us into one of the old families — one of the F.F.C.'s. And then we could abandon Presbyterianism and go to the Church of England. For as the Argyles say — if we are to go to Heaven at all, we might as well go by the first-class route, and having in hand, an aristocratic prayer-book with a nice Puseyite cover.

MCPETERSON: How foolish you talk. If old St. Clair would consent to have his son marry the daughter of a Grit, John A. would never speak to him again; and if my daughter were to marry a Tory, George B. would read me out of the party.

MRS. MCPETERSON: Then Liny I'm afraid we must leave out St. Clair.

ANGELINA: I don't care.

MCPETERSON: You don't care? Do you suppose I forget his seranading of you?

ANGELINA: Well, I think we have finished now.

MCPETERSON: No we haven't. Teach your mother how to bow, and how to walk across the room. *Mrs. McPeterson doing the Grecian bend a good deal, strides across the room, and bows in an awkward fashion; the daughter teaches her, and at each bow old McPeterson bows too.* You improve daily, my dear. Now, I must go and order wine. I think the $1.50 sherry will do.

MRS. MCPETERSON: Yes, and have a few bottles of Moet's to mix with the cheap champagne. And if you could find one of the Government clerks that we could borrow to act as my equerry, and groom of my chamber, and my lad-in-waiting, it would be very nice. Some fellow who is useful for nothing else.

MCPETERSON: I will make inquiries; shall be sure to find somebody now that the Civil Service is being made a system of out-door relief for the incompetent relations of wire-pullers. I must go to my wine merchant.

ANGELINA: And I must do some shopping.

McPeterson and Wife exit. Angelina and St. Clair enter.

ST. CLAIR: Oh Angelina!

ANGELINA: This is too daring. If you were to meet papa —

GEORGE: I'd risk my life for you. I cannot live without you. You are the ocean to the river of my thoughts. You haunt me with your beauty and persecute me with anxiety. In every sweet sound is your voice. The light of your eye is in every star. How can I overcome your father's objections?

ANGELINA: Have you not likewise your father's objections to overcome?

GEORGE: Yes, but I think an article in the *Dasher* would change his views.

ANGELINA: You have hit on the only way you can move my father. You know in the Roman Catholic Church they get dispensations for irregularity from the Pope. Now the *Smasher* is the great Grit pope, and if you could get an article in the *Smasher* saying that in an exceptional case a Grit and a Tory might marry — as, for instance, when they are very fond of each other as we are — all might be well on our side. If the *Smasher* gave him directions, my father would eat five dollar bills and sleep on a bed of walnuts. But would you marry me without your father's consent?

GEORGE: I am prepared to defy my father. They say John A. nearly fainted with horror when he heard that the son of a Tory wanted to marry a Grit. But though a person of such extreme sensibility, he would probably survive the shock of our marriage. If I may make a pun, he has though a Tory a great deal of grit in him, and he is specially strong on virtue.

ANGELINA: No; let us not think of marrying without our fathers' consent. I will never marry any one but you; let that be enough. But if we are forced to desperate courses, my Highland blood will not shrink from a bold step. For I, too, am proud of my race. That race so strong, so many-sided, so thrifty, and yet so generous and tender where they love; so full of purpose and of power; hard as the wave-beaten granite, and soft as the moss which grows on the brow of the steep; prickly as their thistle, but with the heart and beauty of its crimson flower. They gave me a spirit as free as the streams of their native hills; John Knox's strength and Burns' liberal heart; and Marie Stuart's fiery fervour without her falseness.

GEORGE: My heroine! Ronald was right. You should have been serenaded not with the fiddle but the bagpipes, and I can see a glory in them now I never saw before. Yes; not only Marie Stuart's fervour, but her beauty too. *He embraces her. Enter McPeterson.*

MCPETERSON: You Tory scoundrel! *George throws himself on his knees, but McP. only belabours him with his stick, and George flies, while Miss McP. cries "Don't Papa!" They all exit.*

SCENE V

The same. George St. Clair and Angelina.

GEORGE: I heard your father and mother were out and I bribed Bridget to let me in again. I have been to both newspapers and have met with nothing but discouragement.

ANGELINA: Then we are indeed undone.

GEORGE: Yes. On entering the office of the *Smasher* I saw a small boy engaged in sorting papers, and I asked him who he was. He replied "A devil". I started, but suddenly remembered all about printer's devils, and said, "Oh! can I see the editor?" He asked what editor? Was it the night editor, or the city editor, or the political editor, or the transcendental editor, or the theological editor, or the fighting editor, or the blackguard editor, or the editor-in-chief? In my utter bewilderment I asked for the blackguard editor, and the devil shouted out, "Our own blackguard — to the front". Immediately there appeared an elderly gentleman with spectacles, and having the appearance of a Sunday school teacher. Having told him my business he informed me that a matrimonial question like mine would only come under his cognizance if I were a candidate for a seat in Parliament. He added that my case was one partly theological, partly political, in the purest sense, and that I had better see the political editor, whereupon the devil cried out — "Kohinoor to the front". Again I was in the presence of a model of respectability, and he informed me that he thought I had better see the editor-in-chief at once. "Then enter there," cried the devil, pointing to a door on his right, and on opening which I saw the editor-in-chief dictating how a Tory should be roasted to one "amanuensis", and then turning to another and telling him whether hell had or had not an existence. "The fact is," he concluded, "if they could knock the bottom out of hell we would re-create it with an article. All Canada is at our feet, and we can do as we please, and we are determined to have a hell. We are just as strong as the convict Davis on future punishment." At last he turned to me, and having heard my story he said no word but rang for his brother, told the devil to summon "our own blackguard," the "transcendental," the "theological," and every editor and clipper in the establishment. "Theological, sing a hymn," said the editor-in-chief. Scarcely had the sacred strains sounded when I heard a war-whoop from the brother of the editor-in-chief, and the whole pack made at me. When I found myself at the door half alive I was thankful.

ANGELINA: My poor George!

GEORGE: I went and recruited my strength with oysters and wine, and then repaired to the *Dasher* office. About the personnel of the *Dasher* staff I know nothing, for I happened to meet the editor-in-chief on the stairs, and having told him my story, he looked at me with a frank expression, and merely said: "You're mad! You're mad!" and on my honour I thought I must be, ever to enter a newspaper office again, after running such a risk as I ran in the office of the *Smasher*.

ANGELINA: Those papers are dreadful things.

GEORGE: As I turned to leave, the editor-in-chief of the *Dasher,* fixing me with his glittering eye, said with the utmost courtesy: "Follow me and I will show you our inquisitorial chamber." I followed him. At the touch of a secret spring a door flew open, and we found ourselves in a room kept with scrupulous neatness. On all sides were implements of torture: boots, thumb-screws, Procrustean beds, ankle-chains, hand-cuffs, rapiers, daggers, and many other cruel instruments, the very names of which have escaped my memory. "This," said my guide, taking down an auger of huge dimensions, "this is the augur with which we bore into a fellow's vitals." I shuddered. "And this," he said, taking down a rapier, "is what we thrust under a person's fifth rib. Of late it has been used on a learned subject. You see the blood has an Oxford hue." On a slow fire at the end of the room a figure lay which I was informed belonged to one Robert Pinchbeck. "That is a process," said the editor-in-chief, "which is supposed to be understood at the *Smasher* office, but we understand it too." And he smiles on his victim with the enthusiasm of an artist. He then threw open a large cupboard in which hung the skeletons of those who had been tortured to death, with their names and pedigrees, and the date of their demise, pasted on a little beam overhead. "The owner of this skeleton," said he, pointing to the second one, "gave us more pleasure than perhaps any other of our subjects, and we tried on him nearly every instrument of torture in our possession." Here a radiant light of inspiration glowed on his face, and "with gentle voice and soft, angelically tuned," he sang as follows, all the skeletons keeping time with their gaunt bones, and grinning a horrid laugh:

McK___r has gone like a light o'er the wave,
When night clouds are gathering o'er the dark sea,
No more will he gladden great M___t's conclave,
No more will he madden the patient Pardee.

We called him with fondness 'the blundering child,'
For with the best of intentions he never did right,
And a beam o'er the waters when tranquil and mild,
Best emblemed his smile when just up for a fight.

Unless 'twas in coin, all that's golden he hated,
And kid gloves would tear, if one dared them to show,
Nor cared he how heavily the people were rated,
Could he draw but the long, and play the sweet beau.

But he's gone! oh, he's gone like a light o'er the wave —

Here he was interrupted by the figure of Robert Pinchbeck, who asked him if he was singing a hymn, adding that if so he would like to join in, but the only answer he received was — it has escaped my memory — but I remember well the editor-in-chief seizing on a poker, which he told me was a Thalberg poker, and stirring up the fire with considerable energy. He then turned to me and asked me if I should like to have a pair of wrist crushers placed on me, "or, perhaps," he added with the utmost politeness, "you would wish to try the boot on? or would you prefer to be placed on this Procrustean couch? Would you like to be bound to one of those skeletons? We'll do anything to oblige you." I begged of him to let me go. "Then go," he cried, "but beware of marrying the fair Grit."

ANGELINA: O, George, what a country is this Canada of ours.

GEORGE: Come; I have prepared everything. Run away with me to that land of peace and newspaper propriety below the line.

ANGELINA: What if we should be stopped by detectives like Mr. Arches and Mrs. McTrieb?

GEORGE: I'll take care that will not happen and even if we were we should cut no ridiculous figure. There's a great difference between running away with another man's daughter and stealing another man's wife and not only his wife but his children too. I don't know which to think the greater fool.

ANGELINA: How can women do such things?

GEORGE: My Dearest — There are women of a certain type who are always sporting on the brink of the precipice. We need not wonder if some of them go over. Any woman who acts so as to deserve the name of flirt is an enemy to herself and to her sex. But the married flirt is an enemy of the whole race. She is an unmitigated nuisance. She destroys her husband's peace, disgraces her children, and mars the opening of some eager young fool. Such scandals would be rarer if artificial obstacles were not thrown in the way of the union of such hearts as ours.

ANGELINA: I pity the poor young fellow.

GEORGE: It is the foolish woman that is most to be pitied. He deserves to be censured and laughed at as he will be. He was more like the leader of family exodus than the organizer of an elopement, a beardless Abraham migrating with his household Gods than a Paris of the new world. The grip of Montreal detectives was worse than the upbraiding Nereus.

ANGELINA: Of whom?

GEORGE: Oh, an old sea deity. But be sure I will prevent all danger of capture. Nor can I believe but that Heaven will smile on our attempt to escape into virtuous freedom.

ANGELINA: I could not go today.

GEORGE: When then?

ANGELINA: I am full of fears.

GEORGE: Dismiss them. The fates fight for lawful, even as they fight against unlawful loves. To the devotees of these Cupid is constantly transformed into a policeman and his little dart into a truncheon; to those who follow the better path the gay heathen little God becomes a veritable angel of light beckoning them onward not merely to greater sensuous happiness, but to higher planes of moral, intellectual and spiritual being. Dismiss your fears and lean on my faithful heart.

ANGELINA: I am resolved. Come here tomorrow at this hour. Papa and mamma will both be out, and I'll be ready to start with you for that land of correct clergymen and pure politicians. *They exit.*

SCENE VI

The same. Angelina. Enter St. Clair.

GEORGE: Have you seen the *Smasher* and *Dasher?* Both have articles on the question this morning.

ANGELINA: What question?

GEORGE: Our marriage, which they treat as an accomplished fact; it is dreadful. The *Smasher* says my youth has been steeped in dissipation; hints that you are a weak vessel; and thus concludes: "Never since John A., in an evil hour for Canada, entered public life, has he done anything so nefarious, so ruffianly and so traitorous, as concocting this marriage. A nice person he is to play the servitor to Cupid. He ought to be caricatured as a link-boy to Hymen. Away with such immoral coalitions. Talk not to us of the happiness of young people. Happiness indeed! Preposterous! Puling nonsense! when the interests of a great party are at stake. Before happiness — before individual peace of mind stands the great party of purity." The *Dasher* says: "There has always been something of the sly schemer about George B., but the most devilish guile with which he has set on foot this marriage surpasses all his achievements."

ANGELINA: Dreadful! *Bursting into tears.*

GEORGE: Follow me. Let us leave this region of newspaper oppression and erotic despair.

ANGELINA: I'll follow you to the ends of the earth. *As they go forth enter McPeterson and old St. Clair.*

MCPETERSON: Where were you going?

ANGELINA: *Falls at his feet and says* — Papa, I was going to marry him.

MCPETERSON: Suppose there is no necessity of your going away. Mr. St. Clair has always at heart been a sound Grit. The moment he was offered a good place he discovered this, and tomorrow morning the *Smasher* will have an article explaining to the world his true character, and saying that the marriage between you and his son is one of the most auspicious events that could happen. You see there are coalitions and coalitions. All coalitions that suit the Tories are damnable: all coalitions that suit us are divine.

ANGELINA: Do I dream?

OLD ST. CLAIR: No! Embrace me, my daughter. *Angelina throws her arms around his neck and kisses him. Enter Ronald.* There, that's nice, that's nice, that's nice. 'Gad, I'm not surprised at my son. What trouble we have given these young people and all for humbug. I wish I knew any way of lessening the humbug in the world.

RONALD: Commit suicide.

OLD ST. CLAIR: Commit suicide!

RONALD: Yes. I thought you wanted to decrease the humbug in the world. That would be an effectual way.

GEORGE: Don't be cynical at this hour. I have some reason to be morose. My body is still black and blue from the blows of the *Smasher* editors. "Our own Black-guard," or "Our Special Blackguard," whichever he was, hit specially hard, and under the belt too; in fact, his blows have made it impracticable to sit down with comfort. But when my heart is full of joy, what care I —

OLD ST. CLAIR: Ah, well, all is over now. I was born and bred a Tory, but I was really *au fond* a Grit.

MCPETERSON: Yes, he was always a fond Grit.

RONALD: A contract or a good place has a wonder potency of conversion. *Enter Servant.*

SERVANT: The editor-in-chief of the *Smasher* and his staff are come to congratulate you, sir.

MCPETERSON: Show them in. *Enter Mrs. McPeterson from one side and the Editors from the other.*

MRS. MCPETERSON: O, Liny, kiss me; we shall now belong to one of the F.F.C.'s. *To George.* My son!

GEORGE: My mother!

EDITOR-IN-CHIEF: *Sings.*

Tomorrow this couple will happy be:
Tomorrow must ring the marriage-bell,
And whoever with this does not agree
We'll roast him slowly, but roast him well.

SECOND EDITOR: We'll roast him nicely,
We'll roast him neatly;
We'll do it politely,
We'll do it featly,
And all in Christian love.

THIRD EDITOR: Away with love, away with sorrow,
Give me but plenty of good abuse,
For if I live on each tomorrow,
Some public character I must traduce.

THE WHOLE STAFF: *Sing in chorus.*
Roast him slowly, roast him slowly, roast him slowly,
But roast him well;
For he's a Tory, for he's a Tory, for he's a Tory,
O roast him well.

RONALD: O, most sweet voices!

EDITOR-IN-CHIEF: I have not yet shaken hands with the bride. May you have every blessing, dear Angelina, and be the mother of a stalwart race of Grits. I suppose there is no difficulty about your future husband. He's sound?

GEORGE: I take my politics from Angelina's eyes.

RONALD: Better teachers than most men have in that corrupting science.

EDITOR-IN-CHIEF: And her eyes like the stars which guide the Dominion, borrow their light from the *Smasher.* That will do.

GEORGE: But I hope, sir, she will acquire none of the enlightenment of your "special blackguard." It is, I assure you, almost as impossible for me to sit down at this moment as it would for one of those cherubs who are represented all head and wings, and who, holy though they be, have one characteristic of hell, as described in the sacred writings.

EDITOR-IN-CHIEF: Now that you are in our party, remember that you have no business to think for yourself, sir. We'll do all that for you.

GEORGE: I am too happy to fight on that argument. Come, Angelina, and let us seek to realize the unexpected turn events have taken.

ANGELINA: O George, how happily everything has turned out! May the union between your honest father and the party of purity be symbolical of ours. *Advancing to the footlights.*
Nay, do not wonder that both hurled us to perdition,

For our policy undoubtedly was — *coalition.*
Nor could he or I be said to be
Impartial — since each was *parti-pris.*
Can *we* be harsh on parties — one or both,
That to coalesce — they were nothing loth?
Yet as so ruthlessly young hearts they'd crush,
Ere on one side a factious straw they'd brush.
The sad suspicion will force itself unbidden
That by both parties country's overridden.

H.M.S. Parliament

or The Lady Who Loved A Government Clerk

By William Henry Fuller

Ottawa, Citizen Printing And Publishing Company, 1880
Copyright 1875

PREFACE

The adapter of this piece of extravagance begs to disclaim any political proclivities. He has attempted, he hopes not unsuccessfully, to get a little harmless fun out of political peculiarities and weaknesses, irrespective of party — in fact, he has endeavoured to act as much as possible after the pattern of the Irishman at Donnybrook Fair, and wherever he has seen an available head has tried to give it a good-humoured tap, not out of any animosity, but simply for the fun of the thing. If any head should appear to come in for more than its fair share of taps, it must be attributed solely to the particular prominence of the said head, and not to any other cause. If any expression or allusion in this extravaganza should give reasonable cause of offence to any person, he will be sincerely sorry, and hereby apologizes for it in advance; but, as the epidermis of politicians is proverbially tough, he feels convinced that no offence will be taken where none is meant.

DRAMATIS PERSONAE

Sir Samuel Sillery, K.M.G.	*Chief Financier of H.M.S. "Parliament"*
Captain Mac. A.	*Commander of H.M.S. "Parliament"*
Sam Snifter	*Clerk in the Sealing Wax Department*
Alexander MacDeadeye	*A Misanthropic Member*
Tom Black	*A Statistical Member*
Ben Burr	*A Poetical Member*
Angelina	*The Captain's Daughter*
Mrs. Butterbun, a Monopolist	*Purveyor of refreshments to H.M.S. "Parliament"*

The Chief Financier's little ring of Senators and Members

Members, Clerks, Etc., by a full Chorus.

ACT I

A chamber or Committee Room in the House of Commons. Members discovered grinding axes; others turning grindstones. On some of the axes are painted in large letters, "Section A," "Section B," "Nut-locks," "Printing Contracts," etc.

CHORUS: *Sung.*
　We sail the ship of State,
　Tho' our craft is rather leaky;
　Our grindstones swift revolve,

159

Tho' at times they're rather creaky.
We grind away the livelong day,
And talk in the house all night,
But if we're in luck and don't get stuck,
Our axes will soon be bright.

Enter Mrs. Butterbun with large basket on her arm.

MRS. BUTTERBUN: *Recitative.*
Hail! gallant Members, safeguards of your nation,
I'm glad to see you at your proper station;
Relax your labours — I'll refreshments *set,*
Your axes will grind better for a *whet.*
Produces bottles of ginger beer, apples, etc. Sings.
Aria.
I'm called Mrs. Butterbun, *Dear* Mrs. Butterbun,
'Tho I could never tell why,
For I sell my refreshments at very low prices,
So I'm *cheap* Mrs. Butterbun, I.
I supply all the Members and lobby attenders
With ginger pop, flavoured with rye;
I've apples so fruity, and oranges juicy,
For members to suck when they're dry.
Then buy of your Butterbun, cheap Mrs. Butterbun,
Members should never be *shy.*
'Tho *indeed that's a failing not often prevailing,*
Then buy of your Butterbun, buy.

TOM BLACK: Well, Mrs. Butterbun, how are you today? I think I'll take a bottle of ginger pop, with the old rye flavour. How much is it?

BUTTERBUN: Fifteen cents!

TOM BLACK: Fifteen cents? Why, it used to be only ten.

BUTTERBUN: Ah! but Mr. Black, you forget the <u>N.P.</u> — everything has gone up.

TOM BLACK: Now, Mrs. Butterbun, allow me to inform you that the additional duties imposed by the N.P. on the imported articles which enter into the composition of your ginger beer, amount exactly to one and one-thirty-second of a mill on each bottle, and, consequently, you are not justified in increasing your price fifty per cent. I showed this clearly in my last leading article.

BUTTERBUN: Can't help that, Mr. Black. I've got a monopoly like some of the big manufacturers, so, if you don't like to pay fifteen cents, you'll have to go without.

TOM BLACK: *Aside.* Oh! confound the N.P. if this is going to be the game — it's all very well in theory, but I don't see the fun of paying fifteen cents instead of ten for my ginger beer — they'll have to increase our sessional allowance at this rate.

BEN BURR: What about apples, today, Mrs. Butterbun?

An apple sweet,
I think 'tis meet
That I should eat.
That's poetry, Mrs. B. You ought to give me one for nothing for such an exquisite stanza.

BUTTERBUN: Certainly, Mr. Burr; here is one.

BEN BURR: But this is rotten, Mrs. Butterbun.

BUTTERBUN: So is your poetry, Mr. Burr, so that's all right.

BEN BURR: Are you aware, profane woman, that I am the Poet of Canada? that the roar of the mighty cataract, beside which I have been nurtured, finds an echo in my verses? Do you not know that I am to be appointed the Poet Laureate of the Dominion?

BUTTERBUN: Very likely, Mr. Burr; they've been making a many queer appointments lately, but if you want the apples you had better take them; they are two for ten cents.

BEN BURR: Two? Why, they used to be three.

BUTTERBUN: Dear me, gentlemen, I'm surprised at you. You seem to forget all about the N.P. Why, what was it for if not to put up the price of everything?

BEN BURR: Oh! this is too much.   *Aside.*   I begin to think the N.P. is a sell, only I don't like to say so.

Enter Alexander MacDeadeye.

MacDEADEYE: I have thought it often — the N.P. is a sell. —   *All recoil from him, with expressions of horror.*

BUTTERBUN: Why, what's the matter with the man? He looks miserable.

TOM BLACK: Don't take any notice of him, it's only poor Alec MacDeadeye — he's rather cantankerous. He used to be commander of this ship, but now he's degraded, and he's only an ordinary chap like the rest of us, and it preys upon him.

MacDEADEYE: Preys upon him! nae doot it does. How would you like it yoursel, after being captain of the ship to step down to be joost a common member of the crew?

TOM BLACK: Well, Alec, you ought to have been more civil when you were skipper, and then, perhaps, you'd have been in command now.

MacDEADEYE: Ah! that's it! — Joost because I would na condescend to humbug ye, ye turn me oot! Weel, weel, ye'll get enough humbug before ye're done, and as for the N.P., I'm joost fairly sick of it.

ALL: Oh! oh! oh!

BEN BURR: MacDeadeye, I would not wish to be hard on a man that's down, but such sentiments as yours are a disgrace to the ship.

BUTTERBUN: *Recitative.*
But tell me who's yon clerk, whose roseate nose
Bespeaks a love of beer — or something worse?

TOM BLACK: That is the smartest clerk in all the House,
Sam Snifter.

BUTTERBUN: Oh that name! Remorse! Remorse!   *Enter Sam Snifter.*

SAM: *Madrigal.*
The Government clerk
Loved the great chieftain's daughter.
He daren't propose,
For he could not support her,
He sang "my scanty pay."

ALL: He sang "his scanty pay."

SAM: The lowly youth
For his love did vainly sigh,
And spent too much
On bitter beer and rye.
He sang "my scanty pay."

ALL: He sang "his scanty pay."

SAM: *Recitative.*
Thanks, gentlemen, for this your kindly chorus,
But choruses yield little sustentation;
If you would kindly get my *pay* increased,
That would indeed be genuine consolation.

BUTTERBUN: *Aside.*   Beer and old rye must be his consolation.

ALL: Yes, yes; old rye must be his consolation.

TOM BLACK: But, my dear fellow, you are *too* ambitious. You can't expect the Captain's daughter to look favourably on a third-class clerk in the sealing wax department.

MacDEADEYE: If ye'd ony perlitickal influence, noo, there might be a chance for ye; but, the Captains of such craft as ours don't give onything away unless they get some votes for it.

ALL: *Recoiling.*   Shame! shame!

SAM: It's strange that the daughter of a man who commands H.M.S. "Parliament" may not love another who is in the same service, although in a humble capacity. For a man in this great and glorious country may rise to any position, — *if he's only got cheek enough.*

MacDEADEYE: Ah! mon, cheek's a grand thing. If I'd had mair cheek I might have been Captain still.

TOM BLACK: MacDeadeye, I don't want to be hard on a man who has seen better days; but such a sentiment as that is enough to make an honest politician shudder.

BEN BURR: But see, our gallent Captain approaches — *"bring on the banquet"* — I mean, let us greet him as so great a chieftain deserves. *Enter Captain — Cheers.*

CAPTAIN: *Song.* I am the Captain of the "Parliament."

ALL: And a right good Captain *he.*

CAPTAIN: You're very, very good,
And be it understood
I've a large majori*tee.*

ALL: We're very, very good,
And be it understood
He's a large majori*tee.*

CAPTAIN: In debate I'm never slack,
Howe'er the foe attack;
And I'm good at repar*tee,*
I never, never say
A thing that's not *O.K.*
Whatever the temptation be.

ALL: What! never?

CAPTAIN: No; never.

ALL: What! *never?*

CAPTAIN: Hardly ever.

ALL: What he says is always quite O.K.!
Then give three cheers to show our senti*ment.*
For the truthful Captain of the "Parlia*ment."*

CAPTAIN: I do my best to satisfy you all.

ALL: But some of us are *not* content.

CAPTAIN: I'll anticipate your wishes,
And see some loaves and fishes
Are served out to the malcontent.

ALL: He'll anticipate our wishes,
And see some loaves and fishes
Are served out to the malcontent.
All rub their hands rejoicing.

CAPTAIN: The position which I fill
Abuse I never will
Whatever the emergen*cee.*
Corruption is a thing
I detest like anything —
And it never has been charged to me.

ALL: What! never?

CAPTAIN: *Confidently.* No; *never.*

ALL: What! *NEVER?*

CAPTAIN: Well, *very seldom.*

ALL: Very seldom has been charged to *he,*
Then give three cheers to show our sentiment
For the *moral* Captain of the "Parliament."
Exeunt all but Captain. Enter Butterbun.

BUTTERBUN: *Recitative.*
Sir, you seem anxious; the sad expression of your engaging countenance denotes a more than common sorrow. Here, take a doughnut.

CAPTAIN: Thanks, Mrs. Butterbun. Yes, I *am* anxious. The fact is that our party has of late shown signs of weakness — they've such large appetites, the public manger scarcely can contain sufficient fodder to supply them all; added to this, our great Financier, the party's backbone, has lately seemed inclined to put his back up; and so to bind more closely to my cause, I had agreed to wed him to my daughter; but sad to say, she doesn't seem to hanker after him.

BUTTERBUN: Ah! poor Sir Samuel; but no doubt a man like him, who understands all about *duties* will soon be able to convince your child that 'tis *her duty* to obey her Pa. But see, here comes your daughter. I go. Farewell! *She exits.*

CAPTAIN: *Looking after her.* Her doughnuts are delicious. *Takes a bite. Enter Angelina.*

ANGELINA: *Ballad.*
Sorry her lot who gives her heart
To a young man who can't support her;
Whose hopes of advancement are sadly dark
For lack of interest in the right quarter.
Oh! if that *bonus* they'd only give,
Hope would have something whereon to live.

Sad is the fate of a third-class clerk
Who loves his chieftain's only daughter;
No wonder the poor fellow shirks his work,
And drowns his grief in whisky and water.
Oh! if that bonus they'd only give,
Hope would have something whereon to live.

CAPTAIN: My child, I grieve to see you are still pensive. When I left you Sir Samuel's budget speech to read, I hoped it would have cheered you; in fact that it would have sent up your depressed spirits as it has done everything else. Sir Samuel would be grieved to see you a prey to melancholy and you know he will be here presently to claim your promised hand.

ANGELINA: Ah! papa, your words cut me to the quick. I esteem and venerate Sir Samuel, for he is indeed a wonderful man, and there must be a tender place in the *chests* (I should say the bosom) of everyone for the great inventor of the N.P.; but, alas! my heart is given to another.

CAPTAIN: Given? horror! Not to one of the Opposition?

ANGELINA: No, papa; do not think so meanly of your daughter; but, oh! pity me! for he is but a humble clerk in this very house.

CAPTAIN: Great Caesar! *a common clerk.*

ANGELINA: *Spiritedly.*   Not a *common* clerk, papa; there are no common clerks in Government employ.

CAPTAIN: True, my child; but still — yet, stay, *eagerly*   has he any political influence?

ANGELINA: Alas! no, papa. If he *had,* he would have been a Deputy Head at least, by this time.

CAPTAIN: True.

ANGELINA: But I assure you, dear papa, he is most accomplished — he moves in the very best circles — he dances divinely, and he sings comic songs in a way that would bring tears to your eyes. *Beseechingly.*   Oh! Papa, with your interest, who knows what he might rise to?

CAPTAIN: No doubt a young man who can sing comic songs in the way you describe would be very useful to the party. But come, my child; you know how important it is that I should consolidate our interests by attaching Sir Samuel firmly to us, and surely you would not let a mere sentimental objection stand in the way of so noble an object.

ANGELINA: Oh! I have thought of this: — but fear not, Papa; I know well how important it is for the interests of the country that *we should remain in power,* and though my heart should break, I will never betray my love. Besides, he has only $400 a year!

CAPTAIN: My noble-minded daughter! — but see, here comes Sir Samuel surrounded by the admiring ring of Ministers and Senators, who attend him in his journeys throughout the country in search of the great Boom.

ANGELINA: *Looking off.* — But, dear Papa, the Senators are all dressed like elderly ladies! — why is this?

CAPTAIN: That, my dear, is to enable the audience to recognize them. But retire, my child, and take with you this last speech of Sir Samuel's on the sugar question, so that you may be able to compliment him on his latest eloquent utterance.

ANGELINA: My dear unsophisticated Pa! *Exit Angelina. Enter Sir Samuel, Ministers, Members, Snifter, MacDeadeye and Chorus.*

Barcarole.
Up from St. John. N.B.
Comes Sir Samuel Sillery, K.M.G.
Wherever he may show,
Up, up the prices of all things go.
Shout! for the great N.P.
And Sir Samuel Sillery, K.M.G.

CHORUS OF MEMBERS: We sail the Ship of State,
And gallant Members *we are,*
We're ready in debate,
And quite devoid of fe-*ar.*

Our foes may rail, but they can't prevail
Against our majori*tee,*
And we'll have the sway for many a day,
All along of the great N.P.

CAPTAIN: Now, let us all give three-times-three
For Sir Samuel and the great N.P.!
Hooray!

SIR SAMUEL: *Sings.*
I'm Sir Samuel Silleree,
Inventor of the great N.P.
Whose praise Canadians loudly sing.

MINISTERS: And we are the ministers who form his little ring. *Repeat.*

SIR SAMUEL: When in Council I preside,
My bosom swells with pride,
For I see prices rising for almost everything.

MINISTERS: And so do the Ministers who form his little ring.

SIR SAMUEL: But if wages don't rise too,
I fear I shall look quite blue,
And seek the seclusion which private life will bring.

MINISTERS: And so will the Ministers who form his little ring.

SIR SAMUEL: *Sings.*
   When I was a lad, in the year '34,
   I was errand boy in a druggist's store;
   I washed out the bottles and I rolled the pills,
   And I dunned the patients for their little bills.
   I washed out the bottles so careful*lee,*
   That now I am a Minister and K.M.G.

CHORUS: He washed out the bottles so carefullee,
   That now he is a Minister and K.M.G.

SIR SAMUEL: As errand boy I made such a mark
   That they gave me the post of dispensing clerk;
   I mixed up medicines and pills so blue,
   And pasted the labels on the bottles too.
   I pasted on the labels so careful*lee,*
   That now I am a Minister and K.M.G.

CHORUS: He pasted on the labels so careful*lee,*
   That now he is a Minister and K.M.G.

SIR SAMUEL: As dispensing clerk I made such a name
   That a partner in the firm I soon became;
   I prescribed for my customers' little ills,
   And totted up the totals of their yearly bills.
   I totted up the totals in a way so free,
   That now I am a Minister and K.M.G.

CHORUS: He totted up the totals in a way so free,
   That now he is a Minister and K.M.G.

SIR SAMUEL: At totting up totals I made such a pile,
   That I thought into politics I'd go for a while;
   I talked about figures so very glib*lee,*
   That they thought a great financier I must surely be.
   I talked about figures in a way so free,
   That now I am a Minister and K.M.G.

CHORUS: He talked about figures in a way so free,
   That now he is a Minister and K.M.G.

SIR SAMUEL: Now, Government clerks, whatever your degree,
   If you wish to rise to the top of the tree,
   If your soul isn't fettered to an office stool,
   Be careful to be guided by this golden rule:
   Always tot up your totals very careful*lee.*
   And you each may be a Minister and K.M.G.

CHORUS: Always tot up your totals very careful*lee,*

And you each may be a Minister and K.M.G.

SIR SAMUEL: You have a remarkably fine majority here, Captain MacA.

CAPTAIN: It *is* a fine majority, Sir Samuel.

SIR SAMUEL: *Examining a rather seedy looking party.*   A Canadian Member is a splendid fellow, Capt. MacA.

CAPTAIN: He is indeed, Sir Samuel. That gentleman is from one of our *remote* constituencies.

SIR SAMUEL: I hope you treat your crew kindly, Capt. MacA — give them plenty of nice little sinecures, and all that sort of thing, eh?

CAPTAIN: I hope so, Sir Samuel.

SIR SAMUEL: Never forget how much you owe them, Captain MacA., and that they or their friends naturally expect to have the preference in any little matter of contracts, or anything of that sort. They never complain now, eh?

CAPTAIN: Never, Sir Samuel.

SIR SAMUEL: What! *never?*

CAPTAIN: Hardly ever, Sir Samuel.

SIR SAMUEL: *Looking round.*   Desire that remarkably fine-looking young clerk to step forward.

CAPTAIN: Mr. Snifter, Sir Samuel desires to speak to you.   *Sam Snifter steps forward.*

SIR SAMUEL: You are a very handsome young man, Mr. Snifter.

SAM SNIFTER: Yes, Sir Samuel.

SIR SAMUEL: I hope you work very hard for the Government?

SAM SNIFTER: Very hard, Sir Samuel.

SIR SAMUEL: What department are you in?

SAM SNIFTER: The Sealing Wax Department, Sir Samuel.

SIR SAMUEL: I should like you to explain to me in detail your duties.

SAM SNIFTER: Well, Sir Samuel, I come every morning punctually at half-past nine and sign the book.

SIR SAMUEL: Very good. And then what do you do?

SAM SNIFTER: Then I take a rest, Sir Samuel.

SIR SAMUEL: Quite right — Government officials should always be careful not to overwork themselves; the strain of official duties on the mind is very wearing. What next?

SAM SNIFTER: Then I read the papers, Sir Samuel.

SIR SAMUEL: Very proper; Government officials should always keep themselves acquainted with the events of the day; — but I trust you never read the Opposition journals?

SAM SNIFTER: *Never,* Sir Samuel.

SIR SAMUEL: What! *Stops suddenly.* I mean — Quite right. I presume you read my budget speeches?

SAM SNIFTER: Over and over again, Sir Samuel — *Aside.* over the left.

SIR SAMUEL: This is a remarkably intelligent clerk, Capt. MacA; I trust you will keep your eye on him. — What do you do next?

SAM SNIFTER: *Hesitatingly.* Then I smoke a pipe, Sir Samuel.

SIR SAMUEL: *Doubtfully.* — Smoke a pipe? — I don't know about that.

SAM SNIFTER: *Eagerly.* — I smoke *Canadian* tobacco, Sir Samuel, — I only do it with a view of encouraging home manufactures.

SIR SAMUEL: Oh! that alters the case. Our home manufactures *must* be encouraged — that's one of the chief features of my National Policy. What is your next proceeding?

SAM SNIFTER: Then I go to lunch, Sir Samuel.

SIR SAMUEL: Of course; it is impossible to continue in the performance of such arduous duties without regularity at meals. Well, what next?

SAM SNIFTER: Then I come back, Sir Samuel — *Aside.* Sometimes.

SIR SAMUEL: Naturally. Well?

SAM SNIFTER: Then I smoke another pipe, Sir Samuel.

SIR SAMUEL: *Anxiously.* I hope this laudable devotion to the furtherance of our National Policy has no bad effect on your constitution?

SAM SNIFTER: I *do* feel rather seedy sometimes, Sir Samuel, but the knowledge that I am doing my duty to my country supports me.

SIR SAMUEL: Patriotic young man! such self-sacrifice will undoubtedly meet its reward; after that, what do you do?

SAM SNIFTER: Then it's time to go home, Sir Samuel.

SIR SAMUEL: Of course. And what salary do you get for the performance of these important duties?

SAM SNIFTER: $400 a year, Sir Samuel.

SIR SAMUEL: That's a very liberal salary for a young man. I hope you save money out of it?

SAM SNIFTER: Oh! yes, Sir Samuel; nearly $200 a year.

SIR SAMUEL: Dear me! How do you manage that?

SAM SNIFTER: By a periodical issue of promissory notes, Sir Samuel.

SIR SAMUEL: Quite a financial genius, I observe, Capt. MacA. This young man will make his way in the world. I see you are a youth of ambition; tell me, have you any plans matured?

SAM SNIFTER: Yes, Sir Samuel; I hope to get an interest in a contract some day.

SIR SAMUEL: Very naturally.

SAM SNIFTER: Yes, Sir Samuel; and then I have an uncle who is a Member, and he is going to get the Government to purchase a new patent corkscrew that I have invented.

SIR SAMUEL: A corkscrew! Hum. But would the Government be able to use a sufficient number to make it pay?

SAM SNIFTER: Oh dear, yes, Sir Samuel; every clerk would want a new one every day, and then all the Members and Senators would take home boxes full every Session, along with their stationery.

SIR SAMUEL: I am delighted to see, Mr. Snifter, that you have fully mastered the details of your department. Capt. MacA., if the crew of H.M.S. "Parliament" comprises many such members, the public is, indeed, to be congratulated.

CAPTAIN: Yes, Sir Samuel.

SIR SAMUEL: For I hold that politics
Should be free from any tricks,
And be above suspicion in everything.

ALL: And so do the Ministers who form his little ring.

Exeunt Captain, Sir Samuel and Ministers.

TOM BLACK: Ah! that's something like a Minister. You heard what he said to the captain about treating us properly.

SAM SNIFTER: Yes, and how kindly he spoke about my patent corkscrew. What's to prevent me from making a nice little pot of money out of it, and then I can run for some constituency, and perhaps be a Minister myself some day. That's how they all begin, and why should not I have the same chance as another?

ALL: Well said! Well said!

MacDEADEYE: Hoot! hoot! did ever onyone hear of siccan a thing? Why, ye're all a set of corruptionists, and ought to be ashamed of yersels.

TOM BLACK: Alexander MacDeadeye, if you go for to infuriate this ship's company, I won't answer for holding of them in. What we purpose is perfectly legitimate, and is done by every crew of Her Majesty's ships of State, and you know that just as well as I do; — why, you did it yourself.

ALL: So he did.

SAM SNIFTER: Gentlemen, my mind's made up. I'll take out the patent for my corkscrew tomorrow, and the first opportunity I get I'll tell the Captain's daughter of the fervent love I have for her, and ask her to wait till I get a seat. What say you, gentlemen? do you approve of my determination?

ALL: We do! we do!

MacDEADEYE: I *don't*! Why it's awfu'! — here's a miserable third-class clerk talking about contracts and patents and getting a seat in the Hoose. I ken weel he wouldna have talked so when I commanded the ship.

TOM BLACK: What *is* to be done with this hopeless chap? To think of his running down the officers of the craft in this way. Suppose Mr. Snifter, we sing him that song you composed in honour of the service; perhaps it will bring the poor creature to a proper frame of mind.

SAM, TOM: *Glee.*
  A Government clerk is a soaring soul,
  And ought to be his country's pride;
  He will always be genteel, tho' perchance he want a meal,
  And very many things beside.

  His moustache should be waxed, and his hair should curl;
  He should lift his hat to every girl;
  His bosom should heave and his breast protrude,
  And this should be his customary attitude.

CHORUS: His moustache should be waxed, and his hair should curl;
  He should lift his hat to every girl;
  His bosom should heave and his breast protrude,
  And this should be his customary attitude.

SAM, TOM: The "Boston" he should dance with an inborn grace,
　　　　　He should skate, toboggan, and ride;
　　　　　He never should be met beyond the proper set,
　　　　　Nor familiar be with folks outside.

　　　　　He should wear kid gloves, and a cane should twirl,
　　　　　He should break the heart of every girl;
　　　　　His nose should curl, and his lip protrude
　　　　　And this should be his customary attitude.

CHORUS: He should wear kid gloves, and a cane should twirl;
　　　　　He should break the heart of every girl;
　　　　　His nose should curl, and his lip protrude,
　　　　　And this should be his customary attitude.

All exeunt except Clerk, who remains leaning against a desk in a melancholy attitude. Enter Angelina.

ANGELINA: It is useless. Sir Samuel's attentions bore me; — fancy a man whose idea of making love is to explain the effect of the duty on raw materials! And when I asked him if he had seen the new step in the "Boston", he thought I was referring to the movements of the American markets! *Sees Clerk.* Sam Snifter? *Overcome by emotion.*

SAM SNIFTER: Ay, lady; poor Sam Snifter!

ANGELINA: And why *poor* Sam?

SAM SNIFTER: I am, at present, lady, rich only in unrest. I cannot settle to my work. I am perpetually thinking of the last time we circled together in the mazy "Boston".

ANGELINA: *Aside.* Ah, that was a delicious waltz!

SAM SNIFTER: When I take my modest quencher in the morning to allay the fever caused by a sleepless night, it recalls the sweet but exhilarating negus we sipped together; and when in the afternoon I seal the office letters, my emotion causes me to drop the hot wax on my hand instead of on the envelopes — see these blistered fingers. *Extending his hand.* The ribalds in the office say it is screwiness — but *I* know it is sentiment.

ANGELINA: *Looking at his hand.* Poor fellow! have you tried arnica?

SAM SNIFTER: Of what avail is arnica for a wounded heart? *Aside.* I will make the plunge. *To Angelina.* Angelina, your love is the only arnica that can cure my wounds.

ANGELINA: *Indignantly.* Sir; you forget to whom you are speaking. *Aside.* Oh! my poor heart.

SAM SNIFTER: No, lady; I know too well you are my chieftain's daughter, and I only a humble clerk; but I have expectations — my corkscrew!

172

ANGELINA: Sir, I am amazed at your audacity to talk to me of *corkscrews*. I shall begin to think you have been using your corkscrew too much already. *Aside.* Oh! how eloquently he speaks.

SAM SNIFTER: No, haughty lady; nothing stronger than whiskey, I mean *water*, has passed my lips today. I have spoken, and I await your answer.

ANGELINA: You shall not wait long. Your proffered love I haughtily reject. Go, sir; and learn to cast your eyes upon some maiden in your own rank; they should be lowered before your chieftain's daughter.

Duet — Clerk and Angelina.

ANGELINA: Refrain, audacious youth,
　　You're too assuming,
　　And on my condescension
　　Are presuming.
　　You are a humble clerk
　　Who seals the letters,
　　And I the very best
　　Of all your betters.
　　Aside.
　　If cruel fate, my love
　　Did not look cross on,
　　We'd glide through life in one
　　Delicious "Boston".

SAM SNIFTER: Proud lady, cease; refrain
　　My hopes to crumble;
　　I know that, like "Uriah
　　Heep," I'm 'umble;
　　But still, like him, I love
　　My master's daugh*ter*,
　　Although I'm quite aware
　　I didn't ough*ter*.
　　Exit Angelina. Aside.
　　Despite the haughty way
　　The lady snubs me,
　　I have a strong suspicion
　　That she loves me:

　　I'll put it to the test　*Calling off.*

　　My friends, my friends,
　　Come here! come here!

Enter Members, Clerks, MacDeadeye, etc.

ALL: Ay, ay, my lad,
　　What cheer? — what cheer?
　　Now tell us, pray
　　Don't stop, don't stop!

What did she say?
Did you pop? — did you pop?

SAM SNIFTER: The maiden made an awful fuss,
And down my fondest hopes did tumble;
She said I was a cheeky cuss,
And that I'm very much too 'umble.

ALL: The stuck-up thing!

MacDEADEYE: She spurns your suit — it's proper quite;
It sairves you right — it sairves you right.

SAM SNIFTER: *Taking a large ink-bottle from the desk.*
My friends, my friends, my heart is breaking,
With poison now my life I'm taking!
When I am gone, oh! prithee say
He died in the genteelest way.

ALL: *Turning away weeping.*
With poison now his life he's taking,
For oh! his faithful heart is breaking.
When he is gone we'll surely say,
He died in the genteelest way.

SAM SNIFTER: *Uncorks the bottle.*
Be warned my comrades all,
Who love in rank above you,
For Angeline I fall.
Lifts bottle to his mouth.

ANGELINA: *Rushing in* —   Ah! stay your hand — I love you!

ALL: Ah! stay your hand — she loves you!

SAM SNIFTER: *Incredulously.*   Loves me!

ANGELINA: Loves you!

ALL: Yes, yes — ah! yes, she loves you!

*During this, MacDeadeye has taken the bottle from Clerk; he smells it, then tastes it.
Pantomine.*

MacDEADEYE: Why, it's whuskey! — did ever ony one see sic deception?
It's awfu' bad — I mean the deceit, not the whuskey.
Takes another drink.

Ensemble — Sam, Members, Clerk and Angelina sing.

This *denouement* was quite foreseen,

Though some may think the lady green;
Upon the stage, of course, you know,
Such scenes like this do always go,
And lovers fond unite.
But when the honeymoon is o'er,
And poverty comes to (our/their) door,
Instead of kisses, vows and smiles,
And lovers' usual tender wiles,
Of course (we'll/they'll) scold and fight.

ANGELINA: This very night,

SAM SNIFTER: At half-past eight.

TOM BLACK: Just while the House

BEN BURR: Is in debate,

SAM SNIFTER: From the gallery

ANGELINA: I soft will steal.

SAM SNIFTER: To "Alban's" Church

ANGELINA: We swift will go,

TOM BLACK: A clergyman.

BEN BURR: For woe or weal,

ANGELINA: Will make us one;

SAM SNIFTER: And then we can

ANGELINA: Return, for none

SAM SNIFTER: Can part us then.

ALL: This very night,
       At half-past eight,
       Just while the House
       Is in debate,
       From the gallery
       He soft will steal.
       To "Alban's" Church
       They swift will go,
       A clergyman,
       For woe or weal,
       Will make them one;
       And then they can
       Return, for none

Can part them then.
For the Government clerk is a soaring soul,
And ought to be is country's pride,
In spite of low degree, by cheek he wins, you see,
The lady for his bride.
He will wear kid gloves, and a cane will twirl,
His moustache will be waxed, and his hair will curl,
His back will curve, and his chest protrude,
And *this* will be his customary *attitude.*
Embracing the lady. Curtain.

ACT II

Terrace outside the Parliament Buildings — moonlight. Capt. MacA. discovered gazing at the moon, with hurdy-gurdy (practicable handle) slung round his neck. He advances to the footlights and addresses the audience.

CAPTAIN: Ladies and gentlemen, according to received tradition, I ought to sing this song to the accompaniment of a "guitar" or "mandolin", or some such romantic instrument, but, unfortunately, my musical education has been somewhat neglected, and I prefer this sort of thing;   *turns handle*   you see it reminds me of my old political exercises.

Song.

CAPTAIN: Fair moon, I don't intend
To call thee "Heaven's bright regent,"
Though that would be, I know,
Strictly according to precedent.
I merely wished to say
Things are in awful muddle,
And that I quite foresee
Ahead, a precious peck of trouble.
For now Sir Samuel sulks, because
His flame of love my daughter quenches,
And threatens straightway to desert
Unto the Opposition benches.
And so, fair moon, I sing,
These little facts to mention,
And let my audience know
This was my sole intention.
Enter Mrs. Butterbun.

BUTTERBUN: *Aside.*   Ah! here is the Captain. He seems in a sentimental mood —

now is the time to press him for that appointment he promised me. *Aloud.* Good evening, dear Captain.

CAPTAIN: Mrs. Butterbun! and out of the House at this time! This is not right, my good lady; Sir Samuel is now on his legs, and you know how hoarse he gets unless he has some of your oranges to suck. Why, you might be the means of spoiling one of his greatest efforts, and think what a loss that would be to the country.

BUTTERBUN: True, dear Captain, but I was so anxious to speak to you about that appointment — the Session is already far advanced, and you know you promised.

CAPTAIN: *Pettishly.* Of course I promised, we always do; but how can you expect me to anything more than promise, when I have at least a dozen applicants for every post likely to be vacant. *Aside.* And I have promised them all.

BUTTERBUN: *Change of manner.* Ah! I understand. You think your promises to the poor apple woman may be broken with impunity, but beware!! I have influence! Many Members owe me for refreshments! *Pulls out memorandum book, and points to it melodramatically.* I can bring pressure to bear on them — there is danger ahead!

CAPTAIN: Danger?

BUTTERBUN: Ay, danger! Be prepared.

Duet.

BUTTERBUN: Things are seldom what they seem,
Power will pass away like dream;
Once, not many years ago,
Suddenly *you* out did go.

CAPTAIN: *Reflectively* Yes, I know
I did so.

BUTTERBUN: Constituencies are often fickle
When you cease their ears to tickle;
On a very slight pretence
Members often *jump the fence.*

CAPTAIN: *Sadly.* Very true
So they do.

BUTTERBUN: Though the spoils you may divide
Some must be dissatisfied;
Then majorities we see
Dwindle to minori*tee.*

CAPTAIN: Yes, *I know*
That is so.

CAPTAIN: *Aside.* I am thinking, I am thinking,
This good lady's been a-drinking,
Something strong has been a-drinking.

BUTTERBUN: *Aside.* He is thinking, he is thinking,
That I must have been a-drinking,
Something strong have been a-drinking.

BOTH: Yes, I know
That is so.

CAPTAIN: In this misty style I'm clever,
And could talk like that forever,
To constituents, you know,
We are always talking so.

BUTTERBUN: Very true,
So you do.

CAPTAIN: "If relative or friend has need
At the public rack to feed,
Vote for us; you may depend
We will satisfy your friend."

BUTTERBUN: Yes, I know
You talk so.

CAPTAIN: But when we're in, why then we say,
"Call again another day,
Just now nothing can be done;"
Then they grumble, and look glum.

BUTTERBUN: *Significantly.* Yes, I know.
That is so.
Aside. Though he thinks I'm only fooling,
I'll dissemble, I'll dissemble;
When he sees the wires I'm pulling,
He will tremble, he will tremble.

BOTH: (When he sees/When I see) the wires (I'm/she's) pulling.
(He will/I shall) tremble; (he will/I shall) tremble.
But meanwhile I must dissemble.
Yes, I know
That is so.
Exit Butterbun, tragically.

CAPTAIN: I begin to fear that old lady may be dangerous; I know she has a good
many members on her books. I must try and think of something to keep her quiet
— let me see — there will probably be a Senatorship vacant soon; suppose I
promise her that — or stay; a thought strikes me; I will offer her the Inspector-
ship of the Coteau Bridge, as soon as we have decided to build it; that will give me

plenty of time to look about me. Alas! dangers multiply in every direction.

Enter Sir Samuel.

SIR SAMUEL: Captain MacA., I am greatly disappointed, not only with your daughter, but with you; I am afraid I shall have to go over to the other side.

CAPTAIN: I am sorry to hear that, Sir Samuel.

SIR SAMUEL: The fact is, that although I have paid great attention to the young lady, and have read to her several of my finest speeches, she does not seem much impressed — she actually went to sleep in the middle of them; but this is not all — worse remains behind!!

CAPTAIN: Good heavens! Sir Samuel you alarm me.

SIR SAMUEL: She alarmed *me.* Why, after I had explained to her at great length, and with my usual perspicuity, the exact working of the N.P., she actually said, "Oh, bother the N.P.!" BOTHER THE N.P.!! Surely, Captain MacA., she has never heard *you* speak disrespectfully of my N.P.?

CAPTAIN: I am overwhelmed with amazement. Sir Samuel, I cannot conceive the possibility of any sane person saying "bother the N.P." *Aside.* though, possibly, the N.P. may bother *them.*

SIR SAMUEL: How, then, do you account for this extraordinary conduct?

CAPTAIN: I can hardly say, Sir Samuel. She is a very modest girl, and it may be that your massive intellect daunts her.

SIR SAMUEL: That is very probable; but what would you suggest?

CAPTAIN: Well, Sir Samuel, if you would kindly descend somewhat to her mental level, and talk to her of more trivial matters, — the little gossip of society, the latest marriage in high life, the Glengarry caps that young ladies wear now, or something of that sort, — or if you would condescend just to try a few steps of the "Boston" with her occasionally — she would then see that you were mortal like herself, and, I am sure, would yield at discretion.

SIR SAMUEL: It *is* a great condescension, still I will adopt your suggestion. And, see, she is here — let us withdraw and watch our opportunity. *Retire upstage. Enter Angelina.*

ANGELINA: *Confidentially to audience.* This is a scena, and I ought, by rights, to sing it; but really, you know, some of the notes are so awfully high that I *know* I should *squeal,* so I think I had better express my feelings in a soliloquy. *Strikes an attitude a la* Hamlet.
To elope, or not to elope: that is the question
Whether 'tis wiser to endure Sir Samuel,
And put up with his slow and prosy ways,
Or to bolt off this evening with my Snifter,

And, marrying him, to end it? To elope!
To marry! And, marrying him, to have a partner
Always on hand to dance the "Boston" with me:
'Twere a consummation devoutly to be wished.
To elope, to marry, to marry, ay; there's the rub,
For, if we marry, what have we to live on,
Unless papa relents, and raises Snifter's salary?
There's the respect that so long makes the maid
Endure a single life; for who would tread
The long and dreary road of spinsterhood,
But for the dread that matrimony brings
Of debts and duns, and babies without end,
Turned dresses, and empty pockets.

But soft — here comes Sir Samuel.

SIR SAMUEL: Madam, it has been represented to me that you are appalled by my massive intellect.

ANGELINA: Well, Sir Samuel, you *are* rather *heavy*.

SIR SAMUEL: Heavy? I don't quite understand?

ANGELINA: I mean your intellect, Sir Samuel.

SIR SAMUEL: Oh! yes I see. *Aside.* Of course, she means *massive;* the poor girl does not understand these niceties of expression.

ANGELINA: *Aside.* Don't she, though?

SIR SAMUEL: If this is the case I desire to express to you, *un*officially, my willingness to descend occasionally to your mental level.

ANGELINA: You are exceedingly condescending, Sir Samuel.

SIR SAMUEL: Of course, it must be distinctly understood that these descents are to be confined strictly to the privacy of our domestic circle; in public, if you are unable to grasp the full meaning of any remarks, as is most probable, you must listen attentively, and when we are alone together I will explain them to you.

ANGELINA: *Enthusiastically.* This is, indeed, an entrancing prospect you hold out to me. *Innocently.* But does *anyone* ever fully grasp the full force of your remarks, Sir Samuel?

SIR SAMUEL: Very few, indeed!

ANGELINA: So I should think, Sir Samuel.

SIR SAMUEL: *Aside.* There is a good deal of sound common sense in this young lady, even if she is not very brilliant. *Aloud.* I am given to understand that you are particularly partial to a dance which they call the "Baltimore", or the "Philadelphia", or some such name?

ANGELINA: Oh! you mean the "Boston"! Oh yes, I dote upon it.

SIR SAMUEL: In that case, if you are quite sure there is no one looking, I shall have no objection to descend to a little "Boston".

ANGELINA: But *can* you dance, Sir Samuel?

SIR SAMUEL: The man who could invent the N.P. is *capable of anything.*

ANGELINA: But, Sir Samuel, you don't dance with your *intellect,* you dance with your *legs.*

SIR SAMUEL: It is the same thing.

ANGELINA: *Aside, looking at his legs.*   At any rate, his legs are not *(Vary, "are" or "are not", according to legs)*   very massive, whatever his intellect may be — however, we can but try. *Aloud.*   Come, Sir Samuel, I am ready. *Dance the "Boston" ludicrously badly. Aside.*   He little thinks how he has confirmed my wavering resolution — to think of going through life with a man who can't dance better than that! *Aloud.*   Sir Samuel, I *did* hesitate, but I will hesitate no longer.

Captain has entered during this speech — he comes down.

Trio.

CAPTAIN: Never mind the why and wherefore,
    Angelina consents, and therefore,
    Thou Sir Samuel's fond of prosing,
    And his N.P. is a bore,
    Though he sets the house a-dozing
    Whene'er he holds the floor.

BOTH: Set the merry bells a-ringing,
    Rend the air with warbling wild,
    For the union of Sir Samuel
    With the Chieftain's lovely child.

CAPTAIN: For a chieftain's duteous daughter;

ANGELINA: For a chieftain's simple daughter;

SIR SAMUEL: For a chieftain's lovely daughter;

ANGELINA: And a clerk not fond of water.

SIR SAMUEL: Never mind the why and wherefore,
    Angeline consents, and therefore,
    Though her intellect's but slender,
    And I fear she's frivol*ous,*
    Yet I think she's young and tender,
    And I might have done much *wuss.*

BOTH: Set the merry bells a-ringing,
    Rend the air with warbling wild,
    For the union of Sir Samuel
    With the chieftain's lovely child.

ANGELINA: Never mind the why and wherefore,
    Angeline consents, and therefore,
    Though they both are quite mistaken,
    And Sir Samuel's not the man;
    To their error they'll awaken
    When they see the other Sam.

BOTH: Set the merry bells a-ringing,
    Rend the air with warbling wild,
    For the union of Sir Samuel
    With the chieftain's lovely child.

CAPTAIN: Sir Samuel, I cannot express my delight at the happy result of your experiment — your dancing was irresistible. I had no idea you could cut such a *figure* in the mazy waltz.

SIR SAMUEL: Capt. MacA., it would be a strange thing if a Finance Minister of my standing could not cut a *figure* in anything. *Exit Sir Samuel.*

CAPTAIN: At length I can see my way clearly. By the aid of my daughter, Sir Samuel will be firmly bound to me; a few fat sinecures, judiciously distributed, will confirm the waverers, and if the "boom" only continues a little longer, I shall be secure. *During this MacDeadeye has entered.*

MacDEADEYE: Captain!!

CAPTAIN: *Recoiling.* MacDeadeye! You here? Ah —

MacDEADEYE: Dinna shrink from me, Captain. I know I'm unpleasant to you, I remind you of some awkward things, don't I? But this time I come out of kindness, I want to give you warning!

CAPTAIN: Warning! You are surely not going to open up another scandal? You haven't been collaring any *more letters of mine,* have you? *Evinces great terror.*

MacDEADEYE: You mistake my meaning, listen!

Duet.

MacDEADEYE: Great Chieftain, I've important information,
    Sing hey! the very awful piece of work,
    About a certain intimate relation,
    Sing hey! your artful daughter and the clerk!

BOTH: The artful, artful daughter and the clerk!

CAPTAIN: MacDeadeye, in connundrums you are speaking,
And keeping me entirely in the dark;
The answer to them vainly I am seeking,
Sing hey! the artful daughter and the clerk!

BOTH: The very artful daughter and the clerk!

MacDEADEYE: Great Chieftain, your young daughter is a trying
Her engagement with Sir Samuel to burk —
She means this night with Snifter to be flying;
Sing hey! your artful daughter and the clerk!

BOTH: The very artful daughter and the clerk!

CAPTAIN: MacDeadeye, you have given timely warning,
The obligation I'll not try to shirk;
I'll talk to Master Snifter in the morning,
Sing hey! the sack I'll give to that young clerk!

BOTH: The very artful daughter and the clerk!

CAPTAIN: MacDeadeye, I thank you for your warning; I will at once take measures to arrest their flight. This will afford me ample concealment — *no one will be able to see through this!*

Lets fall a sheet of white calico on which is painted the words "Ministerial Policy". Holds it up before him.

MacDEADEYE: *Aside.* Ha! ha! he don't see my little game. I've given Sir Samuel notice, and he'll drop on them just at the nick of time; and when he sees the Captain here he'll think he's in the plot too, and then he'll come over to our side of the hoose! How's that for a conspiracy?

Enter Snifter, Angelina, Butterbun, Clerks, etc. Captain at back, shrouded, unnoticed.

ALL:
Carefully on tiptoe stalking,
Moving gently as we may;
While Sir Samuel is talking,
We will softly steal away.
Trombone note.
Alarmed. Goodness, me!
I hear them come;

MacDEADEYE: Silent be,
It was the "Hum".
Here the cover of a magic lantern arranged at wings or in front, so as to throw the shadow of a large "bug" on the back scene, is withdrawn, the figure of the "bug" is seen at back.

ALL: Yes, yes; it was the "Hum",

CAPTAIN: They're right — it is a "Hum." *Pointing to bug.*

ALL: Call a sleigh — the fare's a quarter,

SAM SNIFTER: *Feeling pockets.*   Yes, but who'll defray the fare?

ALL: For a clergyman is ready
To unite the happy pair.
Trombone note.
Goodness me,
I hear them come;

MacDEADEYE: Silent be,
Again the "Hum."

ALL: Again it was that "Hum."

CAPTAIN: They're right, it is a hum.   *Shadow as before. Uncovering.*   Hold!
All start.

CAPTAIN: Silly daughter of mine, I insist upon knowing
What you may be doing with this Government clerk,
For these officers of mine, though highly respectable,
Are scarcely fit company, my daughter, for you.

CHORUS OF CLERKS: Now, hark at that, do. Though highly respectable
We're scarcely fit company for a lady like you.

SAM SNIFTER: Proud Pre-mier-er, that haughty lip uncurl,
Vain man, suppress that supercilious sneer,
For I have dared to love your matchless girl,
A fact well known to all my comrades here.

CAPTAIN: Oh! horror!

Duet.

CLERK AND ANGELINA: Yes (I/he) a humble third class clerk,
Who's chief employ is sealing letters,
Forced to such poor, degrading work
By those whom fate has made (my/his) betters.
(Have/has) dared to rise (my/his) wormy eyes
Above the sphere to which you'd mould (me/him)
In manhood's glorious pride to rise,
(I am/He is) a Civ-il-i-an, behold (me/him).

CHORUS: He is a Civ-il-i-an,
For he himself hath said it,
And it's greatly to his credit
That he is a Civ-il-i-an;

For he might have been a Draper,
A Grocer or a Baker,
Or perhaps a Hardware man.
But in spite of all temptations
To other occupations
He remains a Civilian.
Hurrah! hurrah!
For the Government Civ-il-i-an.

ANGELINA: Dearest papa, do not be angry, we only came out to listen to the "Hum."

CAPTAIN: The Hum?

ANGELINA: Yes, papa, the "Hum" you know, of the N.P. — it is to be heard very plainly in the evening at this time of year.

CAPTAIN: *In a passion.*   Oh, this is too thin — blow the Hum and the N.P. too!

MacDEADEYE: Hear! hear! blow the N.P.

ALL: Oh! oh!

CHORUS: Did you hear him? did you hear him?
Oh! the monster overbearing!
Don't go near him! don't go near him!
He is swearing! he is swearing!
He "blowed" the N.P. — he "blowed" the N.P. —
Yes, he "blowed" the N.P.
During this Sir Samuel has entered and comes down.

SIR SAMUEL: My pain and my distress,
I find it is not easy to express;
To abuse my great N.P.
Is a thing incomprehensible to me.

CAPTAIN: Sir Samuel, one word — The facts are not before you;
The word was injudicious I allow;
But hear my explanation I implore you,
And you will be indignant too, I vow.

SIR SAMUEL: I will hear of no defence —
The expression was too awful —
I question very much
If it was not unlawful.

Not many days from hence
I promise that you *shall* see
What is the consequence
Of thus speaking of the N.P.

ALL: This is the consequence

185

Of thus speaking of the N.P.

SIR SAMUEL: For I'll teach you that the great N.P.
Must be spoken of respectful*lee*,
And always be regarded as a sacred thing.

CHORUS: And so say the Ministers who form his little ring.
Etc., etc. Captain retires back of stage.

SIR SAMUEL: Come here, my worthy young man, — for you *are* a very worthy young man, I am sure.

CLERK: Very much so, Sir Samuel.

SIR SAMUEL: How came your chief so far to forget himself as to use such horrible language?

CLERK: It was in this way: You see, Sir Samuel — I am only a third-class clerk —

SIR SAMUEL: Don't be ashamed of that; you may rise. You will probably scarcely believe it, but I myself was at one time in a comparatively humble position: — The force of genius, Mr. Snifter — the force of genius!

CLERK: Exactly so, Sir Samuel — that is just what I said to Angelina. Angelina, I said, Sir Samuel has risen to the top of the tree, and why should not I?

SIR SAMUEL: Stop — Angelina? I don't quite comprehend — To whom do you allude?

CLERK: To the captain's daughter — We love each other, Sir Samuel! She is the seal which has stamped an indelible impression on the wax of my heart! — *Rush to each other's arms.*

ALL: A very pretty simile!

SIR SAMUEL: Wax indeed! — Insolent subordinate! you shall feel the consequence of putting *me* in a *wax*. Let the Sergeant-at-Arms arrest this insubordinate clerk instantly. *Sergeant-at-Arms arrests him.*

CLERK: A moment ago you said I was a subordinate — now you say I am *in*subordinate! — This is another specimen of Ministerial inconsistency.

SIR SAMUEL: Away with him! Captain MacA., have you such a thing as a *cell* — a dungeon *cell* — in this building?

CAPTAIN: Oh dear! yes, Sir Samuel — the whole institution is a *series of sells*, in fact the *whole concern is one gigantic sell!*

SIR SAMUEL: Then *cell* him at once.

MacDEADEYE: Yes, as he has sold a mony mair in his time.

Octet and Chorus.

CLERK: Farewell, my own
An-ge-li-na, farewell;
This is, I own,
An extremely awkward *sell.*

ANGELINA: Oh, were it known
Who it was pa did tell,
He should atone
To me for this horrid *sell.*

SIR SAMUEL: The sack, the sack,
I'll give to this clerk so fell,
And he'll confess
That it is indeed a *sell.*

MacDEADEYE: If *he* gets the sack,
And loses his love as well,
It will, in fac'
Be a terribly awkward *sell.*

BUTTERBUN: But, when is known
The secret I have to tell,
All will be thrown
On their beam ends by the *sell.*

SIR SAMUEL: Angelina, I can hardly express to you my annoyance at this painful revelation. *You,* who might have been the bride of the financial genius of the age, to throw yourself away upon a third-class clerk!

BUTTERBUN: Hold! I have something to say to that!

SIR SAMUEL: You!!

BUTTERBUN: Yes, I. Prepare for the revelation!!
Song — Butterbun and Chorus.
Air — "My love he is a sailor boy."
You remember, Sir Samuel, you once had a nephew
Who, like little Charley Ross, was stolen away;
And where he was taken to,
Or who did abduct him,
You never had no notion,
Up to the present day.
Oh! his uncle he did value him
Just as if he was his own,
And his name it was Samuel,
Just the same as your own.

CHORUS: Oh! his uncle he did value him
Just as if he was his own,

187

And his name it was Samuel,
Just the same as your own.

BUTTERBUN: Well, I'm sorry to say that I am the very person
Who abducted that infant, at thirteen months old,
And I brought him up most careful,
And I got him in the Government,
And he is the very party
Which now you behold.
Oh! his uncle he did value him
Like silver or gold,
And his name it is Samuel,
Now twenty-one years old.

CHORUS: Oh! his uncle he did value him
Like silver or gold,
And his name it is Samuel,
Now twenty-one years old.

SIR SAMUEL: Then I am to understand, Mrs. Butterbun, that this young gentleman is my nephew who was stolen by you at the early age of thirteen months, and has since been brought up secretly by you?

BUTTERBUN: That is the idea I intended to convey.

SIR SAMUEL: This is very remarkable — in some respects it is almost as remarkable as the National Policy; but, I confess, I should like some further proof of identity. Are you in a position to furnish any? If not, it is of no consequence; as a politician, I am aware that a great deal must be taken on trust.

BUTTERBUN: I can furnish you with indisputable proofs, Sir Samuel; you remember that your nephew had a large pimple on his nose?

SIR SAMUEL: *Reflectively.* Let me see! He was thirteen months old — yes, if my memory serves me, his nose *did* look remarkably like a large pimple.

BUTTERBUN: *Tragically.* Examine, for yourselves, the nose of Mr. Snifter — there is no deception, ladies and gentlemen — tell me if you observe a pimple.

ALL: *Examining nose.* Yes, several.

SIR SAMUEL: In that case, there can be no doubt about the identity. Mr. Snifter, I should say Samuel, I am aware it would be the correct thing to request you to come to my arms, but, as I observe you have your arms full already, *Clerk is embracing Angelina.* I will content myself with congratulating you on the distinguished relative you have discovered. Capt. MacA., this alters matters entirely.

CAPTAIN: Yes, Sir Samuel, but I hope you mean to marry Angelina, all the same.

SIR SAMUEL: It would be impossible for me to marry my nephew's wife — or, at any rate, his promised wife; that would be bigamy, or something equivalent.

Besides, I don't think she is *massive* enough for me. I think that, under the circumstances you had better marry your daughter to my nephew; and, of course, as a near relation of mine, and a Lower Province man, he must be provided for comfortably.

CAPTAIN: Of course, Sir Samuel. *Aside.* We will get him into the House, and that will be another vote on our side.

SIR SAMUEL: MacDeadeye, you must consider our negotiations at an end. My principles will not allow me to come over to your party.

MacDEADEYE: Hoot, mon — ye're *principles?* Ye mean ye're *interest* — *To audience.* — he calls himself a Finance Meenister, and canna' distinguish between *principle* and interest.

ALL: *Song.*
    Oh! joy; oh! rapture unforeseen,
    Our prospects now are all serene;
    (Papa/Uncle) a settlement will make,
    And we a stylish house will take,
    And entertain our friends.
    And every one on (us/them) will call;
    And every week (we'll/they'll) give a ball;
    The "Boston" (we/they) will dance all night,
    Nor go to bed till broad daylight;
    And thus (our/their) time (we'll/they'll) spend.

CAPTAIN: For I am the Captain of the Parliament!

CHORUS: And a right good Captain *he.*

MacDEADEYE: But keep a sharp lookout,
    And mind what you're about,
    Or you'll lose your majori*tee.*

CAPTAIN: I acted on the square
    All through the whole affair,
    And it turned out right, you see;
    I was very nearly stuck,
    But I had my usual luck,
    Which never has deserted me.

CHORUS: What, never? *etc., etc.*

CAPTAIN: *Laughing.* Well, it did *once.*

CHORUS: It only *once* deserted *he;*
    Then give three cheers to show our sentiment
    For the *lucky* Captain of the "Parliament."

Air — "The sea, the sea, the open sea."

SIR SAMUEL: The P., the P., the Great N.P.
    That lets nothing into the country free,
    Nothing into the country free.
    It sends up the price of everything,
    And makes the producers merrily sing,
    The producers merrily sing.
    Oh! if ever we have prosperi*tee*
    It will come on account of the Great N.P.,
    On account of the Great N.P.

MacDEADEYE: I have sat in the Hoose for many a year,
    But sic rubbish as this I ne'er did hear,
    Sic rubbish I ne'er did hear.
    For *producers,* nae doot, it's all verra weel,
    But how do the puir *consumers* feel?
    The puir consumers feel.
    Oh, we ne'er shall have real prosperi*tee*
    Till we knock on the head the horrid N.P.,
    This horrible sham, the N.P.

ANGELINA: The P., the P., the Great N.P.,
    Of opinion there seems much diversi*tee*
    Regarding this strange N.P.
    But when Doctors like these do disagree —
    Points to MacA. and MacDeadeye.
    So very decidedly disagree —
    About the effect of this queer N.P.,
    There is no other course, it seems to me —
    No other course seems open to me
    But to YOU to leave the *Decree.*

CHORUS: He is a Ci-vil-i-an;
    For he might have been a Draper,
    A Grocer, or a Baker,
    Or perhaps a Pub-li-can.
    But, in spite of all temptations
    To other occupations,
    He remains a Civ-il-i-an.
    Hurrah! hurrah!
    For the Government Civ-il-i-an.

Curtain.

Closing Scene and Tableau

A noise of altercation is heard behind scenes. Enter "Canada", followed by "Britannia."

CANADA: It's no use your talking like that mamma. I won't be dictated to. I'm quite old enough to manage my own house. Anyone to hear you talk would think I was not even *grown up.*

BRITANNIA: There is no doubt, my dear, about your being grown up; the only dread in my mind is whether you are not *outgrowing your strength.*

CANADA: You needn't be anxious about that, mamma; I. assure you my *constitution is quite sound.*

BRITANNIA: I am very glad to hear it, my dear, but you must admit you have been very extravagant lately — building all those long railways. Why, when I was your age, a few stage coaches were quite good enough for me. Where *do* you expect all the money is to come from?

CANADA: *Indignantly.* The idea of talking like that! It's all very well for you, mamma, in your little poky house, but in this great big place of mine I shouldn't see some of the children from one year's end to the other if I didn't build railways. *Bursts into tears.* I never would have thought it of you, mamma, wanting to keep me away from the dear children all the way off in British Columbia! *Cries bitterly.*

BRITANNIA: *Comforting her.* There, there, don't cry my pet, I wouldn't keep you apart from your children for the world; but you know, really, you have been drawing on me for a great deal of money lately.

CANADA: I am sure, mamma, I haven't spent nearly so much as sister "Zealand" or sister "Australia" has — and see what a lot of beef and things I sent you last year! — but there, I always thought you liked them better than me; and if you don't want to give me any more money I can borrow it from "Cousin Jonathan." I know he'll lend it to me.

BRITANNIA: *Reproachfully.* Now, Canada, this is very ungrateful of you. You know you have always been my favorite daughter. Didn't I send you Lord Dufferin and his darling wife to help you manage the House, though I could ill spare him?

CANADA: Well, mamma, you can't say we did not appreciate him.

BRITANNIA: Of course you appreciated him, child; how could you do otherwise? and when he came back didn't I send you my favourite Princess and her husband? and yet you have the face to say I don't love you as well as I do the others!

CANADA: *Coaxingly.* So you did, dear old mammy, and it *was* naughty of me to say you didn't love me. But see, Mamma, here are quite a number of the gentlemen of my household. I mean my present household, for you know I have had to make a change lately. This, mamma, is Captain MacA., my superintendent.

BRITANNIA: I am glad to see you, Captain MacA. You are remarkably like one of my own people, and I fancy you resemble him somewhat in other respects besides personal appearance. Benjamin is a very clever man, but, as I have had occasion to tell him, there is such a thing as being *too* clever. I hope you won't be too clever, Captain MacA.

CAPTAIN: I shall endeavour not to be, madam.

BRITANNIA: There is one good thing I have heard about you, Captain MacA., and that is, that, although you are said to be a little too fond of your party, yet that, personally, you are remarkably free from reproach. This is a very good thing, but you must remember that to a great extent, you are responsible for the good conduct of your subordinates, and I am not too well satisfied with the behaviour of some of your provincial coadjutors. Will you bear this in mind, Captain?

CAPTAIN: Yes, madam.

CANADA: This, mamma, is Sir Samuel, who manages my money matters.

BRITANNIA: How do you do, Sir Samuel? I think I had the pleasure of seeing you lately in my money market, and a very good bargain you seem to have made. We are very glad to see you, provided you don't come *too* often. So I see you are going to make Canada a great manufacturing country, Sir Samuel?

SIR SAMUEL: We hope so, madam.

BRITANNIA: Well, well! I should have thought that with nearly three million square miles of territory and only about four millions of people to occupy it, that it would have been better to have devoted your attention in the first place to developing your agricultural resources. However, as I tell my daughter here, I am not going to interfere with your domestic arrangements, and I hope the experiment will answer your expectations.

CANADA: Now, mamma, I must introduce to you Mr. MacDeadeye, my *old* superintendent. I liked him very much, mamma, and I am quite sure he was very honest, but somehow he didn't get on with the family. I fancy it was the hard times, as much as anything else, that made them quarrel.

BRITANNIA: I am very happy to make your acquaintance, Mr. MacDeadeye. I have heard much good of you. I am sorry that you would not allow me to confer on you the same distinction that I have conferred on some of your brethren. Sir Alexander MacDeadeye would sound very prettily.

MacDEADEYE: Ye're verra kind, ma'am, but I dinna pretend to be onything mair than a honest working mon, and I take no heed of ony empty titles.

BRITANNIA: Tut! tut! Mr. MacDeadeye, that is all very well, but it is not very complimentary to me, and I fancy that sort of talk has done you some harm. However, no doubt you mean well, so we will say no more about it.   *Turns to Canada.*   Now, my child, there is one thing I must really speak to you very seriously about. I don't want to meddle with your domestic affairs, and, although I can't say I approve of your going back on your *mother's free trade principles* in the way you have done, still I don't feel called upon to interfere, but I am told you are carrying on a flirtation with your "Cousin Jonathan," and some people are even talking about an alliance between you.   *Reproachfully.*   Oh! Canada, *I would never have believed it of a well-conducted girl like you!*

CANADA: *Indignantly.   It's a horrid story mamma,* I like "Jonathan" very much as a near neighbour and a cousin, but I should never dream of a closer connection,

and I don't believe he desires it either. It is people like that horrid "Bystander" who have been setting these stories about. *Believe me, mamma, there's nothing in it. Breaks off into the following song.*
For I'm very, very fond of my dear mamma.

CHORUS: And a right good "ma" is she,

CANADA: And believe me when I say, those who think the other way
Are a very small minori*tee.*

CHORUS: And believe us when we say, those who think the other way,
Are a very small minori*tee.*

CANADA: To help I'll ne'er be *slack,* whatever foe *attack,*
Let him come by land or sea;
I may flirt a bit, *of course,* but for better or for *worse*
I will never be untrue to *thee.*
Addressing "Britannia".

ALL: No; never!

BRITANNIA: What, never?

ALL: No; NEVER!!
We will never be untrue to thee.

Air — "Rule Britannia"

Hail Britannia! the ruler of the sea,
Canada to Britain ever true shall be.

Wave flags, Union Jack and Canadian Ensign. Tableau.

Curtain.

2

"LETTY SALAD" Gavotte.

J.E.P. ALDOUS.

Ptarmigan
or A Canadian Carnival
An Original Comic Opera in Two Acts
Written by J.N.McIlwraith Composed by J.E.P.Aldous, B.A.

Dedicated to the Canadian Club of Hamilton, Ontario
Hamilton Spectator Printing Company, 1895

DRAMATIS PERSONAE

Ptarmigan	*an Unconscious Villain, in love with Maple Leaf*
Bob O'Link	*of the Bank of Montreal, also in love with Maple Leaf*
Robin	*a Muscular Musician, in love with Trillium*
Hy Holder	*Lieutenant of Volunteers, in love with Blue Belle*
Dick Cissel	*a Medical Student, in love with his Profession*
Al Louette, Corbeau	*French Canadians, in love with British Rule*
Wis-Ka-Tjan	*the Canada Jay — an Indian*
Trillium	*a Cultured Amateur, in love with Beethoven*
Blue Belle	*a Wealthy Widow of literary tastes, in love with Browning*
Hepatica	*representing the "Herald" — a "New Woman"*
Maple Leaf	*an Athletic Canadienne, in love with her Country*

Chorus of Snow Shoers, Tobogganers, Soldiers, etc.

The action takes place during an afternoon and evening of a Canadian Winter Carnival.

ACT I

Scene: Wintry Landscape near Toboggan Slide. Campfire in background. A light snow falling. Enter Hy Holder, Dick Cissel and Snow Shoe Club.

CHORUS:
> All Hail to the season that hides the ground
> 'Neath a comforter deep of snow!
> With our snow shoes on we can tramp around
> The fields and the forests where health is found,
> And merrily sing as we go.

> Here's that! For the man who can stay indoors
> When the crust will bear his weight.
> He's in love with the books over which he pores,
> But far above learning our spirit soars,
> For the snow shoer's lord of his fate.

> O'er the snow-covered fences we gaily speed,
> O'er the frozen ponds and creeks.
> When we come to an icy hill — take heed!
> Drop down on the snow shoes, they're wings indeed —
> 'Tis the jolliest one of our freaks.

Now gather around our gay bon-fire,
And whatever else we do,
In this bracing air let us all conspire
To sing a song, while the flames leap higher,
To the trusty old snow shoe.

HY HOLDER: This is all very well when we're off by ourselves, but some of us will sing small enough when the ladies appear.

DICK CISSEL: Why so, Hy Holder? Your learned madame would never dream of driving out here with the other girls for tobogganing. She'd as soon go to a P.M.

HY HOLDER: But she is coming — under protest. She has the idea that if she humours me a little in this way during carnival, I'll oblige her afterwards by reading Browning. She is indeed a *Blue* Belle.

DICK CISSEL: If that's all, I can prescribe for her. Having almost completed my first year at the Medical College, I confidently affirm that there is nothing better for her complaint than a course of outdoor sports. Take her snow-shoeing three times a week, before meals, skating twice —

HY HOLDER: It's no use, Dick! The fact of the matter is, the women of this country are being educated far beyond us. We shall soon have nothing whatever in common with them. Ah! Here comes a fellow sufferer.

DICK CISSEL: His temperature appears to be abnormally low. Doesn't he look blue? *Enter Robin.*

CHORUS: "Won't you tell me why, Robin?"

ROBIN: *Recitative.*   My comrades dear, your sympathy unloosens
The tongue I swore should fettered be for aye.
Song.
I always did think I could sing,
Till Trillium came home from the College.
She told me, "You can't do a thing
That needs any musical knowledge."

CHORUS: Rude Trillium!
What will become
Of the whole country,
If such effrontery
Makes Robin mum?

ROBIN: I wrestled with Schubert and Franz,
To Schumann and Grieg I was springing,
But Trillium led me a dance
And told me to practise sight-singing.

CHORUS: Fiddle-de-dee!
How could we see

Rob, our best cricketer,
Snubbed by a wicketer
Maiden than she?

ROBIN: I studied the tonic-sol-fa,
Joined a choir and the new Philharmonic.
"Sing in tune!" cried my love, "Or papa
Must speedily give me a tonic!"

CHORUS: Never mind, Rob!
Her we shall bob
Down on this slippery
Hill, and for snippery
We'll make her sob.

HY HOLDER: Alackaday! Robin, you're no worse off than the rest of us. Is Trillium coming out to the Slide this afternoon?

ROBIN: She said she'd try to come, if she could get in her practising in the forenoon and postpone the meeting of the Ophocleidium Harmonaical Symphony Club.

DICK CISSEL: Cheer up! We'll back our Winter Carnival to amputate both Browning and Beethoven. *Enter Ptarmigan in distress.*

PTARMIGAN: Help! Help! Help! Help! A persecuted creature,
I see your fire and run here hard's I can;
I'd soon be left without a decent feature
By which you'd know your old friend Ptarmigan.

CHORUS: Ptarmigan!

PTARMIGAN: Ptarmigan!

Ensemble.

ROBIN, HY HOLDER, DICK CISSEL: PTARMIGAN:

Dear boy! It is glorious again to see	Dear boys! It is glorious again to see
The face of our school fellow!	The face of my school fellows!
Happy we	Happy me
To welcome him back to Canadian soil,	To be welcomed back to Canadian soil,
And never abroad may he have to toil.	And never abroad may I have to toil.

Enter Al Louette and Corbeau in pursuit of Ptarmigan. They denounce him in patois.

Ensemble, with change of key.

ROBIN, HY HOLDER, DICK CISSEL:	PTARMIGAN:
False one! Wretched man! We now know your crime, We've been told of your perfidy just in time! We'll lynch you here without more delay, You'll hang by the neck till you're dead as clay.	False ones! Wretched men! I don't know my crime, Nor what is my perfidy. Give me time! If you lynch me here without some delay You're hanging an innocent man, I say

Robin, Hy Holder and Dick Cissel take off scarves to hang Ptarmigan. A sound of sleigh bells is heard.

DICK CISSEL: Good gracious! The ladies! They'd think it awfully ungentlemanly of us to proceed with this operation before them.

HY HOLDER: They'll find out that Ptarmigan has been abroad, and set him up a model of "culchaw."

ROBIN: They won't let us hang him, anyway, for didn't he — yes, he did — sing in tune.

DICK CISSEL: Let us tie him up to this tree back here, and leave the Frenchies to look after him. There is a body of men to whom properly belongs the honour of carving up this subject.

ROBIN: You mean?

DICK CISSEL: I mean the force that will never shirk a disagreeable duty, though millions — of bacteria — stand in the way — the — Regiment of Volunteers.

HY HOLDER: I suppose it would be better to do the business in an orthodox manner. After the girls have had enough tobogganing, I'll go and call out my company.   *Enter Ladies, led by Trillium and Blue Belle.*

LADIES: Here we are — all of us — plain ones and beautiful,
Sober and gay,
Stupid and wise.
When there's tobogganing, e'en the most dutiful
Can't stay away,
Hither she hies.

Sleigh riding pleases the best of our quality;
Skating we love,
Hockey we've tried;
But when we seek for the essence of jollity,
Give us a shove
Down a long slide.   *Dance to sleigh bells.*

Duet — Trillium and Blue Belle.

BLUE BELLE: I can write a verse in Latin or in Greek,

TRILLIUM: I can sing my best when critics cram the house,

BLUE BELLE: But to tell the truth I'm much inclined to shriek,

TRILLIUM: And I'm as timid as a tiny mouse,

BLUE BELLE: When I reach the very top

TRILLIUM: Of that awful, awful drop!

BLUE BELLE: To be shot out into space,

TRILLIUM: Where the ice spray cuts your face,

BLUE BELLE: Isn't really half so charming

TRILLIUM: As it truly is alarming.

BLUE BELLE: Will you risk it?

TRILLIUM: Yes! I'll risk it!

BOTH: Oh, my brave, heroic friend!

They fall upon each others' necks and embrace with tears.

TRILLIUM, BLUE BELLE, HY HOLDER, ROBIN: *Sung as a quartet.*
See! Through the pine trees, the sun is sinking low,
The night will be upon us soon, then homeward we must go.
We'll try to descend to (your/our) lowly plain.
(You'll/We'll) take (us/you) up to yonder height.
And flash (us/you) down again.

CHORUS: Hurry up!
The carnival won't last,
But while it's here,
It cannot go too fast.
Hold on tight!
But if you do let go,
Roll quickly off the track into the deepest snow.

Hurry up!
Your lovers' talk can wait
Till summer comes.
You're keeping us too late.
En avant!
Let's see who'll first be there,
To break the track who will boldly dare?

Off to the slide, side by side,

(We'll/You'll) take (you/us) down. Hurrah!
On to the slide, danger defied,
We shall go down. Hurrah!

Here's that! For the girl who can stay indoors
With a novel or fancy work gay,
We all of us dare to trust to your care,
We've taken a holiday,
So off to the slide we go,
Come, along! Here we are!
We're off to the slide, all danger defied,
Hurrah for our carnival! Hurrah!

Al Louette and Corbeau lie down by camp fire and go to sleep.

PTARMIGAN: *Song.*
So this is then a sample of Canadian hospitality;
In my unhappy case it soon will end in a fatality.
Of all the scrapes I've got into in many years of travelling,
I've never been in one that was beyond my wits unravelling,
That snow shoe club seemed most unlike committing an atrocity,
But here am I, tied hand and foot, witness of its ferocity.
My voice you may admire, but there's sameness in my attitudes,
I'm humourous when I'm at large, but now I think in platitudes.
No prophet has a chance to get his longed for notoriety
Where he was born, but all *I* wished was civilized society.
I longed to breathe my native air and see the life Arcadian,
But I am not allowed to join in any sport Canadian,
If I've been rude I'm sure they'd see it was quite intentional,
For as a rule my manners are decidedly conventional.
Well! If I'm doomed to single bliss and solitude perpetual,
Farewell, ye stalwart muscle men, I quickly shall forget you all.
Spoken.   Hello! Who's this coming? Well! If it ain't my old flame, Maple Leaf. Of
course, she wouldn't condescend to be *driven* out here like the rest. Many a mile
she's tramped me. Who's that with her now? If I know the specie he's a bank clerk.
Ah! These blasted bonds!   *Enter Maple Leaf and Bob O'Link trailing toboggan.*

Duet — Maple Leaf and Bob O'Link.

BOB O'LINK: O wait, I pray you, Maple Leaf,
To hear my heart's fond story.
You need not frown, I shall be brief,
I'll cause you not a moment's grief,
For coldness is your glory.

DUET: Cold, cold the day has been,
And colder still the night will be,
But what care we, for bright will be
The heart that's warm within.

MAPLE LEAF: Don't look so doleful, Bob O'Link,
The walk I fear has tired you,

Lie down there, and before you think
I'll whisk you to that very brink
Where we have oft admired you.

DUET: We love the manly men,
And if you search this country all,
Within the Bank of Montreal
You'll find them — wielding Pen.

BOB O'LINK: You always change the subject, dear,
When I would fain be saying
That life for me, without you near,
Is what I cannot face. Then hear
Me out, your step delaying.

DUET: Like wines the ____* above
In it our hearts luxuriate.

MAPLE LEAF: But why will you infuriate,

BOB O'LINK: But why do I infuriate

MAPLE LEAF: Me with your rant of love?

BOB O'LINK: You when I speak of love?

MAPLE LEAF: Forgive me, friend! I only chide
Because the time you're wasting.
What matters love, or aught beside
Our grand, old, icy Mountain Slide,
Whose joys we should be tasting?

BOTH: Then onward we shall move.

BOB O'LINK: Still longer must I sigh for you.

MAPLE LEAF: I'm not inclined to sigh with you.

BOB O'LINK: How gladly would I die for you.

MAPLE LEAF: I'll not agree to die for you.

BOB O'LINK: You love me? Time will prove.

MAPLE LEAF: I love you? Time will prove.

PTARMIGAN: Encore!

Trio — Maple Leaf, Bob O'Link and Ptarmigan.

This word is indecipherable in the original edition (Editor).

MAPLE LEAF: Oh! Horror! What is that I see?

PTARMIGAN: 'Tis Ptarmigan tied to a tree.

BOB O'LINK: His accent is enough for me.

ALL: O Whirra, Whirra, Whoo!

Maple Leaf hastens to untie Ptarmigan.

MAPLE LEAF: Why, 'tis indeed my early friend!

PTARMIGAN: Good fortune you to him did send!

BOB O'LINK: I don't approve! No help I'll lend.

ALL: O Whirra, Whirra, Whoo!

MAPLE LEAF: Strange welcome home from foreign lands!

PTARMIGAN: Indeed, I fell in with brigands.

BOB O'LINK: I'm not sure that I should shake hands.

ALL: O Whirra, Whirra, Whoo!

MAPLE LEAF: We'll dance to warm you, if you choose.

PTARMIGAN: I've not got on my dancing shoes.

BOB O'LINK: And I suppose I can't refuse.

ALL: O Whirra, Whirra, Whoo!

WIS-KA-TJAN: "Hurruld a Cent!"

Enter Hepatica and Wis-Ka-Tjan.

HEPATICA: *Recitative.*   Wis-ka-tjan! Quickly turn away your face!
   I never should have brought you to this place.
   I'm educating him to sell the papers,
   Escort me through the slums and cut no capers
   The ordinary youth I view with loathing,
   But Whiskey Jack will shine — in proper clothing.

   I see no criminal, nor sign of one!
   These giddy three are going in for fun;
   So long's my noble red man's not corrupted
   I'll join the dance that we have interrupted.

   Spoken.   Have any of you seen a desperate criminal that I hear is at large in this neighbourhood?

MAPLE LEAF: No, indeed! What has he done?

HEPATICA: That's what I came to find out.

PTARMIGAN: We haven't seen any such person about.

BOB O'LINK: Pardon my curiosity, but ah — why should you — a lady — seek the society of one whom you know to be a "desperate criminal?"

Solo — Hepatica and Quartet — Maple Leaf, Hepatica, Bob O'Link and Ptarmigan.

HEPATICA: My name's Hepatica — don't laugh —
And writing's my profession,
I'm working on the "Herald" staff —
But pardon this digression.

QUARTET: The earliest of the flowers of spring,
A dainty, modest, little thing;
She's here when snow
Decides to go —
But pardon this digression.

HEPATICA: If I can of this ghastly crime
But be the first reporter,
I'll think I've had a better time
Than she has when you court her.

QUARTET: For Love's a very fickle boy.
He brings much pain and little joy.
In (her/my) own way
(She's/I've) more to say
Than (we/you) have when (we/you) court her.

Whiskey Jack in the act of scalping Al Louette and Corbeau wakens them and they denounce Ptarmigan to Hepatica, who proceeds to interview him, while Maple Leaf runs off for help to rescue him.

HEPATICA: Now then, you may as well save time by making a clean breast of it right away, and telling me what you've done, for I'll get it out of you if I have to sit here all night.

PTARMIGAN: Well, mawm, I was just hopin', as you're one of them newspaper ladies who know everything, that *you'd* be able to tell *me* what I done.

HEPATICA: What do they *say* you've done?

PTARMIGAN: I can't tell you that neither, until you teach these two pinions of mine   *Indicating Al Louette and Corbeau*   to talk English.

Enter Chorus of Girls, who release Ptarmigan.

CHORUS: Ptarmigan! Our
Brightest fellow,
More of gumption
Than the others.

Ptarmigan! Our
Maple's "Hello!"
Roused compunction
In our brothers.

They are racing
To the city
For the guard of
Honor due you.

Danger facing,
Full of pity,
They will ward off
Who pursue you.

Quartet — Trillium, Blue Belle, Maple Leaf, Hepatica and Chorus of Girls.

QUARTET: The loves that we love in our later life
Are most common-place of men.
When one of them asks us to be his wife,
We are quickly wed — but then!

How our fancy returns to the love of our youth,
And we picture him always young.
He's the lofty mind and the soul of truth,
Unlike those that we're cast among.

CHORUS: How our fancy returns to the love of our youth,
And we picture him always young.
He's the lofty mind and the soul of truth,
Unlike those that we're cast among.

QUARTET: The loves that we love in our later life
Have of worldly goods a store.
They are stout and bald, but without *much* strife
They will yield us gold galore.

CHORUS: Still our fancy returns to the love of our youth,
And we picture him always young.
He's the lofty mind and the soul of truth,
Unlike those that we're cast among.

BLUE BELLE: You poor, dear, old fellow! Don't tremble any more, you are quite
safe with us. We will never see the humblest wretch abused, for we all belong to the
National Council of Women.

TRILLIUM: Besides, we've formed ourselves into a Ladies' Auxiliary for the P.P.A.

PTARMIGAN: The — ah — which?

HEPATICA: Ptarmigan Protective Association.

PTARMIGAN: That's a *game* law!

MAPLE LEAF: Hark! There comes your guard of honour.

Enter Hy Holder's company of volunteers, who crowd round Ptarmigan?

PTARMIGAN: Oh, I say! Is this a closed season for Ptarmigan?

Solo and Chorus for 13th Batallion (Written by the late Captain J.B. Young)

VOLUNTEERS: "In days of yore, the man of Gore
    Show'd pluck and valour bold,
    As Stoney Creek and Lundy's Lane
    The story well have told;
    The land they left us then we'll guard,
    And show that lapse of years
    Can find the muscle to fight as hard
    In the 13th Volunteers."

FULL CHORUS: "Then hurrah! hurrah! for the scarlet coat,
    And hurrah for the rifle true,
    Hurrah for the colours we'll ne'er desert,
    The Red, the White, and the Blue."

VOLUNTEERS: "Should we be called, as they were then,
    By war to take the field,
    Oh, may we not disgrace those men
    Who knew not how to yield,
    But may we win ourselves a name
    The foe shall ever fear,
    And Canada shall proudly claim
    Each 13th Volunteer."

FULL CHORUS: "Then hurrah! hurrah! for the scarlet coat,
    And hurrah for the rifle true;
    Hurrah for the colours we'll ne'er desert,
    The Red, the White, and the Blue."

VOLUNTEERS: "When duty calls and danger lowers,
    Then let us boldly stand,
    And prove that every man of ours
    Dare die for his native land,
    Let all who dread to meet that day,
    And all with coward fears,
    Fall out of the ranks — as well they may —
    Of the 13th Volunteers."

FULL CHORUS: "Then hurrah! hurrah! for the scarlet coat,
And hurrah for the rifle true;
Hurrah for the colours we'll ne'er desert,
The Red, the White, and the Blue."

VOLUNTEERS: "We tempt no foe — but none we fear;
We stand but in our right,
To guard our homes, our loved ones here,
Our maids with eyes so bright.
Then in his heart let each one bear
An image fond and dear,
For whom all dangers quick he'll dare,
Each 13th Volunteer."

FULL CHORUS: "Then hurrah! hurrah! for the scarlet coat,
And hurrah for the rifle true;
Hurrah for the colours we'll ne'er desert,
The Red, the White, and the Blue."

HY HOLDER: Ladies! Will you kindly retire? Your presence distracts us from accomplishing the ends of justice.

TRILLIUM: Indeed! Why, Justice herself is a woman.

HY HOLDER: Please go, girls! Do you suppose we tramped all this way just to march about and sing?

BLUE BELLE: You don't generally do any more than that, do you? *Enter Robin.*

ROBIN: Ah, there he is, the shameless, fallen creature,
Whose presence doth pollute the air
Of this fair Canada of ours.

GIRLS' CHORUS: What has he done?

Solo — Robin.

ROBIN: You ask me what he's done? I'll tell his story,
Although the tale corrupts my wholesome tongue
We all knew him of old, but never more he
Shall be our guest, nor join our friends among.

GIRLS' CHORUS: We'll listen if we can,
Speak out then like a man,
For we've no fear of what we hear
Against our Ptarmigan.

ROBIN: He left his father's house for sake of money —
Alas! His crime will turn you into Fates —
Lower he sank, until, the trait'rous one, he
Signed papers to be fused into the States.

Robin being overcome with emotion, mumbles his last line, and Hy Holder commands Dick Cissel, Sergeant of Volunteers, to explain.

DICK CISSEL: "Be it known that on the 29th day of February, 1893, P. Tarmigan, a native of Ottawa, Canada; reported himself for naturalization, and declared his intentions preparatory to being admitted a Citizen of the United States."

PART CHORUS: Oh, horror without name!
Unutterable shame!
Our highly prized! He's naturalized
And now must bear the blame.

DICK CISSEL: He proves, by the examination of two competent witnesses, his residence in the United States more than five years, his attachment to the principles of the Constitution of the United States, and favourable disposition to the good order and happiness of the same.

PART CHORUS: Oh hateful, perjured hand!
With us you cannot stand.
We'll let you know before you go
You've got a native land.

DICK CISSEL: Thereupon, said Ptarmigan is duly sworn in open Court, and makes oath that he will support the Constitution of the United States, and that he does absolutely and entirely renounce and abjure all allegiance and fidelity to every foreign Prince, Potentate, State or Sovereignty whatever, and particularly to the Queen of Great Britain and Empress of India.

PART CHORUS: You've taken a sacred oath
That you will not be loath
To fight our Queen! Oh dastard! Mean!
You're knave and coward both!

PTARMIGAN: See here! That's coming it rather strong. I ain't no knave nor coward. How was I to know what sort of a boom you were getting on over here? Before I went away these *Indicating Al Louette and Corbeau* were the only Canadians, now you're all "in it."

FULL CHORUS: Cease! Cease your ravings rough,
Your conscience must be tough,
What's to be done with such a one?
There's nothing bad enough!

Enter Bob O'Link running.

BOB O'LINK: A vice-regal dispensation, straight from Rideau Hall! His Excellency, the Governor-General, suggests that the only fitting punishment for such a crime is banishment for life. Ptarmigan shall be condemned to live in the United States, never to set foot in Canada again, and, to make his subjection more complete, he must agree, six months after date, to marry an American girl.

PTARMIGAN: Here! String me up!

BOB O'LINK: What for? Have you not heard that you are free to return to your beloved State of Michigan?

PTARMIGAN: I can't comply with the conditions. What do you suppose I came over here for any how? Just for the carnival, or to see *you?*

Song — Ptarmigan and Chorus.

PTARMIGAN: Swing me round by the heels, till the firmament reels,
Till your arms are played out and your head's in a whirl,
You may e'en take my life, but I'll not have for wife
Anyone but a true blue Canadian girl.

CHORUS: Oh Canada!
(You ever/Your daughters) are so fair.
Dear Canada!
They love the name (you/they) bear,
The Yankee maid,
Or one from South or West,
Doth pale and fade
'Fore her we love the best!

PTARMIGAN: Now what d'ye s'pose always happens to those
Who marry American Girls — "jest as cute?"
They soon solve the riddle, how to play second fiddle,
And are never heard tooting their own little toot.

CHORUS: Oh Canada!
(You ever/Your daughters) are so fair.
Dear Canada!
They love the name (you/they) bear,
The Yankee maid,
Or one from South or West,
Doth pale and fade
'Fore her we love the best!

PTARMIGAN: I am honest, not poor, but of this I am sure,
If I'm jined to a girl over there in the States
I should never be able to keep up her table,
Her theatres, party gowns, backs, chocolates.

CHORUS: Oh Canada!
(You ever/Your daughters) are so fair.
Dear Canada!
They love the name (you/they) bear,
The Yankee maid,
Or one from South or West,
Doth pale and fade
'Fore her we love the best!

PTARMIGAN: She would tease for an hour to get off on a tower,
And never think twice of me left in the shop.
When she'd spent all my cash she would lay on the lash,
And divorce me quite gaily — I'd never cry "Stop!"

CHORUS: Oh Canada!
(You ever/Your daughters) are so fair.
Dear Canada!
They love the name (you/they) bear,
The Yankee maid,
Or one from South or West,
Doth pale and fade
'Fore her we love the best!

ROBIN: Poor chappie! You almost make one sorry for you. Is there no lady here who will take pity on him and sacrifice herself to go as a missionary into the United State of Michigan?

GIRLS: Not one!

ROBIN: What's to be done with him?

HY HOLDER: We can't put him in any ordinary jail, for that would raise a mutiny among the other prisoners. They could not endure being under the same roof with him for, whatever their crimes, they are all Canadians!

DICK CISSEL: There is room in the new Small-pox Hospital, but the patients would object. His disease is worse than theirs.

BOB O'LINK: I have an idea.

ALL: No! How strange!

BOB O'LINK: Strange, but true. Let him be confined in the Ice Palace, where by midnight he'll be frozen to death. There let him remain — a monumental warning to youthful Canadians so long as the ice palace itself shall endure.

HY HOLDER: The very thing! I'll leave a guard to see that he does not escape and we'll join you later at the home of Blue Belle.

CHORUS:
Oh Wretched Man! your doom we seal,
So hide your guilty face.
From our decree there's no appeal,
We'll take you to a place
Where you will shiver and shake and sneeze
Until, Oh Monster of Vice!
As solid as Ottawa Rock you'll freeze
Within our Palace of Ice.
And such befall
The traitors all

Who do as you have done;
They are the most
Obnoxious host
That dwell beneath the sun!

Tableau with Ptarmigan tied to a toboggan, and the centre of fixed bayonets. End of Act I.

ACT II

Scene: Madame Blue Belle's Drawing Room, to which tobogganing party has adjourned to dance. Bob O'Link and Maple Leaf withdraw to front.

BOB O'LINK:
    Ah! Maple Leaf, you lightly dance
    As if you had no heart at all,
    But while my feet keep time by chance,
    The crowd, the laughter on me pall.
    Come, sit you here and let me try
    To make you feel when I am nigh
    That all the rest may go their way
    If Bob O'Link shall with you stay.

    Oh, my dearest sweetheart!
    Turn you again to me.
    Show me your hazel eyes, full
    Of the love light I long to see.

    Thy name by all men is revered
    As emblem of our own countree,
    But how my hopeless heart were cheered
    Could I but pluck thee from the tree
    To wear thee, shelter thee, my own,
    Thou shalt not wither all alone
    No autumn blast shall blow thee down,
    Thou'lt come to me my life to crown.

    Oh my dearest sweetheart!
    Turn you again to me
    Show me your hazel eyes, full
    Of the love light I long to see.

AL LOUETTE: *Announces at door.* Mademoiselle Hepatica et Monsieur Purple Martin. *Enter Hepatica and Ptarmigan, the latter disguised.*

HEPATICA: *To Blue Belle.* To a cultivated woman of the world, such as yourself,

210

the name and works of our great Canadian painter are doubtless well known, and therefore I have taken the liberty of bringing him here this evening to introduce him to you. I am sorry that we have come when you are not alone, for I daresay not one of your guests has ever heard of M. Purple Martin. *Company indignantly protest.*

CHORUS: We are no Philistines!
  Our own Composer shines!
  Our native Poet's lines
  With ardour drive us frantic.
  The country, as a whole,
  Adores the artist soul,
  From frontier to the Pole,
  Pacific to Atlantic.

  Then cheer for him
  With strongest vim,
  The Great Canadian Painter.
  We'll sing our lays
  And dance to praise
  The Great Canadian Painter.
  Our citizen who paints
  We place among the saints,
  He never has complaints
  Of any local strictures.
  Before his canvas dries,
  One with the other vies
  To seize the honoured prize.
  We buy up *all* his pictures!

  Then cheer for him
  With strongest vim,
  The Great Canadian Painter.
  We'll sing our lays
  And dance to praise
  The Great Canadian Painter.

PTARMIGAN: Ah! Really! I had no idea that the few little things I've struck off would win me so speedy recognition.

BLUE BELLE: Tell me about your master piece, do. You call it — the name escapes me!

PTARMIGAN: Modesty forbids me to talk shop. *He and Blue Belle promenade and Ptarmigan looks at paintings.* Are these all Canadian artists?

BLUE BELLE: Every one! We wouldn't give space on our walls to any man who was not a Canadian.

PTARMIGAN: Wonderful! Wonderful! And are you so far advanced in the other arts? Excuse my ignorance. I've been abroad, you know, and find things greatly changed on my return.

BLUE BELLE: No doubt. Canada is now synonymous with culture. Beethoven will
   soon be studied in all our kindergartens and Browning used as a first reader. As for
   singing, excuse me a moment and you shall hear what we can do.   *Ptarmigan gets
   Hepatica to introduce him to Maple Leaf.*

BLUE BELLE: *To Robin.*   Our distinguished guest would like some music. Will
   you kindly sing?

ROBIN: I should be most happy, but I'm really too nervous to venture alone. Do
   you — do you think — ah — that Trillium would — ah — object *very* much to
   singing a duet with me?

BLUE BELLE: Not if *I* ask her, I'm sure, to oblige our famous countryman.

Duet — Trillium and Robin.

ROBIN: My humble song —

TRILLIUM: There now, that's wrong!

ROBIN: Your window at —

TRILLIUM: You're singing flat!

ROBIN: I make my moan —

TRILLIUM: Oh! What a tone!

ROBIN: I'm yours till death!

TRILLIUM: Now! Watch your breath.

BOTH: Oh pardon, friends,
   We'll make amends,
   No errors more (I'll/she'll) mention,
   We needn't mind,
   They're deaf and blind,
   They're paying no attention.

ROBIN: Then Trillium, darling, it is our fate
   To be *tête à tête.*
   We are alone completely
   Do you not see
   I've changed the key —
   Thanks all to your instruction!

*During first part of duet, company promenade, talk and laugh. Gradually they leave
the room.*

TRILLIUM: It seems indeed a *tête à tête*
   Is ever my fate.

212

You think I'm singing sweetly,
You cannot tell
Exactly how well,
Nor praise my tone production.
The man I wed must be able to play
The piano all day,
The flute and 'cello nightly
My accompaniments
At all events
Must never fail to inspire him,

Enter from different directions Ptarmigan and Maple Leaf, Hy Holder and Blue Belle, Dick Cissel and Hepatica, Bob O'Link by himself and disconsolate. They steal up behind Trillium and Robin and listen with smiles.

ROBIN: I know I am not worthy of you,
    But what can I do?
    Treat not my case too lightly.
    If ever you find
    The man to your mind,
    I'll do my best to admire him.

HY HOLDER: Come to supper!

DICK CISSEL: Come to supper!

Octet — Maple Leaf, Blue Belle, Hepatica, Bob O'Link, Hy Holder, Ptarmigan, Dick Cissel, and Robin. Soprano Obligato by Trillium.

TRILLIUM: Here's a scene a sweeter than which
    Our great artist could not paint,
    But poor Robin needs a sandwich
    For he looks extremely faint.

    Though your future seemeth murky
    Though your hope and courage fail,
    You'll feel better for some turkey
    And a glass of ginger ale.

    There was never youthful *malade,*
    Wishing Cupid's chain to loose,
    Could resist our Letty Salad,
    Oyster Patty, Charlotte Russe!

    These three maids, with sweet devices,
    Shall make Robin look less glum,
    When we've plied him with ices
    He'll forget his Trillium.

Letty Salad, Oyster Patty, Charlotte Russe dance a Gavotte. Exeunt all but Hepatica. Enter Bob O'Link.

BOB O'LINK: Will you come to supper? *No answer.* May I have the pleasure of taking you in to supper? *Hepatica still absorbed in writing.* Madame Blue Belle requested me to ask you to favour her with your company in the dining room along with her other guests.

HEPATICA: Excuse me! I don't think you've been introduced.

BOB O'LINK: I — ah — beg your pardon. My name's Bob O'Link.

HEPATICA: And is it Bob O'Link, most charming of singers, I see before me now in black and white?

Duet — Hepatica and Bob O'Link.

HEPATICA: How doth it come to pass
That you've returned so readily,
To light on lowly grass?
You've chosen Maples steadily.

BOB O'LINK: I'm getting old, I fear,
Am troubled with sciatica,
That's why I'm waiting here
Beside the shy Hepatica.

BOTH: When one has not what one loves,
So the poet sayeth,
One must then love what one has,
So the poet sayeth.

HEPATICA: I've heard you sing full oft
To Maple Leaf right royally,
Your tones so rich and soft
Proclaim your heart beats loyally.

BOB O'LINK: T'was e'er my favoured perch
To sing to her diurnally,
She's left me in the lurch;
For him who paints — infernally.

BOTH: When one has not what one loves,
So the poet sayeth,
One must then love what one has,
So the poet sayeth.

BOB O'LINK: But you'll think me very rude to abuse a *protégé* of yours.

HEPATICA: *Protégé* of mine indeed! The Great Canadian Painter!

BOB O'LINK: Oh, Rubbish! I don't believe he's anything of the sort. I've seen the fellow somewhere, but can't for the life of me remember where or how.

HEPATICA: Sir! Do you doubt the authenticity of an introduction from the Press?

BOB O'LINK: No! No! Don't look at me like that! Hepatica! You must help me! Surely the very heart hasn't been squeezed out of you in the Press? Take this long-haired lion back to his lair, or Maple Leaf is lost to me forever.   *Maple Leaf and Ptarmigan appear at back of stage and see Bob O'Link on his knees to Hepatica.*

HEPATICA: Well, I'll do it — on one condition.

BOB O'LINK: Anything! Anything!

HEPATICA: You are on the Carnival committee, eh?

BOB O'LINK: Yes! Yes!

HEPATICA: Well, you will tell me all about the row between —   *As Hepatica and Bob O'Link whisper together Maple Leaf and Ptarmigan retire.*   All right! I'll take Ptarmigan away directly.

BOB O'LINK: Ptarmigan! Impossible!

HEPATICA: Young man! you forget yourself! There's nothing impossible — to the New Woman.

BOB O'LINK: Pray, forgive me. The New Woman! Do you smoke? Where's your bicycle?

HEPATICA: A bicycle in the snow — stupid! I've put it on skates and turned it into an ice-boat. Want to come for a sail to hunt ptarmigan — rare birds?

BOB O'LINK: That villain, Ptarmigan! However did he get out?

HEPATICA: I hypnotized the guards and sent Wis-ka-tjan to change clothes with him.

BOB O'LINK: You must be a very, very accomplished person.

HEPATICA: Oh no! It's quite simple. Would *you* like to be mesmerized?

BOB O'LINK: No violence!   *He picks up large key which she dropped while making mesmeric motions.*

HEPATICA: Thanks. That's my latch-key.

BOB O'LINK: Why did you do it? Were you so disloyal to Canada as to set her foe free?

HEPATICA: I didn't set him free, I brought him here. He's safe enough, he won't leave Maple Leaf.

BOB O'LINK: No, curse him!

HEPATICA: I told him the only way to see her and be welcomed into Canadian society was to don his swallow tail and meet me at my Club —

BOB O'LINK: With a club?

HEPATICA: *At* my Club, I said. I promised to bring him here and introduce him as Purple Martin, the artist. I told him he was sure of a grand reception.

BOB O'LINK: But can he paint?

HEPATICA: I never asked him that question. It's of no importance. He *talks* about Art. Ye gods! How he can talk!

BOB O'LINK: Poor Whiskey Jack! What of him?

HEPATICA: You can't freeze an Indian. A night on the ice will be good for him. I must keep him *fresh.*

BOB O'LINK: Why, oh why, did you do it? Why did you give that traitor a chance —

HEPATICA: I did it for copy, of course. I've a column and a half for our morning edition on Ptarmigan's Escape. None of the other papers will hear of it till tomorrow. See! *She reads off several sensational headings of local interest before she finds the right one.* Now I'm on the spot to report what happens to him next.

BOB O'LINK: I'll let you see that pretty soon — the scoundrel!

HEPATICA: Not yet, if you please. Come and give me full particulars of that Carnival Committee squabble, and you can settle Ptarmigan afterwards. Ladies first!

Exeunt Hepatica and Bob O'Link, as company who have returned from supper begin to dance. Enter Wis-ka-tjan in clothes of Ptarmigan, and covered with icicles.

ALL: Ptarmigan!

PTARMIGAN: Looks to me more like a Jay.

HY HOLDER: So it is! Our Canada Jay — Whiskey Jack!

DICK CISSEL: Who has chloroformed the other bird? O for a chance to vivisect him!

CHORUS: He's fled! How our patriots quiver!
Oh! hasten away
To find him ere day,
Nor let him get over the river.
For you we shall earnestly pray.
What a lasting disgrace to our city
If the awfullest cad,

The worst of the bad,
Isn't captured and killed without pity.
'Twill drive Mayor — mad!
Exeunt all but Maple Leaf and Ptarmigan.

Duet — Maple Leaf and Ptarmigan.

MAPLE LEAF: Ptarmigan!

PTARMIGAN: The eyes of love are keen!

MAPLE LEAF: You mean the eyes of hatred.

PTARMIGAN: Love me again! I crave no greater joy.
Come! Fly with me before the rest return,
The border crossed, how speedily you'll learn
To care for me — your sweetheart since a boy.
Love me again!

MAPLE LEAF: Love me no more! I can treat but with scorn
Your pleading. Where's the woman who could trust
Her future to a turn-coat, one who must
Forget his home, the land where he was born.
Love me no more!

PTARMIGAN: Love me again! The bird from whom I'm named
Each season changes colour — so do you!
The trees and birds to nature's laws are true,
Of being turn-coats they are not ashamed.
Love me again!
Maple Leaf, my own, why will you set up conventional lines of division where none
exist in reality? The same trees grow on either side of the Niagara River, the same
birds sing, the same flowers bloom. Love knows no boundary lines, no tariff laws,
no custom house.

MAPLE LEAF: Hush! What is that?   *Clock strikes twelve. Unaccompanied
double quartet of male voices behind the scenes.*

Clouds with gentle hand are brushing
Wrinkles from the moon's fair face.
Every noisy streamlet's rushing
Has been stilled by frost's embrace.
But our spirits rise with coldness,
We have twice our natural boldness
When the city's under snow,
And the mercury's so low
That it cannot lower be,
Then we tramp abroad with glee.

MAPLE LEAF: Oh, Ptarmigan! Fly! Fly! That's the guard! They must not find you
here! They were to be on duty at the Ice Palace till midnight. By this time they fancy
you're too stiff to move.

PTARMIGAN: So I am! I shan't move a step for one of them.

MAPLE LEAF: My old friend! You say you love me — don't let me see you torn limb from limb before my very eyes.

PTARMIGAN: I'll go — If you will go with me. If not, I don't care what becomes of me.

MAPLE LEAF: Ptarmigan! Go! I beseech you. It will break my heart to see you caught.

PTARMIGAN: You do love me then? I am more to you than friends or native land? *He tries to embrace her.*

MAPLE LEAF: *Song.*
   The only love that's worthy of my heart
   Is one in which man has no part,
   No rival need she fear,
   My country dear!

   When travelling far my weary spirit yearns
   For these broad lakes, my soul returns
   To seek for Nature's land —
   My country grand!

   Her rolling prairies, Rocky Mountains tall,
   Her woods, Niagara's thundering fall,
   Her rivers — all declare
   My country fair!

   No President she needs, nor any Czar,
   Her own brave sons so loyal are,
   She ever more will be
   My country free!

   My fancy fondly rests on bygone days,
   Her record past I proudly praise;
   'Tis borne on high by fame
   My country's name!

   There's naught in history we'd fain forget,
   Our future shall be brighter yet;
   Then go your way, I'm to
   My country true!

While Maple Leaf is singing her last verse, Blue Belle and her lady guests enter from one side and shake hands with guard of eight volunteers, who enter from the other side. All stare suspiciously at Ptarmigan.

PTARMIGAN: Thanks! Lovely song!

MAPLE LEAF: Yes, it is pretty; but, Mr. Martin, did you ever hear one called, "When the Swallows Homeward Fly?"

PTARMIGAN: I know it; but this is not the migration season.   *Aside.*   I mean to stay where I am.   *Enter men who went in search of Ptarmigan, led by Bob O'Link.*

BOB O'LINK: There he is! I told you he was here! Painter? We'll paint him so black and blue you won't know his original colour. What are you waiting for?

HY HOLDER: Bring him outside. We don't like to touch him as long as he is the guest of Blue Belle.

BLUE BELLE: Don't consider me in the least. The enemy of my country is mine!

HY HOLDER: And her lover yours?

BLUE BELLE: *Giving him both hands.*   Though he never translate a line of Browning.

DICK CISSEL: *To Hy Holder and Blue Belle.*   No kissing! Science has declared against it.   *Ptarmigan is seized, but shakes his captors off.*

PTARMIGAN: One moment, please! In that time I can prove that I am no worse than any of the rest of you. Who are these men, Browning and Beethoven, you seem to worship? Are they Canadians?   *Trillium and Blue Belle hang their heads.*   Do you never read anything nor play anything that isn't written by a Canadian? Do you never borrow ideas from the States, nor wear anything that is made there? Do you never smuggle boots from Buffalo? Do you —

ALL: No! No!

CHORUS OF GIRLS:
Every novel that we read's a home production,
Every play we go to see's Canadian,
Every native work we buy — at a reduction,
Every local horse we bet on — if we can.

Oh, we never get a costume from abroad,
To Detroit for our shopping never go;
And we boldly plead not guilty of a fraud,
Such as smuggling Yankee boots from Buffalo.

FULL CHORUS: We can solemnly assure you it is so,
That (they/we) never smuggle boots from Buffalo.

CHORUS OF MEN: Not a man among us searches for a missile
To project upon him who the organ grinds.
When he plays the only airs our boys'll whistle —
Music made up in the best Canadian minds.
Every writer, every artist's a machine,
Caring nothing whether he is paid or no,
Working for our own Canadian Magazine,
They needn't smuggle brains from Buffalo.

FULL CHORUS: We can solemnly you assure it is so,

That we never smuggle (boots/brains) from Buffalo.

PTARMIGAN: Well! All I can say is — Times is changed? *Holds out his arms dejectedly.* Pluck away harpies! *Enter Hepatica.*

HEPATICA: Hands off my property! *Writes some mystic letters on his forehead.*

PTARMIGAN: Manuscript only.

HEPATICA: Touch him if you dare!

ALL: What do you mean?

HEPATICA: What do I mean? I mean that the strongest power in Canada has come to the rescue — the power before which every party, sect and creed must bow — THE PRESS.

BOB O'LINK: Are we to infer that the press of our land approves of annexation?

HEPATICA: How dare you ask me such a question! Where have you been brought up that you don't know that the newspapers try and sentence every criminal out of court? *We* pronounce Ptarmigan Not Guilty!

ALL: Not guilty! Why? On what plea?

HEPATICA: Insanity, of course.

DICK CISSEL: That won't go down. I'm a medical student — first year — and I can give Ptarmigan a certificate for being as sane as I am.

HEPATICA: Not unlikely; but I put it to you all: — Is it possible to conceive of any one, man or woman, in full possession of his or her senses, deliberately renouncing his or her British birthright and electing to become amalgamated with the mobocracy upon our southern boundary?

ALL: You're right! It is not possible! He must have been crazy!

HEPATICA: Since I have demonstrated that Ptarmigan signed those fatal papers during a fit of temporary insanity, will you be satisfied if he here and now destroys them?

ALL: Why, certainly!

HEPATICA: Ptarmigan, to escape the fury of these inquisitors which your own criminal folly, in a moment of mental aberration, has drawn upon you, will you, in the presence of these witnesses, tear up your naturalization papers?

PTARMIGAN: Why certainly! *Tears up whole reams.*

ROBIN: We've saved you from those blessed Yanks,

PTARMIGAN: Oh, thanks!

TRILLIUM: You weep because you've been untrue?

PTARMIGAN: I do!

BOB O'LINK: You'll thank us that we do not kill.

PTARMIGAN: I will!

HEPATICA: You stay here now and don't levant.

PTARMIGAN: I shan't!

Quartet — Trillium, Hepatica, Bob O'Link and Robin.

THE FOUR: The rest of your mortal life
   Endeavour to make amends
   For what you have been.
   If true to our Queen,
   We'll all of us be your friends.

   So here is an end to strife,
   You'll join our volunteers,
   And ever decline
   To cross the line,
   For Ptarmigan then, three cheers.

CHORUS: The wonder of Victoria's reign!
   A renegade won back again!
   Excuse him for he was insane,
   And cheer for him with might and main!

ROBIN: My Trillium!
   I, too, was mad,
   That's why I sang so wildly.
   If you will come
   To make me glad,
   I'll take your training mildly.

TRILLIUM: Dear Robin, first
   'Twas love for me
   That put you out of order.
   But in your worst
   Extremity,
   You never crossed the border.

CHORUS: The wonder of Victoria's reign!
   A renegade won back again!
   Excuse him for he was insane,
   And cheer for him with might and main!

PTARMIGAN: Maple Leaf! Every obstacle is removed. Now will you be mine?

MAPLE LEAF: Couldn't think of such a thing, really.

PTARMIGAN: Tell me why? Would you not be happy with me — your own old lover?

MAPLE LEAF: I might for awhile; but if I ever saw you look melancholy — at spring cleaning time, for example — I'd imagine you were longing to be like my carpets — over the line!

PTARMIGAN: Nonsense! Where you are will be carnival for me all the year round.

MAPLE LEAF: At first perhaps; but in time you would forget your duty to me if you had to pay duty on your cigars.

PTARMIGAN: I'll give up smoking. I'll give up —

MAPLE LEAF: No, you won't! If you did, you would just sit round and mope and wish you were making more money. What is money? Vile money! I despise it.

BOB O'LINK: Take me! I have none!   *Maple Leaf does so.*

PTARMIGAN: Well, if you marry Bob O'Link
We all may say Ta! Ta!
The far Northwest
Will claim our best —

MAPLE LEAF AND BOB O'LINK: *Embracing.*
'Twill still be Canada,
My love!
'Twill still be Canada.

FULL CHORUS: While they are under British rule
They'll never feel the cold.
While they are under British rule
They'll want but little gold.

PTARMIGAN: You'll have to be your own house maid,
Your cook, your doctor, nurse,
Bank clerks are sent
To banishment.

MAPLE LEAF AND BOB O'LINK: They might do something worse,
My dear!
They might do something worse.

FULL CHORUS: The athletic Canadian girl
Is never known to shirk.
The athletic Canadian girl
Is not afraid of work.

PTARMIGAN: Here's a conundrum. Will any one guess
What's to become of me?

ALL: Give it up!

HEPATICA: No, I'll not give it up. It belongs to me.

PTARMIGAN: What are you going to do with me?
Marry me?

HEPATICA: Marry you — the New Woman? Not very likely! I mean to take you on
in place of Whiskey Jack. Since that aboriginal youth has tasted the aesthetic
delight of modern masculine attire, he's of no further use to me. He's become a
dude! I must have the raw material, and, next to the Noble Red Man, the
naturalized American citizen is the nearest approach to the primeval specimen to
be found upon our Western Hemisphere.

PTARMIGAN: But I'm not one now!

HEPATICA: Never mind! You're the best I can do at present. I'll make good copy
out of your experiences of low life. There! Carry these.   *Handing him camp stool
and bundle of papers*   Now shout, "Herald, a cent!"

PTARMIGAN: Hurruld, a cent!

FULL CHORUS: We shall not remember the crime that is past,
Since Maple Leaf's left him lamenting;
No slur on his future career shall be case,
The criminal truly repenting.
Our ladies take in
The fact that the sin
Of loving th' American vulture,
Is worse beyond doubt than being without
A fraction of what they call culture.
You may come from the land of the heather and cakes,
You may be a native of Chile,
Your parents may live beside Italy's lakes,
Per adventure you've even been silly
Enough to be born
In the country we scorn,
If now you will join in our party.
We'll make you a friend. To you we extend
A Canadian greeting most hearty.

Curtain.